This new book from Mary Brady is unique in that it addresses a subject on which psychoanalytic publications are scarce. The reader will find thirteen chapters written by very distinguished analysts practicing in different parts of the world who bring their clinical experience together with some theoretical proposals.

For the title of this book, Mary Brady skillfully put together key psychoanalytic clinical concepts like 'erotic transference and counter-transference' and the *field theory* coined by Madeleine and Willy Baranger in 1961–62.

Today, it is even more evident that the analytical situation now hinges on two centers: the patient and the analyst. The latter is not considered now the privileged observer. From this perspective, an analytic process is conceived as a total situation in which the focus is the transference-countertransference relationship.

I would like to suggest another factor: both patient and analyst live in a given culture. This is particularly striking in the treatment of children and adolescents, who are the ones most impacted by changes in society and culture. Nowadays we are contemporaries of a series of transformations in subjectivity.

This book is a must for child and adolescent analysts as it sheds light on the changes in sexuality that happened after psychoanalysis was born during the Modern Era, and the importance of being aware of the erotic feelings that arise during work with young patients. But I think that therapists treating patients of any age will benefit from this immersion in the clinic of eroticism in the analytical session.

Virginia Ungar, M.D.,
International Psychoanalytic Association President

As if eroticism wasn't already elusive, child and adolescent work presents thornier problems still, so erotics in this clinical arena have been particularly absent, indeed taboo. Not so in this volume. Here is a collection of scholarly, intuitive, passionate and playful, chapters reflecting a brave and daring foray into the erotic field of child and adolescent analysis. Constituted in a *suspended real*, play therapy (child, adolescent and adult) elevates persons to characters dramatizing this hidden, passionate world. A co-created theatre, this is the *real* real; with courage and deft awareness, these papers show how play depicts it and what to say and do.
Read this book, learn from the best among us and find the child analyst within you.

Andrea Celenza, Ph.D., *Author of:* Transference, Love, Being: Essential Essays from the Field *(forthcoming from Routledge)*

The essays chosen by Dr. Brady compel us to explore the ways in which we can keep alive the erotic encounter with our analysands. The essays utilize theory to be present in the encounter rather than to keep our distance. Given the often deep uncertainty we have about our own capacities to encounter eros in our relationships, the book is a powerful help in demonstrating how, from various theoretical positions, it is possible to explore our own awakened erotic countertransference in service of its awakening in the life of our analysands. This is a book to be read and thought about multiple times.

Ray Poggi, M.D., *Training and Supervising Analyst, San Francisco Center for Psychoanalysis and Psychoanalytic Institute of Northern California*

Braving the Erotic Field in the Psychoanalytic Treatment of Children and Adolescents

Braving the Erotic Field in the Psychoanalytic Treatment of Adolescents and Children is a groundbreaking collection of chapters by an international group of analytic authors. The book addresses the general lack of psychoanalytic writing on working with erotic feelings in the consulting room when treating children and adolescents. This lack is doubly odd given Freud's emphasis on childhood sexuality as well as the intensities of the adolescent body/mind.

This book takes the view that the subtle interchange of feelings, dreams, narratives and images that arise when erotic feelings are in the fore is better conceptualized as an *erotic field*, than with the binary of transference/countertransference. In contemporary psychoanalysis the idea that transference love offers the possibility of knowing the other in the deepest possible way is supplanting an attitude of suspicion. Clinical work with small children to late adolescents will be offered, including gay and gender-fluid adolescents.

This book makes a decisive contribution to assist clinicians to brave the erotic field with children and adolescents.

Dr. Mary T. Brady is an adult and child psychoanalyst in private practice in San Francisco. She is on the Faculty of the San Francisco Center for Psychoanalysis and the Psychoanalytic Institute of Northern California. Her books, *Analytic Engagements with Adolescents: Sex, Gender and Subversion* and *The Body in Adolescence: Psychic Isolation and Physical Symptoms* were published by Routledge in 2018 and 2016, respectively.

Braving the Erotic Field in the Psychoanalytic Treatment of Children and Adolescents

Edited by Mary T. Brady

LONDON AND NEW YORK

First published 2022
by Routledge
4 Park Square, Milton Park, Abingdon, Oxon OX14 4RN

and by Routledge
605 Third Avenue, New York, NY 10158

Routledge is an imprint of the Taylor & Francis Group, an informa business

© 2022 selection and editorial matter, Mary T. Brady; individual chapters, the contributors

The right of Mary T. Brady to be identified as the author of the editorial material, and of the authors for their individual chapters, has been asserted in accordance with sections 77 and 78 of the Copyright, Designs and Patents Act 1988.

All rights reserved. No part of this book may be reprinted or reproduced or utilised in any form or by any electronic, mechanical, or other means, now known or hereafter invented, including photocopying and recording, or in any information storage or retrieval system, without permission in writing from the publishers.

Trademark notice: Product or corporate names may be trademarks or registered trademarks, and are used only for identification and explanation without intent to infringe.

British Library Cataloguing-in-Publication Data
A catalogue record for this book is available from the British Library

Library of Congress Cataloging-in-Publication Data
Names: Brady, Mary T., 1959- editor.
Title: Braving the erotic field in the psychoanalytic treatment of children and adolescents / edited by Mary T. Brady.
Description: Milton Park, Abingdon, Oxon ; New York, NY : Routledge, 2022. | Includes bibliographical references and index. |
Identifiers: LCCN 2021048301 (print) | LCCN 2021048302 (ebook) | ISBN 9781032210018 (hardback) | ISBN 9781032210025 (paperback) | ISBN 9781003266303 (ebook)
Subjects: LCSH: Child psychotherapy. | Adolescent psychotherapy. | Psychoanalysis.
Classification: LCC RJ504 .B736 2022 (print) | LCC RJ504 (ebook) | DDC 618.92/8914--dc23/eng/20211103
LC record available at https://lccn.loc.gov/2021048301
LC ebook record available at https://lccn.loc.gov/2021048302

ISBN: 978-1-032-21001-8 (hbk)
ISBN: 978-1-032-21002-5 (pbk)
ISBN: 978-1-003-26630-3 (ebk)

DOI: 10.4324/9781003266303

Typeset in Bembo
by MPS Limited, Dehradun

For Dallas

Contents

Foreword: Eroticism in Psychoanalytic Theorizing and Process by Andrea Celenza	xii
Acknowledgements	xvii
Contributors	xviii
Introduction: Braving the erotic field in the psychoanalytic treatment of children and adults MARY T. BRADY	1
Editor's Introduction to: **Types of sexual transference and countertransference in psychotherapeutic work with children and adolescents**	8
1 Types of sexual transference and countertransference in psychotherapeutic work with children and adolescents ANNE ALVAREZ	10
Editor's Introduction to: **Braving the erotic field in the treatment of adolescents**	26
2 Braving the erotic field in the treatment of adolescents MARY T. BRADY	28
Editor's Introduction to: **Traversing challenging terrain: discussion of Mary Brady's 'Braving the Erotic Field'**	47
3 Traversing challenging terrain: discussion of Mary Brady's 'Braving the Erotic Field' DIANNE ELISE	48

x *Contents*

Editor's Introduction to: **On the new semantics of transference love** 57

4 On the new semantics of transference love
GIUSEPPE CIVITARESE
59

Editor's Introduction to: **Child, parents and psychoanalyst: binocular vision in the erotic field** 80

5 Child, parents and psychoanalyst: binocular vision in the erotic field
ELENA MOLINARI
82

Editor's Introduction to: **Elsa's sexual fantasies in a narcissistic and erotic transference** 102

6 Elsa's sexual fantasies in a narcissistic and erotic transference
CHRISTINE ANZIEU-PREMMEREUR
103

Editor's Introduction to: **The tears of a clown: dreaming the erotic in the service of integration** 120

7 The tears of a clown: dreaming the erotic in the service of integration
KIMBERLY BOYD & CHRISTOPHER LOVETT
122

Editor's Introduction to: **A boy's terror and fascination with the male body** 137

8 A boy's terror and fascination with the male body
ROBERT TYMINSKI
139

Editor's Introduction to: **The play of Eros: The story of an adolescent boy, his body, and his analyst's body** 151

9 The play of Eros: The story of an adolescent boy, his body, and his analyst's body
BRUCE REIS
153

Contents xi

Editor's Introduction to: **Too close for comfort: the challenges of engaging with sexuality in work with adolescents** 161

10 Too close for comfort: the challenges of engaging with sexuality in work with adolescents
EMIL JACKSON
163

Editor's Introduction to: **Erotic, eroticized and perverse transference in child analysis** 184

11 Erotic, eroticized and perverse transference in child analysis
N. GRACIELA KOHEN DE ABDALA
186

Editor's Introduction to: **A special boy: melancholic terrors of awakening the erotic man** 198

12 A special boy: melancholic terrors of awakening the erotic man
DREW TILLOTSON
199

Editor's Introduction to: **'Sleeping Beauties': avoidance of the erotic in adolescence** 216

13 'Sleeping beauties': avoidance of the erotic in adolescence'
MARY T. BRADY
217

Index 229

Foreword: Eroticism in Psychoanalytic Theorizing and Process

Andrea Celenza

The place of sexuality in psychoanalysis is like the lost city of Atlantis, shrouded in mystery, fantastic and ideal, yet uncannily disappeared and dismissed (as if) lacking in evidence. Despite that psychoanalysis was founded, then elaborated on this fundamental drive (Freud being our Plato), the dimensions of Eros are eternally evanescent, ultimately erased in our discourse, found and refound along the way only to be lost again. Now is a time of its reemergence, yet even in current day practice there is a constant shying away.

A legend of an ideal city, Atlantis was first described in Plato's *Timaeus*.[1] The story is told through the words of Timaeus (a fictional Pythagorean philosopher from Southern Italy) to Socrates in a monologue on the creation of the world. He describes Atlantis as 'a vast power … that sprang forth from beyond, larger than Libya and Asia … a great and marvelous royal power … set out to enslave all … reach[ing] a point of extreme peril … [the entire] force sank below the earth all at once … and disappeared … now unnavigable and unexplorable'.

The parallels to erotic life are apparent. Eroticism creates the world, internally structuring our vision of externality. Its inherent affective power threatens enslavement, we risk extreme peril seeking its ideal and it regularly disappears from view.

Freud eventually saw the global reach of the sexual, first focusing on the erogenous zones of infantile sexuality, then moving to a broad, vitalizing instinct including 'all manner of tender feeling … *lieben*, to love' (Freud, 1910). In the words of Merleau-Ponty (1962), 'The sexual is not the genital. It is what causes [one] to have a history … provides a key to one's life'. And further, 'The body of the other is not perceived as an object, but rather as inhabited by a secret perception, by a sexual schema that is strictly individual … the body [of the other] is enigmatic'. Thus, Eros ignites life and with every desire comes a dread, a threat to one's being and very existence, because to encounter the other is to encounter a mystery. The mystery of the unknown, the challenge of separateness and difference and the threat of the other's intentionality. Larger than Libya and Asia, indeed.

Foreword: Eroticism in Psychoanalytic Theorizing and Process xiii

The desexualization of psychoanalytic theorizing, therefore, is especially surprising. It is not solely a contemporary phenomenon, and yet it is only in the past several decades that papers focusing on the centrality of sexuality have emerged in our literature (Laplanche, 1989, 1997; Green, 1995; Fonagy, 2008; Celenza, 2014; Elise, 2019, to name a few). Interestingly, this desexualization is not solely the province of psychoanalysis, but goes back to ancient times in other fields as well. It is rooted in a tendency toward dualism that long predates Descartes, derived from a desire to transcend the body – to segregate and idealize pure reason and linear, abstract thought.

This dualism arises inevitably from fearing sexuality itself, not only because we are afraid of incest (as in sexual boundary violations) but because sexuality is inherently threatening. We resist erotic transferences and erotic countertransferences because we resist the exposure of narcissistic, oedipal-level wounds, our patient's as well as our own. Psychoanalytic authors (Klein, 1930; Britton, 1992) have written about the epistemophilic impulse and its inhibition due to traumatic experiences revolving around a child's curiosity of the primal scene. But perhaps most threatening is the mysterious other … sexuality is transgressive – we cross the boundaries of the unknown and penetrate a new frontier. Our vulnerability *is* our body, our nakedness, our desires in the face of the unknown other.

Hence, the desexualization of psychoanalytic theorizing continues to perplex and remains a missing aspect of the treatment situation as our anxieties and unconscious prohibitions inevitably move us away from erotics. This, despite that the clinical situation is an intimate relationship that easily lends itself to sexual metaphor. As I have written elsewhere (Celenza, 2014), the dialectic between holding and penetration fosters a mutual deepening as intimacy deepens – knowing the other is dialectically related to desiring the other; a mutual enhancement, one seemingly defining the other through opposition yet each paradoxically intensifying the other. To hold is to grasp; to penetrate is to transgress. Our work is penetrating and enveloping, incisive and containing, a firm receptivity that retains, envelops and holds the other in mind. The word *is* the touch is the affect is the knowledge.

In clinical work, erotic erasure can be easily seen in contemporary theorizing of maternal transferences, reflected in the tendency to interpret downward (down and away, so to speak) from oedipal to pre-oedipal conceptualizations of sexuality,[2] resulting in a desexualization of the maternal erotic transference. There has been a tendency to interpret away from oedipal erotics toward a de-erotized maternal, to avoid the intensity of erotic transferences at both the oedipal level and within the maternal transferences. Contemporary writings that correct this erasure include the work of Chassaguet-Smirgel (1970), McDougall (1992), Balsam (2012, 2019), Benjamin (1995), Dimen (2003), Wrye and Welles (1994), Salamonsson (2012), Elise (2002, 2015, 2019) and Celenza (2014, 2017, *in press*).

xiv *Foreword: Eroticism in Psychoanalytic Theorizing and Process*

At the other end of the developmental continuum, erotic and loving transferences are not acknowledged as well, especially in the final phases of a successful psychoanalysis and here I am referring to Bolognini's (1994) loving transference and affectionate transference. He describes erotic transferences along a continuum (from erotized, to erotic, to loving and finally affectionate), comprising a broader range of meanings for erotic transferences.[3] I see Bolognini's attempt here not to delineate variations along the dimension of real/unreal but rather mature and less mature forms of attachment and love, yet transferences all the same.

We now generally accept sexuality as fundamental to the structure of the mind (Green, 1995; Laplanche, 1989, 1997). For example, Laplanche's (1997, 1999) general theory of seduction depicts the mother as the universal driving force of all scenes of seduction, presenting the infant with her enigmatic, sexual unconscious. The infant *takes in* and translates these mysterious messages, constituting its unconscious. These affects and longings are then rekindled in later genital sexuality yet retain the maternal–infant dyad to serve as their template.

Despite these considerations, the metapsychological theorizing continues to be hidden, submerged or lost when discussing clinical work. Now that countertransference is legitimated, viewed as a critical channel for unconscious communication, can erotic countertransference enter our discourse, i.e., the embodied and sexual analyst? This volume addresses these questions and takes them a step further still, wondering if there can be a place for an embodied analyst *with children and adolescents*. One might ask how it might be possible to do play therapy without the analyst's embodiment. Wouldn't sterilized play suffer from restriction …. making the term 'erotic insufficiency' (Brady, this volume) particularly evocative of this missing dimension.

As current theorizing enlarges our frame from discovery to elaboration, from two-person to the analytic field, this volume expands the erotic horizon to include a vision of the *erotic field*, including not only erotic transferences but erotic *counter*transferences, especially as emergent in treatments with children and adolescents. As analysts, we are the objects that will not be had, upholding the incest taboo and thereby cultivating a setting where early forms of desire can safely emerge. We must have the full range of affectivity at our disposal, but we must also help our patients reckon with, interpret and be unafraid to experience the excitements and mysteries of the unknown other.

We don't go willingly into this terrain, for fear of its power, our own vulnerability in relation to it, the helplessness, excitement and ignitability surrounding it. What if he says….? What if she wants….? What would I say? What will he feel? What might I *do*? As I mentioned, we avoid this terrain not only due to the fear of sexual boundary violations, but also for fear of evoking oedipal rejections and vulnerabilities.

Not coincidentally, sexuality in all its erotic dimensions is what adolescents are challenged with during this developmental storm of budding sexuality. These authors expertly demonstrate how to create a safe analytic space to

Foreword: Eroticism in Psychoanalytic Theorizing and Process xv

contain and explore these newly emerging excitements without frightening, over-stimulating, or avoiding these insistently intruding, unfamiliar feelings. They expose the hidden sufferings that emerge in play and inevitably revolve around the erotic dimension of living and growing.

As if eroticism wasn't already elusive, child and adolescent work presents thornier problems still, so erotics in this clinical arena have been particularly absent, indeed taboo. Not so in this volume. Here is a collection of scholarly, intuitive, passionate and playful, chapters reflecting a brave and daring foray into the erotic field of child and adolescent analysis. Constituted in a *suspended real*, play therapy (child, adolescent and adult) elevates persons to characters dramatizing this hidden, passionate world. A co-created theatre, this is the *real real*; with courage and deft awareness, these papers show how play depicts it and what to say and do.

Read this book, learn from the best among us and find the child analyst within you.

Notes

1 Cartwright, M. (2016). *World History Encyclopedia*. https://www.ancient.eu/atlantis/
2 I realize this assumes a linear developmental trajectory, which is problematic in itself.
3 Subsequently, Bolognini (2011) delineated multiple roles of the analyst in concordant relation to these transferences.

References

Balsam, R.H. (2012). *Women's Bodies in Psychoanalysis*. New York, NY: Routledge.
Balsam, R.H. (2019). On the natal body and its confusing place in mental life. *Journal of the American Psychoanalytic Association*, 67(1), 15–36.
Benjamin, J. (1995). *Like Subjects, Love Objects: Essays on Recognition and Sexual Difference.* New Haven, CN: Yale Univ. Press.
Bolognini, S. (1994). Transference: Erotised, erotic, loving, affectionate. *International Journal of Psychoanalysis*, 75, 73–86.
Bolognini, S. (2011). The analyst's awkward gift: Balancing recognition of sexuality with parental protectiveness. *Psychoanalytic Quarterly*, LXXX, 33–54.
Britton, R. (1992). The Oedipus situation and the depression position. *New Library of Psychoanalysis*, 14, 34–45.
Celenza, A. (2014). *Erotic Revelations: Clinical Applications and Perverse Scenarios*. London: Routledge.
Celenza, A. (2017). Lessons on or about the couch: What sexual boundary violations can teach us about everyday practice. *Psychoanalytic Psychology*, 34(2), 157–162.
Celenza, A. (*in press*). *Transference, Love, Being: Essential Essays From the Field*. London, England: Routledge.
Chassaguet-Smirgel, J. (1970). *Female Sexuality: New Psychoanalytic Views*. London, England: Karnac.

xvi *Foreword: Eroticism in Psychoanalytic Theorizing and Process*

Dimen, M. (2003). *Sexuality, Intimacy, Power*. Hillsdale, NJ: Analytic Press.

Elise, D. (2002). The primary maternal Oedipal situation and female homoerotic desire. *Psychoanalytic Inquiry*, 22, 209–228.

Elise, D. (2015). Eroticism in the maternal matrix: Infusion through development and the clinical situation. *Fort Da*, 21(2), 17-32.

Elise, D. (2019). *Creativity and the Erotic Dimensions of the Analytic Field*. New York: Routledge.

Fonagy, P. (2008). A genuinely developmental theory of sexual enjoyment and its implications for psychoanalytic technique. *Journal of the American Planning Association*, 56, 11–36.

Freud, S. (1910). Wild psychoanalysis. *SE*, 11, 219–228.

Green, A. (1995). Has sexuality anything to do with psychoanalysis? *The International Journal of Psa*, 76, 871–883.

Klein, M. (1930). The importance of symbol formation in the development of the ego. In Mitchell, J. (Ed.) *The Selected Melanie Klein*, pp. 95–114. New York: Free Press.

Laplanche, J. (1989). *New Foundations for Psychoanalysis*. London: Blackwell.

Laplanche, J. (1997). The theory of seduction and the problem of the other. *International Journal of Psychoanalysis*, 78, 653–666.

Laplanche, J. (1999). The drive and its source-object: Its fate in the transference. In *Essays on Otherness*, pp. 117–132. London: Routledge.

McDougall, J. (1992). *Plea for a Measure of Abnormality*. New York, NY: Brunner/Mazel.

Merleau-Ponty, M. (1962). *Phenomenology of Perception*. New York, NY: Routledge.

Plato, *Timaeus*. Cartwright, M. (2016). https://www.ancient.eu/atlantis/World History Encyclopedia

Salamonsson, B. (2012). Has infantile sexuality anything to do with infancy? *The International Journal of Psa*, 93(3), 631–647.

Wrye, H.K., & Welles, J.K. (1994). *The Narration of Desire: Erotic Transferences and Countertransferences*. Hillsdale, NJ: Analytic Press.

Acknowledgements

Most of the chapters in this book were generously written by their authors especially for this project. There are four exceptions: Anne Alvarez's 'Types of sexual transference and countertransference in psychotherapeutic work with children and adolescents', published in the *Journal of Child Psychotherapy*, 2010, 36(3), 211–224; Emil Jackson's 'Too close for comfort: the challenges of engaging with sexuality in work with adolescents', published in the *Journal of Child Psychotherapy*, 2017, 43(1), 6–22 and my two papers: 'Braving the erotic field in the treatment of adolescents', published in the *Journal of Child Psychotherapy*, 2018, 44(1), 108–123 and 'Sleeping Beauties': succession problems of adolescence', 2017, published in the *Journal of Child Psychotherapy*, 43(1), 55–65. I am grateful to the Journal of Child Psychotherapy for the permission to reproduce these works.

Eros can thrive in the intercourse of ideas and the pleasure of relationships, not only in the sexual or sensual realms. The friendship or friendly collegiality of all the authors in this book animated this project. Such relationships are also part of what accompanies me in and nourishes my clinical work. I am also indebted to Ray Poggi, my consultant, who is an ever-vigorous source of ideas and to my friend Cathy Witzling who took a look at some of these pages with her writerly eye.

In this strange and ghastly pandemic year I have been enriched to have some extra and precious time with my son Danny Cole and my partner Dallas Sacher.

Contributors

Anne Alvarez, Ph.D., M.A.C.P. is a Consultant Child and Adolescent Psychotherapist (and retired Co-Convener of the Autism Service, Child and Family Dep't. Tavistock Clinic, London, where she still teaches). She is author of *Live Company: Psychotherapy with Autistic, Borderline, Deprived and Abused Children* and has edited with Susan Reid, *Autism and Personality: Findings from the Tavistock Autism Workshop*. A book in her honour, edited by Judith Edwards, entitled *Being Alive: Building on the Work of Anne Alvarez* was published in 2002. She was Visiting Professor at the San Francisco Psychoanalytic Society in November 2005 and is an Honorary Member of the Psychoanalytic Centre of California. Her latest book, *The Thinking Heart: Three Levels of Psychoanalytic Therapy with Disturbed Children* was published in April 2012 by Routledge.

Christine Anzieu-Premmereur, M.D., Ph.D. is an adult and child psychiatrist and psychoanalyst. Member of the Société Psychanalytique de Paris and at New York Psychoanalytic Institute, she is faculty of the Columbia University Psychoanalytic Center, where she directs the Parent–Infant Training Program. She published 'The Process of Representation in Early Childhood', 'Attacks on Linking in Parents of Young Disturbed Children', 'A Psychoanalytic Exploration of the Body in Today's Psychoanalysis', in French on play in child psychotherapy and on psychoanalytic interventions with parents and babies.

Kimberly D. Boyd, M.D. is a graduate and faculty member of the Boston Psychoanalytic Society and Institute where she is a Training and Supervising Psychoanalyst and a Supervising Child and Adolescent Psychoanalyst. She has served there as Co-Chair of the Child Analysis Committee, which oversees the institute's child training programs. She is also on the faculty of the Massachusetts Institute for Psychoanalysis. She is in private practice in Newton, Massachusetts, where she treats children, adolescents and adults.

Mary T. Brady, Ph.D. is an adult and child psychoanalyst in private practice in San Francisco. She is on the Faculties of the San Francisco Center for

Psychoanalysis and the Psychoanalytic Institute of Northern California. Her books, *Analytic Engagements with Adolescents: Sex, Gender and Subversion* and *The Body in Adolescence: Psychic Isolation and Physical Symptoms* were published by Routledge in 2018 and 2016 respectively. She is North American Co-Chair of the Committee on Child Analysis (COCAP) of the International Psychoanalytic Association. She co-leads a private study group on *The Treatment of Adolescents and Young Adults* and another group, *Trauma on Film*. ORCID: 0000-0001-9128-1810

Andrea Celenza, Ph.D. is a Training and Supervising Analyst at the Boston Psychoanalytic Society and Institute and Assistant Clinical Professor at Harvard Medical School. She is also Adjunct Faculty at the NYU Post-Doctoral Program in Psychoanalysis. She has written numerous papers on love, sexuality and psychoanalysis. She has two online courses and is the recipient of several awards. Her writings have been translated into Italian, Spanish, Korean, Russian and Farsi. Her third book, entitled, *Transference, Love, and Being: Essential Essays from the Field*, is forthcoming from Routledge. Dr. Celenza is in private practice in Lexington,Massachusetts, USA.

Giuseppe Civitarese, M.D., Ph.D. is a training and supervising analyst of the Italian Psychoanalytic Society (SPI), and a member of the American Psychoanalytic Association (APsaA) He lives and is in private practice, in Pavia, Italy. Among his books are: *The Intimate Room: Theory and Technique of the Analytic Field* (2010); *The Violence of Emotions: Bion and Post-Bionian Psychoanalysis* (2012); *The Necessary Dream: New Theories and Techniques of Interpretation in Psychoanalysis* (2014); *Losing Your Head: Abjection, Aesthetic Conflict and Psychoanalytic Criticism* (2015); *The Analytic Field and Its Transformations* (with A. Ferro, 2015); *Truth and the Unconscious* (2016); *An Apocriphal Dictionary of Psychoanalysis* (2019); *A Short Introduction to Psychoanalysis* (with A. Ferro, 2018); *Sublime Subjects: Aesthetic Experience and Intersubjectivity in Psychoanalysis* (2018). ORCID: 0000-0002-3466-4329

Dianne Elise, Ph.D. is a Personal and Supervising Analyst and Faculty member of the Psychoanalytic Institute of Northern California, a Training Analyst of the International Psychoanalytic Association and has served on the Editorial Boards of the *Journal of the American Psychoanalytic Association* and *Studies in Gender and Sexuality*. Her over 30 psychoanalytic publications include wide-ranging papers and book chapters on the subjects of gender, sexuality, and erotic transference. Elise's 2019 book with Routledge, *Creativity and the Erotic Dimensions of the Analytic Field,* expands her work in innovative ways and presents her contemporary thinking on erotic life in psychoanalysis. She has developed the concept of *analytic eroticism* to portray the role of libidinal vitality in clinical treatment. She is in private practice in Oakland, California. https://orcid.org/0000-0002-1659-6908

Emil Jackson, M.Psych., is a Consultant Child and Adolescent Psychotherapist and Adult Psychotherapist with over 30 years' experience of therapeutic work with adolescents. His clinical and management base is at the Tavistock & Portman NHS Foundation Trust in London, where he is Head of Child & Adolescent Psychotherapy in the Adolescent and Young Adult Service. For many years, Emil has also been centrally involved in teaching and supervising on the Tavistock's professional doctorate in child and adolescent psychotherapy. Alongside his clinical work, Emil is also an accredited executive coach and coaching supervisor. For the past 20 years, he has been involved in a wide range of coaching and consultancy across public and corporate sector organizations – from FTSE 100 companies, to global social media firms, to family businesses to schools.

Norma Graciela Kohen-Abdala, M.D. is a Psychiatrist and Psychoanalyst. She is a Training Analyst Apdeba, Full Member of IPA, Specialist in Children and Adolescents IPA, Professor of: (a) Melanie Klein and English School and (b) Great Teachers: W. Bion, Iusam-Apdeba. Former Head of the Department of Children and Adolescents, Apdeba. Former Head of the Department of Children and Adoldescent Psychopathology at the British Hospital of Buenos Aires Argentina. Former Coordinator of the Psychopedagic Cabinet of Pestalozzi College, Buenos Aires. Liberman Award Winner Apdeba.

Christopher Lovett, Ph.D. trained at The Boston Psychoanalytic Society and Institute. He is member of the board of directors of the Boston Group for Psychoanalytic Studies and a member of the editorial board of The Journal of the American Psychoanalytic Association. He has written and presented papers on a range of subjects in the field, including the analytic frame, Green's concept of the 'Dead Mother'. Most recently he presented a paper, 'Disappearance in the Analytic Field: An Inquiry into Psychic Immobility, Elasticity and the Nature of Reverie' at the Annual Congress of the Canadian Psychoanalytic Society in 2019 and, also in 2019, the paper 'The Erotics of the Container' at the Congress of the International Psychoanalytic Association in London. He is private practice in Newton Centre, Massachusetts.

Elena Molinari, M.D. Paediatrician, Psychoanalyst, Full Member SPI and IPA, expert in psychoanalysis of children and adolescents. Since 2004 she has been teaching 'Children Neuropsychiatry' in the Postgraduate course of Art Therapy at the Academy of Fine Arts of Brera in Milano. She is currently board member in charge of Scientific Research of the Italian Psychoanalytic Society SPI. She has written numerous contributions in international and national journals. She published in 2017 for Routledge *Field Theory in Child and Adolescent Psychoanalysis. Understanding and Reacting to Unexpected Developments.* https://orcid.org/0000-0002-5135-4584

Bruce Reis, Ph.D., FIPA, is a Training and Supervising Analyst and Faculty Member at the Institute for Psychoanalytic Training and Research, New York; an Adjunct Clinical Assistant Professor in the New York University

Postdoctoral Program in Psychotherapy and Psychoanalysis; and a member of the Boston Change Process Study Group. He is Regional North American Editor for the International Journal of Psychoanalysis as well as the North American book review editor. He has previously served on the editorial boards of The Psychoanalytic Quarterly, and Psychoanalytic Dialogues. He is the co-editor (with Robert Grossmark) of *Heterosexual Masculinities* and author of *Creative Repetition and Intersubjectivity* (2020). https://orcid.org/0000-0002-1572-5229

Drew Tillotson, PsyD, FIPA, BCPsa is a board-certified psychoanalyst maintaining a full-time private practice for adults in San Francisco, California. He is a graduate member and Past President of the Psychoanalytic Institute of Northern California (PINC) and teaches widely in the Bay Area. He has published on aging, intercultural phenomena, book reviews for *Fort Da* and the *International Journal of Psychoanalysis*, and is co-editor and a chapter author for the forthcoming Routledge publication, *Body as Psychoanalytic Object: Clinical Applications from Winnicott to Bion and Beyond*.

Robert Tyminski, D.M.H. is an adult and child analyst member of the C.G. Jung Institute of San Francisco and a past president; he teaches in the Institute's analytic training programme. He is a Clinical Professor in the Department of Psychiatry at the University of California at San Francisco. He is the author of *Male Alienation at the Crossroads of Identity, Culture and Cyberspace* (Routledge, 2018) and *The Psychology of Theft and Loss: Stolen and Fleeced* (Routledge, 2014). He is a 2016 winner of the Michael Fordham Prize from the *Journal of Analytical Psychology*. ORCID: 0000-0001-6324-8052

Introduction

Braving the erotic field in the psychoanalytic treatment of children and adults

Mary T. Brady

Doing dissertation research in dusty stacks 35 years ago, I came upon Harold Searles' (1958) paper, 'Oedipal love in the countertransference'. I still recall vividly how touched I was at Searles' description of finding himself choosing his tie in the morning for a paranoid-schizophrenic man hospitalized at Chestnut Lodge. Searles adds, the patient:

> ...referred to us, now in the third and fourth years of our work, as being married, and at other times expressed deeply affective fantasies of our becoming married. When I took him out for a ride in my car for one of the sessions, I was amazed at the wholly delightful fantasy and feeling I had, namely that we were lovers on the threshold of marriage, with a whole world of wonders opening up before us; I had visions of going upon innumerable rides with him, going to look at furniture together, and so on. When I drove home from work at the end of the day I was filled with a poignant realization of how utterly and tragically unrealizable were the desires of this man who had been hospitalized continually, now, for fourteen years. But I felt that, despite the tragic aspect of this, what we were going through was an essential, constructive part of what his recovery required; these needs of his would have to be experienced, I felt, in however unrealizable a form at first, so that they could become reformulated, in the course of our work, into channels which would lead to greater possibilities for gratification. And I felt a solid sense of personal satisfaction that I was able, now, to go through feeling-experiences with a male patient which years before, even in much lesser degree than this, would have scared me away.
>
> (1958: 185)

What stays with me is the freedom and mobility of Searles' and his patient's psychic experience: the deepest and most lovely of feelings can occur in the most unlikely of circumstances. We love whom we love, when we love. It is always an opportunity to love, though often also a challenge. Searles himself contrasts his relative comfort with sexual and loving feelings towards this male patient with an earlier experience when he too readily agreed to a male

DOI: 10.4324/9781003266303-101

2 Mary T. Brady

patient's plan to move during a period of the treatment when the patient was expressing erotic feelings towards Searles. My hope in this book is that we can accustom ourselves to thinking and feeling in this territory so that we do not have to 'abandon ship' and leave our patients either literally (as Searles did in his earlier treatment) or emotionally (in various forms of distance or withdrawal) – but rather move around with some freedom in the erotic, sensuous and loving feelings in the field.

Searles' paper inspired my doctoral dissertation (completed in 1988) entitled, 'Oedipal love in the countertransference: Variations related to gender'. Today, I wonder if Searles' and his patient's feelings could be better seen as an 'erotic field', not quite so pinned down into 'these <transference> needs of his', and Searles' <countertransference> feeling of satisfaction of being less scared of same sex erotic feelings. At any real depth and intimacy of psychoanalytic work it can be difficult to pin down 'whose feeling is it?' (see Chapter 2 of this volume). Instead, I suggest the fluidity and subtlety of these shared feelings are better characterized as part of an 'erotic field'. Field theory (see Chapters 4 and 5 this volume) seems to particularly lend itself to this subtle interaction, as does Ogden's (1994) concept of the 'analytic third'.

To return to my younger self in the stacks: my dissertation research was also stimulated by Ethel Persons' (1985) writing about gender differences in the expression of erotic transference. She saw male patients as potentially more 'resistant to the expression' of erotic transference and female patients as more 'resistant to the resolution' of erotic transference. Certainly, the topic of erotic transference coincides with whom and how we are allowed to love societally. In the current moment, at least in certain cultural arenas, more diversity in loving is allowed (in terms of gender identity and object choice). This greater freedom also allows analysts to reimagine aspects of ourselves as we work in intimate contact with our patients. To my 35-year older ears, the concept of 'resistance' now seems restrictive. Rather: 'What did these pairings imagine, dream or allow?' 'What fears and dangers were the pair unable to transform?'

Over the past 20 years (having become a child/adolescent analyst as well as an adult analyst), my writing has turned primarily to urgent subjects involving adolescents (Brady, 2016, 2018). Both the immediacy and the challenges adolescents pose evoke my desire to write (in order to think) while in deep waters. Likewise, I have been particularly compelled to write about the delicate issue of working with the erotic as it arises with adolescents. In presenting on this topic (Brady, 2019: <International Psychoanalytic Association with Anne Alvarez, Kim Boyd & Christopher Lovett – who have contributed Chapters 1 and 7 respectively to this volume>), I have been impressed with the level of interest, concern or anxiety regarding how to deal with the erotic with children and adolescents. As I describe in Chapter 2, despite Freud's pivotal discovery of infantile sexuality, talking about sexual feelings with children and adolescents can feel taboo – thus all the more important to discuss frankly. That is why I decided to write/edit this book. My goal is to lend an international group of analysts with varied theoretical perspectives to each reader, in order to sift through your own experiences. I have chosen to broaden the book from my emphasis in Chapter 2 on adolescents to include the treatment of younger children. Alvarez's chapter is focused mainly on children. Molinari's and Anzieu-Premmereur's chapters are focused on young female patients, while Kohen-Abdala's chapter is focused on a young boy. (My Chapter 2 as well as those by Boyd and Lovett, Reis, Tyminski and Tillotson focuses primarily on adolescent boys, while my Chapter 13 as well as the chapter by Jackson focuses on late adolescent females.) Working with the erotic in child and adolescent treatments is the overarching theme of this book, as opposed to working with sexual trauma specifically. That being said, Chapter 1 (Alvarez) and Chapter 11 (Kohen-Abdala) take up this issue.

Children's minds can allow a unique view into sexuality. In Chapter 2 I note that 'Naomi', a pubertal girl came to a session after the 'sex ed' talk at school. With utter sincerity she asked me, 'What is puberty for?' I was struck that while I could answer the question biologically, I could not answer what puberty would mean for her. What had it meant for me? What would the resonances of my pubertal self be in relation to her pubertal self?

We could equally ask, 'What is sexuality for?' The answers that emanate from an adult mind would certainly be different than those from a child's or an adolescent's mind. While children and adolescents are referred to treatment for myriad reasons, I agree with Ogden (1995) that psychic aliveness is an over-arching measure of analysis. Erotic aliveness in the broadest sense *is* aliveness (Elise, 2019 and Chapter 3 this volume).

As I describe in Chapter 2, my 'discovery' of the usefulness of Field Theory in erotic territory emerged in a clinical moment with a patient, when I felt the impossibility of extricating 'whose feeling was it?' I foreshadow this moment here in order to raise the question of how different theories help us to see or can even impede us from seeing. As an edited book, the reader will encounter different theoretical views here. I consider it of value to not homogenize these views, but to raise questions about what each theory helps us with (or how it fails us) as the reader moves from chapter to chapter.

Several writers in this volume refer to Bolognini's (1994) influential paper (in the adult literature) differentiating erotized, erotic, loving and affectionate transferences. I agree with Civitarese (Chapter 4, this volume) that at times calling a transference 'erotized' or 'perverse' can mark our own need to make a distance from a patient. Further, what a particular pair may be able to tolerate/ allow may be much different than for another pair. However, it may also be true that some patients (such as the sexually abused or abusive children whom Alvarez describes, or the sexually over-stimulated child Kohen-Abdala de-scribes) present with organized sexual symptoms/states that have a different flavor than an erotic field that develops well into an analysis (see Chapter 2, this Volume). So, at times, the terms 'perverse' or 'erotized' might allow useful thinking and reflection on certain states in a patient. But I do think it is im-portant to question the distance, or potential for reification, in these terms.

The analytic work with the boy described in Chapter 2 took place when I

4   *Mary T. Brady*

was a child analytic candidate and was supervised by a Freudian analyst. Though the work seemed to me to constitute an 'erotic field', my way of working seemed entirely comfortable to my Freudian supervisor. I believe that the prioritization of sexuality and psycho-sexual development in Drive Theory (most characterized in this volume by Anzieu-Premmereur in Chapter 6) allowed a familiarity and comfort with sexuality. It is an oft cited criticism of contemporary Object Relations theory that sexuality has been unintentionally de-emphasized (see for instance Alvarez's comments in Chapter 1 on Green's critique, as well as Elise in Chapter 2). Any theory can be used defensively to distance ourselves from our patients. Alternatively, my hope in this volume is to use both theory and the authors' imaginative clinical work to help us stay with material that can at times feel too hot to handle.

Field Theory seems to me to allow great fluidity of movement in imagining the erotic. As Civitarese notes in Chapter 4:

> From a field or radically intersubjective angle, the erotic/eroticized transference are addressed as narrative genres unconsciously selected by the 'common' mind of analyst-and-patient-as-a group to make sense of the emotional experience lived in the here and now. If the analyst allows himself to be the critic of a story of which he has the ability to forget *who* wrote it – adopting in this way a true phenomenological stance – and if he concentrates on the truth it contains, whether it is hate or love, *he will not be frightened anymore.*
>
> (Chapter 4, this volume)

Bion prefigures Field Theory by his insight that characters, narratives, dreams and 'holograms' emerge to represent the current emotional interrelationship between analyst and patient.

There are two branches of Field Theory, the first based on the Baranger and Baranger (2008) work which emphasizes the criss-cross projective identifications of the couple, with the greater flow from the patient to the analyst. Italian Field Theory (exemplified by Ferro, 1999; Civitarese, 2010; Molinari, 2017) particularly emphasizes the shared dreaming function of the couple and the use of unsaturated interpretations. From this point of view it is not so much the patient who is ill, perverse or disordered, but that the field 'falls ill', if for instance, the analyst cannot find a way to transform the now shared disturbance through reverie. Field Theory entails a constant attention to the patient's reaction to the analyst's capacity to contain and transform. Whether a particular reverie is shared with the patient in interpretive form is less important than the reverie experience. My meditation on the '*Sleeping Beauty*' fairy tale in Chapter 13, for instance, was not communicated to my patient, but provided a fluidity of imaginative characters (myself as the prince, or as the elder generation king/queen, the good fairy, the evil witch, etc.), which allowed me a mental playfulness in relation to my experience with my patient. The field is co-constructed; a dream or character (such as Sleeping Beauty) is

Introduction 5

not regarded as the product of one mind alone but as the shared projective identifications of the couple, which gathers the emotions in the field.

There are certain pivotal or nodal moments, perhaps moments of acting out described in the following chapters (such as when Anzieu-Premmereur's patient asks to look at her breasts, when Abdala-Kohen's patient asks her to turn her back in order for him to masturbate, or when Tyminski's patient 'rolls over' his forearm) when any analyst would be thinking of our counter-transference experience. I hope as readers you will bring pivotal emotional situations from your own clinical work as you try on each analyst's way of thinking. I would be greatly pleased if a reader found inspiration in how to move around freely with your patients as I did reading Searles' paper on adults.

This book commences with Anne Alvarez's seminal contribution on this topic and is followed by my chapter, introducing the concept of the 'erotic field' in the treatment of adolescents. Dianne Elise then comments on my chapter, bringing in her depth of expertise on sexuality, gender and erotic transference. Her book, *Creativity and the Erotic Dimensions of the Analytic Field* (2019), is a must read for anyone interested in contemporary thinking on erotic life in adult psychoanalysis.

Chapters 4 and 5 bring us to our Field Theorists, Giuseppe Civitarese and Elena Molinari. Civitarese offers us a *tour de force* – a reformulation of the concept of transference love from a Field Theory perspective. Molinari's chapter offers the combined treatment of a four-year-old girl (with compulsive masturbation) and that of her parents. She emphasizes the need for a 'binocular' approach to the subject and the group/family. Her work also entails her use of a reverie involving the painter Egon Schiele's representations of hands as a stimulus to thinking in the parent work. Christine Anzieu-Premmereur then offers us another treatment of a small girl with compulsive masturbation, as well as other somatic disturbances. Anzieu-Premmereur asks the question: 'Is infantile sexuality still a common notion for psychoanalysts?'

The following three chapters convey work with pubertal to late adolescent boys. Kim Boyd and Christopher Lovett ask in Chapter 7: 'What of the erotic life of a child who has not had the benefit of stable caretaking in his early life?' Robert Tyminski likewise addresses himself in Chapter 8 to a profound complication for the erotic – 'How do emerging erotic interests and desires change when a child or adolescent suffers a medical trauma that becomes a chronic condition?' In his chapter the erotic takes the form of a boy's longing both to *see* his male analyst's body and to be with his analyst's body in a vigorous manner in the hope to eventually *be* a healthy man. The form of the erotic between Bruce Reis and his patient in Chapter 9 was of alter-egos who could feel Eros with each other. I would see the 'braving' here in Reis's fluidity in inhabiting his own adolescent self in being with his patient.

Emil Jackson offers his work with two late adolescent females in Chapter 10, which at times felt close to explosive for him. It is an interesting counterpoint to consider the pair male therapist/young female patient here and female therapist/young male patient in my case in Chapter 2. While of course

6 Mary T. Brady

the genders of the pair always have to be seen as unconsciously determined (e.g., when is my patient or am I experiencing myself as a man), the power of cultural forces re gender and sexuality is palpable in this territory. Celenza (2011) reports that 7–9% of male therapists and 2–3% of female therapists acknowledge sexual boundary violations with patients. This is a shockingly high number and the higher prevalence of transgressing male therapists may particularly burden male therapists who are trying to work in a responsible and emotionally open manner with their patients.

Graciela Kohen-Abdala offers us in Chapter 11 the analysis of a four-year-old traumatically sexually over-stimulated child. She poses the challenge that the sexually 'traumatic situation must emerge into the transference in order to be analysed and, at the same time, it generates in us an emotional storm…'. She uses the framework of erotic/eroticized/perverse transferences to consider this material.

I conclude the book with 'brother and sister' chapters on the avoidance of the erotic in the treatment of adolescents. Drew Tillotson's Chapter 12 focuses on a gay male late adolescent and my Chapter 13 on a late adolescent female.

I do not introduce these chapters at length here, because I have chosen to offer the reader some integrating considerations at the beginning of each chapter.

In our work, we accompany a child or adolescent's most nascent thoughts and feelings. Sometimes what we find is delicate and beautiful. The topic of this book is the most sensitive of these nascent thoughts and feelings – the child or adolescent's beginning sexual feelings. Just as there is no infant without a mother, there is no real way for sexuality to develop without an object to receive it. Perhaps to catch it like a ball which has been tossed and to toss it lightly back, up in the air – held by neither, yet belonging to both.

References

Baranger, M., & Baranger, W. (2008). The analytic situation as a dynamic field. *International Journal of Psychoanalysis, 89*, 795–826.

Bolognini S. (1994). Transference: Erotized, erotic, loving, affectionate. *International Journal of Psychoanalysis, 75*, 73–86.

Brady, M.T. (2016). *The Body in Adolescence: Psychic Isolation and Physical Symptoms.* New York, NY: Routledge.

Brady, M.T. (2018). *Analytic Engagements with Adolescents: Sex, Gender and Subversion.* Abingdon & New York, NY: Routledge.

Brady, M.T. (2019). International Psychoanalytic Association Congress, London, U.K. July 26, 2019 Presenter: "The Erotic Field in the Treatment of Children and Adolescents," with Anne Alvarez (London), Chris Lovett & Kim Boyd (Boston).

Celenza, A. (2011). *Sexual Boundary Violations: Therapeutic, Supervisory and Academic Contexts.* New York, NY: Rowman Littlefield.

Civitarese, G. (2010). *The Intimate Room: Theory and Technique of the Analytic Field.* London: Routledge.

Elise, D. (2019). *Creativity and the Erotic Dimensions of the Analytic Field.* London: Routledge.

Ferro, A. (1999). *The Bi-personal Field: Experiences in Child Analysis.* London: Routledge.

Molinari, E. (2017). *Field Theory in Child and Adolescent Psychoanalysis: Understanding and Reacting to Unexpected Developments.* Abingdon/New York, NY: Routledge.

Moss, D. (2012). *Thirteen Ways of Looking at a Man: Psychoanalysis and Masculinity.* New York, NY: Routledge.

Ogden, T.H. (1994). The analytic third: Working with intersubjective clinical facts. *International Journal of Psychoanalysis, 75,* 3–19.

Ogden, T.H. (1995). Analyzing forms of aliveness and deadness of the transference-countertransference. *International Journal of Psychoanalysis, 76,* 695–709.

Person, E. (1985). The erotic transference in women and in men: Differences and consequences. *Journal of the American Academy of Psychoanalysis and Psychiatry, 13,* 159–180.

Searles, H. (1958). Oedipal love in the countertransference. *International Journal of Psychoanalysis, 40,* 180–190.

Editor's Introduction to:
Types of sexual transference and countertransference in psychotherapeutic work with children and adolescents

Anne Alvarez's chapter is first in this volume because it is the seminal paper (Alvarez, 2010) on erotic transference and countertransference with children and adolescents. She notes that her train of thought began when supervising the treatments of sexually abused or abusing children. She noticed moments when hints of 'normal' sexuality developed amidst more disturbed sexuality in the children. She takes up the themes of 'perverse', 'disordered', 'addictive', or 'emerging healthy' sexuality in these children.

For the most part, the children in this chapter arrived at treatment with these troubles and for these troubles. In this way, there is some difference from a field of shared dreaming (such as that I describe in Chapter 2), where it is difficult to say, 'Whose feeling is it?' We could say that depictions of 'perverse' or 'disordered' sexuality are more character studies than ensemble pieces. But Alvarez has a passionate mind, so she is never just standing back and commenting. Alvarez is also sensitive to when such sexual formations are in fact, defensive – the child's effort to scare instead of being scared.

The work in this chapter comes from a Kleinian Object Relations perspective and not from a Field Theory perspective, but one could easily translate it. Alvarez and the other talented therapists in her chapter are aware of 'attracting' their patients out of addictive and stuck states of mind. At other times they are absorbing/bearing the projected disturbance until there can be room for 'attracting' to other possibilities. One could easily begin to imagine a shared sordid dream that briefly yields to a trial romance – or back again.

One of the pleasures of this chapter is that Alvarez brings the sexuality of the infant and the young child to life – in concert with the despair, contempt, boredom or a thousand other states that intermingle with the erotic. Alvarez nods to Freud's 'polymorphous perverse' sexuality of childhood, but does not rest there. Every child analyst or parent knows the delight that accompanies the young child's use of the word 'butt'.

DOI: 10.4324/9781003266303-1

Sexual transference & countertransference 9

Alvarez credits Klein with the move to seeing childhood sexuality in relation to an object. She notes that this focus on the object/breast can't quite capture the object 'whose eyes I want to light up'.

The reader may notice Alvarez's frequent use of questions. It is the way her mind works and why she engages us so. She is always asking, questioning, ever ready to be surprised anew. A receptive mind and eyes for a child to see her/his body/mind reflected in.

1 Types of sexual transference and countertransference in psychotherapeutic work with children and adolescents[1]

Anne Alvarez

I became interested in the whole question of normal sexuality during the supervision of therapists treating severely sexually abused, or in many cases, sexually offending, patients (Woods, 2003; Cottis, 2009). I then began to wonder whether I was recognizing it in my own traumatized or corrupted child patients. It is an interesting and delicate moment during the process of recovery when less perverse, more normal sexuality appears mixed with, or sometimes even disguised by, the more habitual perverse fantasies. I shall have to start with some writings in the adult field first. There is relatively little written about what has been called post-Oedipal sexuality in the child field. A few writers in the field of adult psychoanalytic work have drawn distinctions between perverse, eroticized and normal erotic transferences (Wrye and Welles, 1989; Bonasia, 2001). Some have also distinguished between counter-transferences in the analyst of an erotized versus a normal erotic nature (Davies, 1998; Gerrard, 2004, 2010). I want to think about whether these issues could have any relevance for our child patients. Freud (1905) and Klein (1945) have taught us much about the child's sexuality in relation to his interest in and attraction to his parents as sexual beings. But can we also detect some origins in earlier experiences in infancy of the child's later capacity to feel himself a sexual being capable of being wanted by another? How might such a feeling of sexual self-worth differ from narcissism?

A brief history of psychoanalytic ideas on childhood sexuality

Just as Freud widened the term 'mental' to include processes which took place in the unconscious part of the mind, so did he hugely widen the term 'sexual'. First, he widened it beyond the sphere of the genital, to include various perverse impulses, which he found appearing in the fantasies and dreams of patients who did not practice such pursuits in their actual lives. He concluded that sexuality had many manifestations besides simply the genital union of coitus, and that the origin of these non-genital activities and phantasies lay in a pre-genital period in earliest infancy, a period of what he called polymorphous

DOI: 10.4324/9781003266303-2

perversity. The source or instinct had an aim, and the aim was release of tension. At that early period of psychoanalysis, the objects of the aim, that is, other people, were seen as of relatively little importance (Freud, 1905). Tensions arose, as it were, in their own right, in the erogenous zones, where membranes were sensitive, such as the mouth, the anus and also the genital area: they were described rather like itches that needed scratching. Yet the later case study of Little Hans, like other case histories of Freud's, gives a very different, richer, more subtle impression: we read of painful conflicts between jealousy and tender love, for example (Freud, 1910).

Freud (1905) also identified what he called certain component instincts such as voyeurism, exhibitionism, sadism and masochism which although perverse, only became perversions if they subsequently became fixed and exclusive pre-occupations. Jones (1967: 317) says that Lord Tansey asked why Freud hadn't used a word like 'love' or 'desire for union', where he might have avoided the odium that came down on him for suggesting that infants were sexual, even perversely sexual beings. And in one way, with the hindsight of later studies and later theories, we too can feel irritated at the apparent pathologizing – or even perversizing, if there is such a word – of the love-life of babies. But in another way, Freud was doing the exact opposite – attempting to find the normal elemental threads in the pathological. The problem is that the normal in the normal infant was conceptualized in the language of pathology. We still sometimes do it. We could try some alternatives, to respond to Tansey. Nowadays, instead of polymorphous perversity, we might want to use a word that conveys the global passionateness of babies, the way when they greet someone, their excitement and delight shows in every bit of their bodies. They greet us, as adults do, with smiling eyes and mouths, but they also welcome us most eloquently with their circling hands and wriggling feet.

Freud thought that integration, when it came, arrived through the Oedipus Complex, at around age three, whereas we would nowadays understand that it is the sheer otherness of the parents (even at the two-person, pre-Oedipal stage of earliest infancy) that first induces integration. The normal baby is attracted to his objects, and if they give him time to ponder and linger over his experience, this in itself is highly integrating. I shall also remind us that he is also attractive to them.

But back to some limitations in the Freud's concept of 'component in-stincts'. Here, a century ago, is William James' bow to complexity.

> The traditional psychologist talks like one who says a river consists of nothing but pailsful, spoonsful, quartpotfuls, barrelsful, and other moulded forms of water. Even were the pails and pots all actually standing in the stream, still between them the free water would flow. It is precisely the free water of consciousness (we could add, of unconsciousness too) that psychologists resolutely overlook. Every definite image in the mind is steeped and dyed in the free water that flows around it. With it goes the sense of its relations, near and remote, the dying echo of when it came to

12 *Anne Alvarez*

us, the dawning sense of whither it is to lead. The significance, the value of the image, is all in this halo or penumbra that surrounds and escorts it, – or rather that is fused into one with it and has become bone of its bone and flesh of its flesh.

(James 1992, cited in Crapanzano, 2004)

Even the brain researchers and geneticists are warning us of the danger of thinking too much in terms of pails. The modern brain models and genetic models are extremely detailed, and they are not simple. They describe an awesome complexity (Solms and Turnbull, 2002; Alhanati, 2002). Of course, we cannot entirely dispense with pails either, but a word such as elements or aspects of sexual feeling seems better – or the notion that some feelings and thoughts take place in the forefront of our minds while others remain in the background, not always unconscious, maybe only preconscious as Sandler and Sandler (1994) have suggested. Maybe another term could be paraconscious – existing beside but a bit in the shadow as it were.

Freud, of course, did also have something to say about normal adult sexuality. Although in the *Three Essays* (1905) he did leave room for two currents in human libidinal life, the sensual-erotic and the affectionate. Likierman (2001: 90) points out that he did not regard the affectionate current as a primary, irreducible force. We had to wait for Klein to get that. Fornari has suggested (quoted in Lupinacci, 1998: 411) that the discovery of infantile sexuality dazzled Freud so much that it overshadowed his vision of adult sexuality – specifically of the transition, at the moment of sexual and emotional maturation, from the infantile type of sexuality, 'to the real existence of two genitals bound by a relationship of reciprocal symmetry. Lupinacci (p. 411), agreeing with Fornari, says that 'we have here the idea of a creative and civilized complementary state of structures and functions in the male and female, in which each member of the couple taken individually, is limited and dependent, needs the other and has in turn something to give to the other, to the mutual advantage of both' (1998: 411).

Phillips (1993) makes a related point about the nature of kissing, particularly in adolescents. He points out that there is more to kissing than the elements of sucking or eating. He suggests there is also the return of the primary sensuous experience of tasting another person, and that the kiss is the image of reciprocity, not of domination. 'When we kiss, we devour the object by caressing it; we eat it, in a sense, but sustain its presence. Kissing on the mouth can have a mutuality that blurs the distinction between giving and taking' (1993: 102–103).

Klein, while holding to Freud's theory, in fact replaced the notion of component instincts with the notion of part-objects. The power of the otherness of people to attract us and affect our development was being emphasized. As is well known, the breast as the primary object of need and of desire became the focal point of Kleinian theory, although Klein also said that the baby took in understanding along with the milk.

Later, Bion (1962) wrote of the existence of a preconception in the new-born baby of a mind, what O'Shaughnessy calls an object that gives psychological containment, a psychological object (O'Shaughnessy, 2006). Klein also wrote of the baby's interest in the mother's face and hands, but it is only now that we know that interest in people's faces arrive as early on the scene as the interest in breasts and bottles, that is, immediately after birth on day one (Hobson, 2002). I love the developmental research by Bion, but we can see that moving up the body from genitals to faces and even minds may take us a bit away from sexuality. In any case, Klein taught that these early experiences of love and hate towards the primary object coloured and influenced the later developments in the Oedipal phase (Klein, 1945).

Green (2000), who has questioned whether infant observation and child development research has anything at all to contribute to psychoanalysis, is equally critical of what he sees as the Kleinian emphasis on infancy and what he thinks is its consequent neglect of sexuality. He certainly gets eloquently vituperative on the subject of infant research. He asked, 'What of the researcher who no longer calls the parent of the infant the love object, but rather "the caregiver"? Do caregivers have sexual desires, do they love, do they hate, do they have fantasies, do they dream – who cares?' (p. 58). And in a paper asking whether sexuality has anything to do with psychoanalysis, Green suggests, 'The contemporary and fashionable focus on object relations, pregenital fixations, borderline pathology and theories and techniques drawn from observations of child development have obscured the meaning and importance of sexuality in psychoanalytic theory and practice' (1995: 871). He also says (1995: 876) that even the penis started to be seen as a giving and feeding organ, in other words a breast. He maintains that the role of a sexual relationship is not to feed and nurture but to reach ecstasy in mutual enjoyment. He thinks that the anal, oral, or in other terminologies, the depressive position and the paranoid-schizoid position being seen as older or deeper, means that they are equated with being more important. He says that this reflects 'an anti-sexual attitude which implies that sexuality is superficial' (p. 879). Vituperation aside, Green also makes a very interesting theoretical point. He says, that as a result of Freud's great paper, Beyond the Pleasure Principle (1920), 'We have focussed on death instincts, but Freud, instead of sexual instincts, speaks of life instinct. Life or love instincts' (p. 877). And he says we have neglected this. I think he may have a point there. But Edwards (2010) has pointed out that is not the case in Klein's (1958) paper 'On the development of mental functioning'.

I want to take account of Green's criticisms but to argue that he has left something else important out about Kleinian theory. As is well known, Segal (1957/1981) is responsible for the distinction in psychoanalytic theory between a symbolic equation and a symbol. The symbol is used not to deny but to overcome loss (1957/1981: 57). It is worth mentioning that the concept of symbolization is different from the Freudian concept of sublimation, because symbolization doesn't simply describe a transformation, that is, a change in the form of expression of an impulse or instinct, it involves a more fundamental

14 *Anne Alvarez*

change, that which results from a process of mourning and growth via internalization. It involves facing the pain of the loss that the little girl can never marry daddy, nor be mummy, the little boy can never marry mummy nor be daddy. We have all had patients whose lives have been driven and ruined by a difficulty in accepting such relegation. Symbol-formation is costly: it involves relinquishing possession of, or narcissistic identification with, the primary object, and also, at the Oedipal level, relinquishing the role of being a full intrusive 'member of the wedding' so that, as the American writers I will mention term it, post-Oedipal sexuality can appear in its own right. Even if it is the case that many papers have concentrated on patients whose level of illness involves pre-Oedipal problems, I think Kleinian theory – with its concept of the depressive position, and also its distinction between pathological and healthy types of identification with the sexuality of the parents – leaves plenty of room for sexuality.

One point I do wish to make, however, is that Kleinian thinking tends to lay stress on the self's feelings for the object. But what about the self's phantasies of the object's feelings, even sexual feelings, for it? How are we to think about both aspects of the sexuality of our child patients? Can we distinguish between narcissistic self-evaluation and something like a feeling of sexual self-worth (Gerrard, 2004) which is sufficiently comfortable to enable self-forgetfulness, not narcissistic self-preoccupation?

The question of the normal erotic transference and countertransference

Gabbard (1994: 1083), noted that the psychoanalytic literature (since Searles in 1959) had been remarkably silent on the subject of erotic countertransference feelings. He made the interesting point that sexualization may defend against feelings of love (p. 1091), which he said are relatively more difficult for many analysts to acknowledge than lustful feelings. He said that the value of consultation with a colleague cannot be overemphasized, but that, only by tip-toeing to the edge of that abyss can we fully appreciate the internal world of the patient and its impacts on us.

Davies (1998) a relational analyst, goes into the abyss. She explores the concept of 'post-Oedipal adult sexuality' and suggests that it challenges the fundamental assumption that, whenever erotic feelings enter the psychoanalytic space, the analyst always stands in the role of the Oedipal parent. She says that this can fail to recognize significant developmental changes. Gerrard (2004, 2010), an English adult psychotherapist, takes a line similar to Davies who points out that Oedipal desire is romantic and idealized, whereas post-Oedipal desire tolerates imperfections, and can experience disappointment without the death of desire.

Davies is talking about, not eroticized and therefore pathological infantile transferences, but what she calls 'that form of sexual aliveness that most often … marks the termination phase of an analysis … with the deepening

Sexual transference & countertransference 15

intimacy and potential interpersonal space of successful analytic work'. She agrees with Searles (1959) that this involves a kind of mourning and relinquishment on the part of the analyst, a letting go of the patient to have his own adult sexual life. But she is stressing something more than the letting go: that is, the analyst's responsiveness to the patient's possibly new aliveness, in particular in her paper when the new aliveness first appears in a patient who was previously dead to his sexuality. Something similar may happen in despairing children and adolescents when they experience a new vitality. Davies' patient was an abused and previously profoundly depressed man who pointed out one day after he was finally beginning to show signs of recovery, that she was flirting with him. She became aware that she had been. Then we have to wait to hear what happened.

Davies proceeds to discuss the difference between the Oedipal child and the post-Oedipal child (1998: 753) – who is struggling to experience the self as the object of another's sexual interest when the other is not the Oedipally idealized parent figure (p. 759). Davies suggests that the post-Oedipal parent is in a constant state of experiencing, processing and recognizing his or her child's emerging sexuality and that the child is most acutely tuned into the parents' ongoing struggle. But back to the previously depressed patient who saw she was flirting with him. Davies then disclosed to him that she had indeed been flirting. Her patient asked her what those people who wrote those books behind her would think of that. She suggested they explore this, and then he became nervous and wished to close the door on the subject. They returned to it in subsequent sessions. My own view is that I agree with Davies' suggestion regarding the task of the post-Oedipal parent (in life or in the countertransference), but I think there is a way for the therapist which need not involve actual disclosure. I think Davies could have said something like 'You are beginning to feel you are a person that people feel like flirting with'. I agree with her that a simple falling back on shoulds and shouldn'ts doesn't get us very far with deprived patients, and that it is important to be receptive, but I think myself that it is not helpful to make the situation too over-heated for the patient. I think disclosure could really overburden any patient.

Nevertheless, I think Davies' and Gerrard's ideas on the role of the post-Oedipal parent in development are very interesting. One word about flirting: flirting need not be seen as a purely seductive act. If it is occurring on the symbolic level, it can involve a type of playing, of acknowledging attraction but under safe conditions where the internal Oedipal triangle of which Britton (2003: 55) has spoken of is kept intact, respected and acknowledged.

The question is, is there anything at all relevant in these papers for psychoanalytic work with children? These are clearly delicate issues, especially now that we are so much better informed about the ubiquity of sexual abuse of children. I want to ask some questions, and I shall also offer some speculation about some possible pre-Oedipal origins of sexuality which may link some developmental research with sexuality. The research can be wonderfully illuminating, but much of it (not all) has neglected babies' bodies, and it has

16   *Anne Alvarez*

certainly neglected infantile sexuality. But some of the newer work may have some relevance to these questions.

I shall begin with an attempt, through clinical examples from children, to distinguish perverse sexuality from disordered sexuality, and both of these from normal but delayed Oedipal sexuality. I shall follow this with an example in which a budding adolescent sexuality allowed some important pre-Oedipal history to be rewritten via the post-Oedipal sexuality ... I shall discuss the issue of the developmental implications of the parents' response to all of these levels for the way in which we transform and use the feelings at each of these levels in the countertransference. At the post-Oedipal stage, I am wondering about psychoanalytic technique in the presence of a child's real sexual feelings and sexual self, as opposed to when the child is sexualizing some other feeling for defensive purposes.

An example of perverse sexuality in a child

Seven-year-old 'David' was diagnosed with Pervasive Developmental Disorder with autistic features. He was delayed in language, thinking and symbolic capacities. The therapist gradually learned that he also had a foot fetish. I had noted that several therapists had started wearing sandals during the first warm week of summer, and there had been major reactions from almost all their patients whom I heard about in supervision. Some reactions were more radical than others. This one child, David, began looking at his therapist's feet in sandals with a terrible leer. He accused her of having smelly feet, but he was clearly staring at them with a horrible fascination. Also (and we came to think this was very important), although his leer seemed to accuse her of collusion (i.e., of liking being dirty and disgusting), it also seemed to invite loathing and disgust for him on her part. Thus, there was something cruel and sadistic but also quite masochistic in it. I had seen an almost fetishistic pre-occupation with feet in certain deprived children, and although David's therapist and I discussed the possible origin of the original preoccupation in the history of babies: babies left too much on the carpet watching feet come and go but never seeming to stop long enough, and yet never able to be forgotten about, because the baby was never enough up on the lap and looking at faces. But there was clearly far more to it than a reaction to, or defence against pain. We talked a lot about David's own feeling of being loathed by and disgusting to his mother, which had been real, but also about what now seemed to have become the dangerously addictive quality of his preoccupation. This boy's leer evoked disgust. It was a bit similar to the way in which my own autistic patient 'Robbie' could look at me not lustfully, but so lasciviously that although I felt no fear, I felt a powerful desire to brush him off.

Uriah Heep and Caliban know they are despised. Making yourself ugly and distasteful is better than submitting to seeing that in someone else's eyes, as Sinason (1992: 119) has noted with physically disabled children. The child's pleasure in getting the disgust he expected and what he sought may even, in

Sexual transference & countertransference   17

the worst cases, turn into sexual excitement. We puzzled a lot about this child. We were certain he was not sexually abused, and we wondered a lot, not about how he came to feel disgusting, nor about why he might try to project that feeling into others, but about how he might have discovered the final twist upwards into the excitement.

The following material provides no answers, but it does at least give a sense of the steps in the progression of what amounts to a perversion.

David had been considerably improved in recent months, much less interested in feet, and much more interested in normal, although for his age (which was six and a half), rather immature play: this play had given him genuine pleasure and delight, but not perverse excitement. Sometimes there had even been real symbolic play. On this occasion, he greeted his therapist whom I shall call Cathy, quite normally in the waiting room, with only the briefest of glances at her feet, while the look at her face as he greeted her was more lingering. The session started with one of these new, immature, but more normal pieces of play. He began by sitting on the swivelling office chair in her consulting room. He spun, and the game involved a situation where she would stop it intermittently, and say, 'There you are!' at which point he would giggle and spin it again. It was a kind of peek-a-boo, and Urwin (2002) has suggested the appearance of this game often signals the child's emergence from autistic states. The therapist wrote, 'At times his grin seems somewhat fixed and slightly grimace-like, although his giggle seems more real'. It was vital for her to monitor the difference in order not to collude with or escalate the more perverse moments. However, we must also leave room for our receptive response to more ordinary excitements when they finally come, for children who have previously known only the perverse kind. Otherwise, we collude with the despairing patient's view that there are only two choices, the thrill of perversion or the emptiness of a too sober normality. They play this spinning game for a little while and at one point David spun the chair very fast, thereby bumping his knee on the therapist's chair quite hard. He then squealed in an excited laugh. The therapist knew about David's language delay, and tended to keep her language simple but emotive, so she simply said sympathetically, 'Ohh, ouch'. But David immediately ordered, 'Cry, Cathy!' She said, that 'you bumped your knee, but you want me to cry and that I wonder why you want Cathy to cry'. He says, 'stu-pid' and laughs. She said, 'I think David thinks it's stupid to cry but it's not stupid to cry if it hurts'. She had many times before witnessed his cruel mockery of an injured child doll, but he may also have felt she was stupid not to get it that she was the one who should contain the projective identification, to suffer the hurt and do the crying for him. (Usually, by the way, she did.) In any case, the way in which he responded to her insistence that it was not stupid to cry was to announce with a leer that that he's smelled 'the guinea pig's feet'.

I think we can see here some of the steps in the progression to a fetish fairly clearly. First, David is hurt, then he tries to project the hurt into his therapist, then when she doesn't fully contain it in herself, he feels overwhelming

18 *Anne Alvarez*

self-disgust, and then the smelly feet have to belong to someone else, the guinea pig. A hurt baby self isn't just despicable, it is apparently also disgusting. And what do you do with a profound feeling of self-disgust? One way through is to project and control the disgust. How it got to the final stage of perverse erotization in this child's development, however, we never quite understood. What is clear is that the technical response to a perverse moment needs to be very different from that to a defensive or protective manoeuvre, and certainly from that to more ordinary excitements (Alvarez, 1995).

I want to move on now to two examples of disordered, but not precisely perverse, sexuality. An autistic patient of mine had a repetitive preoccupation with making two dolls dance or jump up and down together while seeming to talk to each other in a pseudo-language. The game was far too private and exclusive to be called real pretend play, the jumps occurred always in one spot, and even the dance involved only the tiniest of circles around the dancers. There were never any leaps, because I think, there was felt to be nowhere interesting to go. Anxiety about the unknown was not the problem, I believe – the deepest of boredoms was. There was simply nothing or nowhere interesting enough to pursue (this may involve the difference between devalued and unvalued or stupid objects: Alvarez, 2006). On one occasion, Joseph came in, in what appeared to be a really quite loving mood towards me, and this time the animals kissed each other very gently on the side of the face, laying their cheeks against each other and murmuring tendernesses. I did not feel this was perverse at all, and not even overly sensuous, but the point was, it didn't stop. It went on and on and on and on, and I began to think, it had started with what seemed like real love, but even Antony and Cleopatra must have got up occasionally and gone out for a breath of fresh air and a good long walk!!! The behaviour was addictive, but not actually perverse, but this certainly raises important technical issues concerning how to unstick the patient from his habitual ways and to help him to move on.

This next example is from another case of my own, where I also think the sexuality is disordered, but not (as yet) perverse. As Viviane Green pointed out (personal communication) this is very much part of the Anna Freudian way of thinking. Disordered would be viewed as a lack of phase dominance where there is no age-related expectable stable dominance of a libidinal phase. This little boy, Michael, was, like David, very turned on by my first sandal day: he lunged across the room, with the set closed grim mouth which I had learned held in a desire to bite I suspect this began to occur when he was two months old and refused feeding when his mother went back to work for a month soon after he had recovered – physically, but not mentally – from a series of traumatizing surgical operations. He had often tried to grab my knees with that look and attempt to press his penis against me. And after a quick glance at my feet, he tried to do the same thing again. I felt he was experiencing a very confused overwhelming, half suppressed and hugely compressed set of impulses – oral and genital all at once but all of it somehow terribly condensed. I tried to clarify this a bit, but he was a child whom it was very difficult to slow down and to help to experience feelings one at a time, as it were. In any case, a few days later, a little calmer, he looked again at my feet very intensely, and asked if he could bite my toes!! There seemed to be no genital excitement this time, and I felt this was a bit of a development – there was only one desire, that to bite, and at least he could allow himself to experience it instead of suppressing it. Subsequently, returning from a summer break, he heard what he took to be a man's footsteps upstairs. He had always scampered to the other side of the room when he heard them. Michael was a very omnipotent and Oedipal child but his fear of a father was compounded, I think, by the early radical and intrusive surgical interventions. I spoke of his fear of the Daddy especially when he was being so possessive and bossy with me today. Towards the end of the session he observed, both that the couch was not really a bed, and that I did actually not go home with him or travel with him on holiday. He also asked a question about what might be upstairs, and I felt that another space/place was opening up. Klein suggested this referred to the mystery of the inside of the mother's body. Crapanzano (2004), an anthropologist, referred to the significance of that which lay beyond the horizon – imaginative horizons (see Britton, 1989; Edwards, 1994 on the sense of space within the Oedipal triangle, opening up). I am suggesting that the powerful compression of Michael's passions was disordered, but not really perverse. When he could slow down to experience one passion at a time, as it were, he could experience curiosity and think.

The normal sexual self and questions of technique: use of our countertransference responses

Lupinacci (1998: 418) offered some interesting ideas on the role of the two sets of parents in the Oedipus myth. She pointed out that the narcissistic egocentric Theban parents tried to kill their infant, out of fear of his hostility, and that the Corinthian adoptive parents, while kind and loving, are somewhat idealized and sexless. She pointed out that both need integrating in the patient, or the child, but also in the analyst at work. She described the need for the analyst to struggle with his own Oedipal impulses and to integrate his or her softer Corinthian aspects with his firmer Theban ones in order to facilitate the patient's integration. Lupinacci, like Klein (1945), locates the origins of the Oedipal fantasies of their patients in earlier pre-Oedipal experiences with the early mother and breast. Her technical recommendations have much in common with Britton's (1989) comments on the parents' response to the child's Oedipal or pre-Oedipal feelings in the course of development. But it is clear that Davies (1998) goes further than attention to a soft warm maternal countertransference response. She is clear that she is speaking of a normal erotic countertransference to the post-Oedipal adult sexuality occurring in the patient.

Up till now, I have been talking about developments in sexual feelings in the self towards a sexual object; now I want to look at the question of the

20 *Anne Alvarez*

development of the self as a sexual being as an object of others' sexuality. I suggest that although this is partly linked to the baby's gradual identification with the parents, it is also likely to be linked with early developments of the baby's feeling of being potent enough to awaken responses, interest, delight in the caregiver. In this view parents do not only satisfy basic bodily needs for food and holding. Nor do they offer only mental containment. Laznik (2009) is interesting on the importance of the normal cannibalistic impulses that parents feel towards the edibility of their babies. Green's (1995) possible contention that this is a privileging of early infancy misses the point that feelings of sexual self-worth in adulthood may have origins in and be traceable back to infancy. Clearly, as I just implied, symbol formation and a resultant capacity for identifications (not pathological over-identifications) with the sexuality of the parents plays a huge part, but is there something else too? Are there some elements which need to be examined in addition to the familiar ones concerning the importance of feelings towards the breast, and the facial and vocal reciprocity we hear so much about from the developmentalists? Is there room for actual infantile sexuality, without reducing sexuality to dependency or infantile needs?

First, I want to mention the sense of agency and potency (not omnipotence) (Alvarez, 1992). Studies have shown that babies enjoy finding that they can be the cause of events and become considerably withdrawn when they fail and experience a feeling of inefficacy (Papousek and Papousek, 1975). The studies let the babies make bells ring and lights come on, but we know that the main causal effects for the baby take place in his interactions with human beings. It is fun to make rattles shake, and any sort of stuff happen, but in the earliest months, one of several things that matters most is to be able to make someone's eyes light up. The capacity to entertain and give delight is being studied by Trevarthen (2001) and by Reddy (2008), and I want to stress that this relationship is different from the need for a feeding or even a containing object in either the Bion (1962) or Bick (1968) sense: it concerns the need for a responsive interested object capable of being delighted. Here is an observation of a baby with a certainly good enough mother, who had in the first seven months of his life seemed a little too passively accepting of his mother's busyness with other things. Around eight months as she prepared to return to work, the two seemed to have formed a stronger and more vital bond. He had found more power to attract and keep her attention through smiles, coos and vocalizations, and she seemed to have more desire to be thus captivated. Then at nine months they were both just beginning to recover from the flu and quite subdued again. The baby tried two different methods of getting his mother to gaze at him and to respond. Both methods failed, but it is the difference in the methods to which I wish to attend. First, he cried a few times, but gave up when his mother carried on with her weary tidying in his room and did not respond. (His cries had never been long or loud.) Then, at a moment when he saw her standing in front of him looking vaguely in his direction, he smiled widely and blew a raspberry; a month before, she would have laughed and/or imitated him, but now she

Sexual transference & countertransference 21

simply continued looking beyond him at something in the room. He then turned over to his dummy and went to sleep. The crying baby asks for comfort, the smiling and performing baby asks for something like delight, to bring a light to someone's eyes. This need not involve a manic defence. He needs comfort, but he also needs an accessible and reachable object; impressible, interested, pleased to be entertained (Trevarthen, 2001; Reddy, 2008). Elsewhere I suggested we need a word for a process which may be a foundation for, and a prelude to reparation – the wish to give something to someone, not in order to repair a damaged object, but to add to the pleasure of an already intact object (Alvarez, 1992).

Trevarthen thinks the emotions of shame and pride shown in infancy are central to development (2001). Bion distinguished between arrogance and pride (1957) as did the Greeks between hubris and philotomo (Lynd, 1958). A very depressed boy had in the past had been very skilled, like David, at getting attention by behaving or speaking in a manner designed to evoke disgust, but did not know how to use more ordinary methods of getting attention. After a few years of treatment where he had given up his old ways, he said one day to his therapist, 'I like it when your eyes are wide'. It seemed to mean that then he could be sure that she was interested. This involves an early integration between both self and object but also within the self – 'I have the power to make an impact (a positive impact) on you'. It arises as an important development in children recovering from lifelong depression, and it is important to be clear when we are seeing simple manipulative and narcissistic seductiveness, and when we are seeing a desire to show and give pleasure rather than simply to show off to make someone else feel inferior or helplessly ensnared. Attracting need not involve seducing.

Childhood sexuality: the question of the parental objects' role

What is the line between an all too seducible parent and one who allows the sexuality without being seduced or seductive? A child, or for that matter, a baby can feel himself capable of giving pleasure to others. How can we respond to showing, without encouraging showing off and narcissism? How can we facilitate self-forgetful showing where the thing or activity being shown is more important than the shower, but the shower is appreciated too?

A clinical example of delayed Oedipal development

A little boy patient of mine, Toby, had been born blind in one eye, a condition which necessitated several operations. He recovered, was cared for by his very devoted parents and his trauma from the surgery and limitations on his early life was not as terrible as it might have been. However, he was a difficult child, and at times his feeling of being extremely precious to his objects was compounded by an arrogant feeling of being special, and all too precious in the

22 *Anne Alvarez*

other sense. However, as he began to feel stronger psychologically (he already was quite recovered physically) his masculine identification started to grow. At age six, just before a break, he developed a taste for pop music, and performed with a great stamping of feet, and a certain macho thrust to his gait, the song, 'Don't stop thinkin' about the S club beat!! Also, he roared, 'Super star, with your big guitar!' not exactly sexily but with a new sort of stomping vitality. He was really monitoring my expression, and I am sure it showed some pleasure; it was so much more spontaneous than his usual very controlling approach in the room. He seemed to be having something of a recovery from a deep sense of damage and helplessness and was showing me his slightly delayed, Oedipal (and still quite narcissistic) potency and sexuality. I found myself thinking that it could be very difficult for the parents of a baby born in such danger to see him as potent and to allow themselves the safety and confidence to dream of his future as a healthy strong and sexy man, a dream every male child probably needs his parents to have for him. Here we need to be interested, not in the acorn in the oak tree, the baby self in the adult, but the oak tree in the acorn. I wonder now if their capacity or his mother's capacity to find him attractive as a baby was limited by his facial imperfection. What you would feel looking at him was concern, which is not the same as the parent's pleasure and pride in her baby's healthy body and face.

I think this raises the question of the importance of the positive counter-transference. I enjoyed this dancing, although my response, though positive, was not particularly erotic. Another child whom I saw some years ago at the clinic, Nicola, had been extremely deprived and rejected in her infancy and had become chronically depressed but also dissociated and hard in spite of having been adopted at eighteen months by very loving parents. There came a point when, after about a year of treatment, at age 11, she showed me a dance she was doing at school and also some steps from the one the older girls were doing. Her dancing gave me a new pleasure – she seemed much softer, shyer and less defended than usual – the dancing was modest, but the lightness and grace and yet sexiness was very attractive, and I am sure my eyes and face – and my words – showed my pleasure and appreciation of this new her. I do not think she was being seductive. I think she was trying out something new in our relationship and trying to give the kind of pleasure she had not been able to give as an infant to her extremely rejecting mother. Puberty was possibly being experienced as a kind of new birth where her painful history could be partially re-written via a tactful appreciation of her newfound attractiveness. Certainly, more work was necessary to move beyond a situation where sexuality could be the main vehicle for positive experiences. She needed to find other ways of opening up and pleasing her objects.

In conclusion, I think there is much work to be done on an exploration of our countertransferences to our patients' bodies, and sexuality, at all the levels, the pre-Oedipal, Oedipal and post-Oedipal. I have speculated on some possible origins of all this in the baby's ability to give pleasure, to make an impact, to entertain by the use of his body, his facial expressions and vocalizations.

I have not had time to discuss his wit and intelligence. When someone makes us laugh or says something intelligent which is not pedantic or exhibitionistic it gives us pleasure and is certainly attractive, and sometimes even sexy. Sometimes the positive transference is harder to take and stay with than the negative – and when it is sexual too, it demands much courage, honesty and respect from us in our countertransference responses.

Acknowledgements

This paper was first presented in a series on *Sexuality* Throughout the Lifespan at the Institute of Psychoanalysis, London in November 2006.

Note

1 I should point out that this chapter was written before I had any acquaintance with Field Theory. It would be interesting if I could relive the sessions with the children described herein to consider how saturated or unsaturated (Bion, 1962: Ferro, 1999) the interpretations made by me and the other therapist might have been in the face of sexual transferences. I would like to think they were fairly unsaturated, as I have for decades been interested in three levels of analytic work, i.e., three levels of ascribing meaning: explanation, description and reclamation/vitalization. The descriptive level relates to questions of ascribing, amplifying or sharing meaning, rather than explaining it. This may bear some resemblance both to the idea of unsaturation and to Winnicott's work in the transitional area where paradoxes are respected.

References

Alhanati, S. (2002). Current trends in molecular genetic research of affective states and psychiatric disorders. In Alhanati, S. (Ed.) *Primitive Mental States. Vol. II.* London: Karnac.

Alvarez, A. (1992). *Live Company: Psychoanalytic Psychotherapy with Autistic, Borderline, Deprived and Abused Children.* London: Routledge.

Alvarez, A. (1995). Motiveless malignity: Problems in the psychotherapy of psychopathic patients. *Journal of Child Psychotherapy, 21* (2), 167–182.

Alvarez, A. (2006). Narzissmus und das dumme object – Entwertung oder Missachtung? Mit einer anmerkung zum Suchtigen und zum manifesten Narzissmus. In Kernberg, O.F. and Hartmann, H-P. (Eds.) *Narzismus: grundlagen – Storungsbilder-Therapie.* Stuttgart: Schattauer.

Alvarez, A. (2010). Types of sexual transference and countertransference in psychotherapeutic work with children and adolescents. *Journal of Child Psychotherapy, 36*(3): 211–224.

Bick, E. (1968). The experience of the skin in early object-relations. *International Journal of Psychoanalysis, 49,* 484–486.

Bion, W.R. (1957). On arrogance. *Second Thoughts.* London: Heinemann.

Bion, W.R. (1962). *Learning from Experience.* London: Heinemann.

Bonasia, R. (2001). The countertransference: Erotic, erotised, and perverse. *International Journal of Psychoanalysis, 82,* 249–262.

Britton, R. (1989). The missing link: Parental sexuality in the Oedipus Complex. In Steiner, J. (Ed.) *The Oedipus Complex Today.* London: Karnac.

24   *Anne Alvarez*

Britton, R. (2003). *Sex, Death, and the Superego*. London: Karnac.

Cottis, T. (2009). *Intellectual Disability, Trauma, and Psychotherapy*. London: Routledge.

Crapanzano, V. (2004). *Imaginative Horizons: An Essay in Literary-Philosophical Anthropology*. Chicago: University of Chicago Press.

Davies, J.M. (1998). Between the disclosure and foreclosure of erotic transference-countertransference: Can psychoanalysis find a place for adult sexuality? *Psychoanalytic Dialogues 8*, 747–766.

Edwards, J. (1994). On solid ground. *Journal of Child Psychotherapy, 20*, 457–483.

Edwards, J. (2010). *Personal Communication*.

Freud, S. (1905). Three essays on sexuality. *Standard Edition of the Complete Works of Sigmund Freud. Vol. VII*, 123–243.

Freud, S. (1910). Analysis of a phobia in a five-year-old boy. *SE, X*, 1–150.

Freud, S. (1920). Beyond the pleasure principle. *SE, XVIII*, 1–64.

Ferro, A. (1999). *The Bi-Personal Field: Experiences in Child Analysis*. London: Routledge.

Gabbard, G.O. (1994). Sexual excitement and countertransference love in the analyst. *Journal of the American Psychoanalytic Association, 42*, 1083–1106.

Gerrard, J. (2004). *Surviving Oedipus*. Unpublished Paper Given to London Centre for Psychotherapy and Lincoln Centre, London.

Gerrard, J. (2010). Seduction and betrayal. *British Journal of Psychotherapy, 26*, 165–180.

Green, A. (1995). Has sexuality anything to do with psychoanalysis? *International Journal of Psychoanalysis, 76*, 871–883.

Green, R. (2000). Science and science fiction in infant research. In Sandler, R., Sandler, R., & Davies, R. (Eds.) *Clinical and Observational Psychoanalytic Research: Roots of a Controversy.* London: Karnac.

Hobson, P. (2002). *The Cradle of Thought*. London: Macmillan.

James, W. (1992). Psychology: A briefer course. *Writings, 1878–1899*, 1–433. New York: Library of America.

Jones, E. (1967). *Sigmund Freud: Life and Work. Vol. II. Years of Maturity*. London: Hogarth.

Klein, M. (1945). The Oedipus Complex in the light of early anxieties. *International Journal of Psychoanalysis, 26*, 11–33.

Klein, M. (1958). On the development of mental functioning. *International Journal of Psychoanalysis, 39*, 84–90.

Laznik, M.C. (2009). The Lacanian theory of the drive: An examination of possible gains for research in Autism. *Journal of the Centre for Freudian Analysis and Research, 19*, 41–62.

Likierman, M. (2001). *Melanie Klein: Her Work in Context*. London: Continuum.

Lupinacci, M.A. (1998). Reflections on the early stages of the Oedipus Complex: The parental couple in relation to psychoanalytic work. *Journal of Child Psychotherapy, 24*, 3409–3422.

Lynd, H.M. (1958). *On Shame and the Search for Identity*. New York: Harcourt Brace and World.

O'Shaughnessy, E. (2006). A conversation about early unintegration, disintegration and integration. *Journal of Child Psychotherapy, 32*, 2153–2157.

Papousek, M., & Papousek, M. (1975). Cognitive aspects of preverbal social interaction between human infants and adults: CIBA Foundation Symposium. *Parent–Infant Interaction*. New York: Association of Scientific Publishers.

Phillips, A. (1993). *On Kissing, Tickling and Being Bored*. London: Karnac.

Reddy, V. (2008). *How Infants Know Minds*. London: Harvard University Press.

Sandler, A.M., & Sandler, A.M. (1994). The past unconscious and the present unconscious: A contribution to a technical frame of reference *Psychoanalytic Study of the Child, 49*, 278–292.

Searles, H. (1959). Oedipal love in the countertranference. *Collected Papers on Schizophrenia and Related Subjects*. New York: International University Press.

Segal, H. (1957). Notes on symbol formation. *The Work of Hanna Segal*. New York: Aronson.

Sinason, V. (1992). *Mental Handicap and the Human Condition*. London: Free Associations Books.

Solms, O., & Turnbull, O. (2002). *The Brain and the Inner World: An Introduction to the Neuroscience of Subjective Experience*. London: Karnac.

Trevarthen, C. (2001). Intrinsic motives for companionship in understanding: Their origin, development, and significance for infant mental health. *Infant Mental Health Journal, 22*, 95–131. (Special Issue: Contributions from the Decade of the Brain to Infant Mental Health).

Urwin, C. (2002). A psychoanalytic approach to language delay: When autistic isn't necessarily autism. *Journal of Child Psychotherapy, 28*: 173–193.

Woods, J. (2003). *Boys Who Have Abused: Psychoanalytic Psychotherapy with Victim/Perpetrators of Sexual Abuse*. London: Jessica Kingsley.

Wrye, J.K., & Welles, J.K. (1989). The maternal erotic transference. *International Journal of Psychoanalysis, 70*, 673–684.

Editor's Introduction to:
Braving the erotic field in the treatment of adolescents

As you will read in the following chapter, I 'rediscovered' Field Theory as I thought about how difficult it was to differentiate my erotic feelings from my patient's. I suggest that the terms erotic transference and countertransference are too static to capture the intense and subtly interactional nature of erotic feelings in a fully engaged analysis and find that the term 'erotic field' better characterizes this development.

The chapter you are about to read differs from the prior one in that sexualized symptoms were not present when Frank entered analysis. Erotic feelings developed in the context of intensive work over a period of years. From a Field Theory perspective this constitutes a 'shared dreaming'[1] of the couple. The use of the terms 'perverse', 'disordered', etc. in the prior chapter describes a symptomatic problem. In that chapter these terms are used to organize the therapist's thinking capacities in order to gather up the emotional distress managed by the symptoms. Civitarese, in Chapter 4, eschews the need for these terms and argues that what one analytic pair may be able to manage and tolerate may be quite different from another pair.

I also introduce the term 'erotic insufficiency' in this chapter. I argue that our rightful concern about sexual boundary violations, (or a timid avoidance of 'taboo' topics), may deprive our child or adolescent patients from an adult mind to accompany them in this territory.

In Chapter 5, Molinari describes her work with an erotic field that encompassed the whole family. She saw unconscious suffering in the parents as highly contributory to their little girl's sexualized symptom and her most important interventions seemed with the parents. Any child treatment (including this treatment which went on from pre-adolescence until age 17) involves a familial field which the analyst joins. In the case you are about to read the mother was chronically depressed and so the boy was lacking a background of erotic vitality with her. Simultaneously, father had been unfaithful and was over-stimulating of his son's sexuality. There was limited headway I could make with these issues in the parents, so the focus of the work was with my patient. I believe that our work allowed an erotic vitality without losing boundaries and so in some ways was a commentary on the

DOI: 10.4324/9781003266303-3

larger familial field, which provided collapsed maternal vitality and insufficient paternal boundaries.

Note

1 In the Bionian sense of 'waking dreaming' (Bion, 1962).

Reference

Bion, W.R. (1962). *Learning from Experience*. London: Heineman.

2 Braving the erotic field in the treatment of adolescents

Mary T. Brady

I have found my patient's body – and my body – to be more directly the subjects of analysis with adolescents than with adults or with younger children. Erotic transference and countertransference can be particularly fraught because of the intensity of emergent bodily sensations in the adolescent and because of her or his normal developmental immaturity. Adolescents need help to name and integrate their newfound bodily experiences. Their minds need to grow into the bodies they now inhabit. It is a challenge for analysts to talk about feelings the adolescent may have barely begun to name. Indeed, budding sexuality and the memories and feelings it stirs in us of our own sexual beginnings are no small things to metabolize. And yet, with rare exceptions, the area of erotic transference/countertransference in the treatment of adolescents is largely ignored in analytic writing.[1]

The catastrophic prospect of boundary violations, particularly with minors, can lead to a timid avoidance of the erotic in our work with adolescents, yielding what I term an 'erotic insufficiency'. The analyst can fear exploiting the trust necessary for an adolescent to bring his or her emerging sexuality into analysis in a lively manner. Feelings that arouse the greatest conflict and guilt in the analyst are precisely those that are most vulnerable to our defensive rejection. In order to consider these ideas, I relate a period in the analysis of a 12-year-old boy when the erotic transference and countertransference were at a height. I also suggest that the terms erotic transference and erotic countertransference do not fully capture the intensely interactional nature of these experiences. I suggest 'erotic field' better conveys this fluidity.

Erotic transferences and countertransferences with younger children can seem comparatively comfortable.[2] One eight-year-old boy fantasized that he was a king, and I, his golden-haired queen, living in a castle together, and that we would never have to part. While the scene I'm describing is only the most conscious aspect of a deeper fantasy, I believe that there are also other reasons why my countertransference response was comparatively easy to bear. I could feel the poignancy of this idyllic picture and sympathize with my patient's frustrations at the inescapable realities of life, such as how old one is, and how old are one's analyst, mother, father, etc. – and how much these exigencies determine. In this familiar oedipal scene, one cannot have what one wants and

DOI: 10.4324/9781003266303-4

yet it is better to have wanted it and even to tolerate knowing that one has wanted it. But, it was also my younger patient's age and related physical immaturity that contributed to a less charged erotic transference/counter-transference than with adolescent patients.

Changing bodies, changing minds

The body of the adolescent is changing radically before his or her own, as well as my eyes. Adolescent boys can shoot up a foot in height over a couple of years. 'Brian', age 13, encountered me in the hallway before a session and said, '(H)ave you always been that short?' His body was new in many ways and led to new experiences in relation to himself and me. Brian and I experienced together his pubertal development and the meanings it shifted within our relationship.

'Naomi', a pubertal girl, having had the puberty/sex talk at school that day, came to her session and asked me with utter sincerity: '(W)hat is puberty for?' I was struck that though I could answer the question in a limited biological sense – the larger psychological and emotional meanings would take years to comprehend.

'Evelyn', a 16–year-old in analysis spoke about being on the verge of having intercourse with her boyfriend. I asked her, '(D)o you think having sex will change anything inside you or between us?' At first, she demurred, but soon said, '(H)aving intercourse will be the end of childhood'. Something would definitely change inside her, as well as between us, and between her and her parents. She would cross a line from her child bodily self to an adult bodily self and there would no longer be a substantive divide between her experiences and those of adults in a sexual sense. Experience would be gained, but a precious boundary that allowed some element of childhood to remain (all too scarce for this girl) would be lost.

Around this time Evelyn asked to use the couch. Her 'use' of the couch[3] was different than any I have experienced. She was in constant motion and reminded me of a seal. She would flip from side to side and then flip over on her stomach to look at me. My experience was of not being able to think with all this motion and I wished Evelyn would just lie still. Evelyn was giving me an experience of how much commotion she felt.

Evelyn had asked to use the couch in order to talk about sexuality. My agreement for her to lie down evoked intimate and erotic feelings in her towards me. Soon after starting to use the couch she told me of making out with her boyfriend in his car for the first time. She said: 'I found myself tracing your initials in the steam on the window'. As we explored this action it seemed that I was both present in Evelyn's erotic feelings *and* that she was summoning me to help her create some 'brakes' to allow thinking space while making out with her boyfriend.

These teens were experiencing rapid bodily changes that they brought to analysis for consideration. I turn briefly to erotic transference and

30 *Mary T. Brady*

countertransference in the psychoanalytic literature on adults in order to create a backdrop from which to consider the far scanter literature on transference/countertransference with adolescent patients.

Erotic transference and countertransference in the adult literature

Person (1985) defines 'erotic transference' as interchangeable with 'transference love', meaning, 'some mixture of tender, erotic, and sexual feelings that a patient experiences in reference to his or her analyst and, as such, forms part of a positive transference' (Person, 1985: 161).[4] She describes the erotic transference as 'both goldmine and minefield' (1985: 163). Passionate feelings are likely to be confusing to patient and analyst and thus their consideration can yield great rewards. Simultaneously, intense feelings in the patient or analyst are also prone to either some form of acting out or defensive avoidance.

A patient's erotic feelings towards an analyst can sometimes be intensely driven and even psychotic in the Kleinian sense of losing touch with reality. Blum describes 'eroticized transference' as a 'particular species of erotic transference, an extreme sector of a spectrum. It is an intense, vivid, irrational, erotic preoccupation with the analyst, characterized by overt, seemingly ego-syntonic demands for love and sexual fulfillment from the analyst' (1973: 63). In my experience there are patients who waver between a capacity to allow strong feelings towards their analyst without becoming psychotic but who may lose hold of reality considerations in the throes of intense feelings.

Person points out that (even in the adult literature) erotic transference 'has always been tainted by unsavory associations and continues to be thought of as slightly disreputable' (Person 1985: 163) compared with other forms of transference. In a sense this is strange, as Freud struggled mightily (in introducing his concept of infantile sexuality) to help us see that there are intense and passionate bodily forces in us all from the beginning. And yet, perhaps we have to accept that passionate and deeply rooted forces always create some defensive alarm. How much more so when the patient has not reached adulthood?

In a well-known and groundbreaking paper Searles (1958) squares off against the orthodox notion, prevalent at the time, that intense emotional reactions on the part of the analyst are pathological:

> (I)n the course of a successful psychoanalysis, the analyst goes through a phase of reacting to, and eventually relinquishing, the patient as being his oedipal love-object; b) in normal personality development, the parent reciprocates the child's oedipal love with greater intensity than we have recognized heretofore; and c) in such normal development the passing of the Oedipus Complex is at least as important a phase in ego-development as in superego development.
>
> (180)

Racker (1953) likewise contends that the Oedipus Complex will express itself in every countertransference, while the form, consciousness of it and intensity vary:

> ...sometimes the analyst loves the patient genitally and desires her genital love towards him; he hates her if she then loves another man, feels rivalry of this man and jealousy and envy (heterosexual and homosexual) of their sexual pleasure. Sometimes he hates her if she hates him, and loves her if she suffers, for in this case he is revenged for the oedipic deceit. He feels satisfaction when the transference is very positive, but also castration anxiety and guilt feelings toward the husband, etc.
>
> (316)

I am using countertransference here to denote the analyst's experience of an intensely interactional transference-countertransference dialogue (Greenberg and Mitchell, 1983; Langs, 1981; Little, 1951; Ogden, 1997; Racker, 1957; Searles, 1958; Winnicott, 1949).[5]

Erotic transference and countertransference, adolescent style

Lena, in a paper discussing the erotic transference of a 16-year-old boy to his female therapist contends:

> Given the centrality of sexual impulses and fantasies in adolescence, one would think that the erotic transference is a common phenomenon in many therapists with adolescents.... (W)hen discussing this topic with colleagues working with adolescents most psychotherapists could think of cases when powerful sexual feelings coloured the transference relationship. And yet little has been written about the erotic transference in childhood and adolescence, even less about the experience of the therapist.
>
> (2017: 43)

Atkinson and Gabbard likewise comment: 'erotic material in an adolescent's transference may create in the analyst a level of concern or even fear of parental retaliation should the parents become aware of the material' (1995: 174). I would add that the fear of the parents' potential response can also be a projection of the analyst's own parental superego, which can lead to repression or avoidance.

Alvarez's (2012) paper: 'Types of sexual transference and countertransference in work with children and adolescents' is a rare and substantive contribution to this topic. She distinguishes among 'perverse', 'disordered' and 'normal' sexual transferences in children and adolescents. Perverse denotes a dangerously addictive sexuality with sadistic and masochistic elements. Disordered indicates an addictive but not fully perverse sexuality.

32   Mary T. Brady

And by normal Alvarez implies the child or adolescent's desire 'to make someone's eyes light up' (2012: 126) and 'the need for a responsive interested object capable of being delighted' (2012: 126).

Paton discusses a scenario when an adolescent sexualizes the therapeutic atmosphere to 'avoid feelings of unhappiness and vulnerability' (2017: 28) which would be similar to Blum's description of eroticized transference and could overlap with Alvarez's perverse or disordered sexual transferences.

Jackson (a male analyst) describes an 18-year-old woman's adjustment to the couch:

> For the first few weeks Sarah seemed tense, lying on the couch with her knees up as if she felt like a terrified virgin on her wedding night. This was poignantly represented when she told me how her new travel card gave her freedom to go wherever she wanted but left her worrying about whether she could manage the increased cost. She was able to recognize how the 'cost' in the transference connected in part to the increased access she had to her fantasies about my 'private life' and her hatred of feeling so excluded from it.
>
> (2017: 18 and Chapter 10, this volume)

Jackson (2017) warns that when sexuality emerges within the transference and countertransference with our adolescent patients: 'threatening to disrupt our thinking and shatter our psychic equilibrium … we should not underestimate our propensity to avoid, negate and defend ourselves against these dynamics, even when we are conscious of them' (2017: 6). He notes that it can be difficult to distinguish between being safe and containing of our adolescent patients' erotic feelings and 'something that is rationalized as safe and containing but which is essentially evasive and defensive on the part of the therapist' (2017: 12). Similarly, Atkinson and Gabbard (1995) describe an erotic transference of a male patient with a female therapist and note that the therapist in such a pairing may be tempted to overemphasize maternal feelings.

Adolescent treatment requires a freedom to experience and tolerate intense feelings, while attempting to be neither over-stimulating nor neglectful of sexual feelings. The following vignette is an excellent example of this. Jackson describes Sarah, an 18-year-old who he sometimes feels to be the 'apple of my eye' (2017: 18). Sarah tells her analyst she has kissed a close friend of her boyfriend.

> The intensity of the impact this had on me was startling. I experienced it like a personal assault – a body blow, affecting my whole physiology and evoking something not far off a sense of outrage as if she had actually been unfaithful to me.
>
> (2017: 18 and Chapter 10, this volume)

The intensity of Jackson's reaction jarred him and gradually led him to understand that Sarah had experienced their recent agreement for her to use the

Erotic field   33

couch as a sexual enactment. Jackson's subsequent vacation break thus felt like a betrayal to her. As he reflected on his intense reaction mentioned above Jackson became more active in interpreting how his breaks, 'could feel like a violation of the therapy and the therapeutic relationship' (2017: 18). Sarah then tells him that she had kissed the boy to hurt *him* more than her boyfriend. Jackson replies:

> I acknowledged the importance of what she was saying about how angry, jealous and cheated on she felt by me over Easter, adding that perhaps now I needed to know what that was like – including what it was like to feel sexually jealous.
>
> (18)

Jackson keeps a close eye to the effect of his comments on his patient. While always important, close attunement to how our words are experienced is only more important in this erotic territory – over-stimulating or insufficient?

Erotic insufficiency/erotic playback

The emerging bodily experiences of the adolescent (first menstruation, first wet dream, first masturbation to orgasm, etc.) are parts of a 'virgin territory' (Holtzman and Kulish, 1997; Kulish, 1998). For the analyst, the patient's pubertal development can rouse feelings of venturing into a particularly forbidden, loaded and vulnerable area. This can create hesitancy and inhibition in the analyst, making her less likely to be able to stand for the acceptance and containment of these sensations and emotions.

Samuels (a post-Jungian analyst) suggests that, 'the subtle damage and deprivation caused by erotic deficit is far less spoken of than what is caused by erotic excess. Physical incest takes place at an appallingly high frequency … but something equally central and much more benevolent in sexuality is being overlooked'. (2000: 278)

I prefer the term 'erotic insufficiency' as 'deficit' implies a lack of capacity, while therapists' avoidance of the erotic with adolescents is often caused more by discomfort and anxiety than incapacity.

Samuels describes 'erotic playback' (2000: 277) in parenting and in clinical processes:

> (I)n the family this is the way in which the parent communicates to children of both sexes that they are admirable, physically desirable and erotically viable creatures. Of course, in a family or in analysis I am referring only to incest fantasy and not to the physical enactment of such fantasy.
>
> (2000: 277)

Samuels adds that the erotic includes more than sex, it also encompasses: 'harmony, relatedness, purpose, significance, and meaning Eros … This means

34   *Mary T. Brady*

of course, that ambivalence, anxiety, jealousy, rivalry, and a sense of lack will also be present' (2000: 278). To translate into my Bionian clinical language – an analyst would need to be emotionally responsive and containing to the erotic (in a broad sense) and also to the related subtleties and problems – what's too much? What's too remote or defensive? What is enlivening or even transformative?

Samuels' concept of 'erotic playback' is not simplistic. He sees sexual identity as not 'unified, fixed, static, eternal, universal' (2000: 278). Erotic playback encourages the individual 'to think of himself or herself in a diversified way, to come alive and hold together in the mind all aspects of the self – body areas, mental areas…' (2000: 278). Samuels acknowledges that erotic playback is vulnerable to mis-attunement as well as to more egregious failures.

Ogden's work on the 'aliveness' of the analytic exchange broadly approximates what Samuels is describing. Ogden advocates the analyst's 'spontaneity and freedom to respond to the analysand from his own experience in the analytic situation in a way that is not strangulated by stilted caricatures of analytic neutrality' (1995: 696). He says:

> I believe that every form of psychopathology represents a specific type of limitation of the individual's capacity to be fully alive as a human being. The goal of analysis from this point of view is larger than that of the resolution of unconscious intrapsychic conflict, the diminution of symptomatology, the enhancement of reflective subjectivity and self-understanding, and the increase of sense of personal agency. Though one's sense of being alive is intimately intertwined with each of the above-mentioned capacities, I believe that the experience of aliveness is a quality that is superordinate to these capacities.
>
> (1995: 696)

More specific to the present discussion, Elise discusses 'analytic eroticism': the 'aesthetic capacity to keep … embodied vitality alive in the analytic relationship' (2017: 34). She compares analytic eroticism to Kristeva's (2014) discussion of maternal eroticism: '(T)he encounter with the mother as erotic being brings into being the child's erotic self, both in the specifically sexual and in the most general sense: vitality in living, a curious and creative engagement with life – Eros' (Elise, 2017: 34). A simple and lovely example comes to mind. Seven-year-old Spencer comes to his session dressed in a collared shirt instead of his usual tee shirts. He tells me that it had been 'picture day' at school and that his mother told him he was wearing his 'handsome' shirt. How beautifully, naturally and subtly she was sowing the seeds of his developing sense as an attractive and desirable boy and future man.

As parents or analysts we do not often consciously set out to provide our children or patients 'erotic playback'. But perhaps we have trouble naming that along with the growth of the mind, we also hope to help free the growth

Erotic field   35

of erotic aliveness in our patients – both sexually and in related forms, such as a passion for ideas, rich sensuality and a broad and complex range of emotional experience and expressiveness.

Timid avoidance of erotic feelings in the consulting room deprives adolescents of sincere adult thinking in relation to allowing and managing sexual feelings. The analyst's capacity to be aware of their erotic feelings but not to act on them, comes across in many ways. If the analyst can feel some ease with sexual feelings alive in the field, then his or her own, as well as the patient's capacity to think about sensual/bodily/sexual feelings can develop in both patient and analyst. This sounds easy in the abstract, but is not so easy in the heat of the moment.

Clinical material – 'pick-up' sticks

'Frank', a sensitive 12-year-old boy with a 'cool', teenage demeanor, appeared at least two years older than his actual age. He was in analysis for depression following his father's death. His mother suffered a chronic depression and was further collapsed in relation to her husband's illness and death. Now two years into the analysis Frank's depression had diminished and an erotic transference developed, partly under the pressure of puberty, and also in response to our having begun a fourth weekly session. Frank had agreed to a fourth session because he could see that our work was helping him to use his mind more actively to sort out his own feelings from his mother's feelings. He observed: '(W)hen my mother is depressed I feel like I can feel her feelings'. His mother accepted my recommendation of a fourth session because she was concerned both about Frank's painful stutter and about some of Frank's 'risky' friends.[6]

Frank felt that I had a special interest in him as demonstrated by my wanting to see him so often. He at first complained that the fourth session was too much time and took away from other things. However, at one point I noted aloud that he seemed distant following my having been away. I commented: '(I)t's easy to feel if someone is not there, that they don't care about you'. He replied: '(I) know you care about me because of the fourth session'. This was the end of the hour, and before he stood up he touched my leg with one of the pick-up sticks we had been playing with and commented that my stockings were 'shiny'. I am reminded of Freud's (1915: 169) comment in 'Observations on Transference Love', that the analyst 'has evoked this love by instituting analytic treatment in order to cure the neurosis'.

At times I noticed Frank looking at my breasts.[7] Another time he looked at my legs and asked, '(A)re they stockings?' I said, '(G)uys your age are often curious about girls' things, like stockings and underwear. Another thing about your age is that there are a lot of intense changes in one's body that can often feel hard to talk about'. Frank replied with emotion, 'I know what you mean. I'm beginning to have acne and other people my age aren't getting it yet'.

36   *Mary T. Brady*

In another session Frank touched my wedding ring and asked:

F: What stone is it?
A: You may be wondering not just what stone, but what the ring means.
F: That you're married.
A: Maybe, but then there's also what that means to you because you're pretty close to me.
F: Have you seen the movie *When Harry Met Sally*? The man in the movie didn't notice the woman at first.
A: You are noticing girls more in general but also noticing me in that way.

It was near the end of the session and Frank was tracing the veins in his forearm with his finger. I was struck by the change in his forearm over the last two years I had seen him – his forearm had changed from that of a boy to that of a man. At this moment I felt attracted to him in the same way as I might towards an adult, masculine man. At 12 he had already largely developed the body of a man.

It has often been observed that it is a challenge for girls who menstruate early to integrate their experiences, having had less time for antecedent emotional and cognitive development. It is also true for boys who have the bodies of men without the same psychological development.

Frank hummed the wedding march under his breath another day, and more than once slipped and asked why we hadn't met on the fifth day, on which we did not have an appointment. I pointed out he might be wishing we met that day as well. I mentioned the possibility of a fifth session to his mother, who spoke of it to an uncle Frank was close to. Frank's mother and uncle seemed to have an underlying suspicion regarding my interest in Frank. Indeed, I had to struggle to sort out my own feelings of attraction to Frank to keep myself from withdrawing from him due to anxiety about my erotic countertransference.

The following interchange seems to capture the incestuous aspects of the transference, and the anxieties surrounding it:

F: I was reading about a Japanese gangster who got shot nine times, shot through the mouth, tongue, teeth. With leprosy could you have a finger fall off?
A: Where did you hear about that possibility?
F: In history class. I think it could happen.
A: It reminds me of an old wives' tale that if a guy masturbates enough his penis could fall off. It's not true, but I guess it comes from that part of a guy's body being really important to him (Frank nods) and worrying something could happen to it.
F: In French tutorial today we were done with work, so we were just chilling, and somebody raised the story of a teacher, who had sex with her 12-year-old student, and he got her pregnant. She was married and

Erotic field 37

had three children. She went to jail, and when she got out, he got her pregnant again.

A: What did you think about that story?

F: It's weird, 24 years older is a little bit of a problem – she was 36. (Frank trails off)

A: Maybe you're uncomfortable talking about it, as I'm an older woman you're close to, and you're 12.

Frank was unable to say any more about this issue, but I felt that it crystallized the transference-countertransference situation. I said, 'I don't think it was good what happened between the teacher and student, but I wouldn't want you to think such feelings are weird'. I gulped internally as I linked this loaded story directly to our relationship. There had been many indicators of Frank's feelings, so it did not feel premature. I felt confident that I was not being seductive but was naming something implicit in order to make it more explicit and thus thinkable. In Field Theory terms the 'impregnating student and pregnant teacher' had become characters in the field (Ferro, 1999) and represented the most intense variation of a 'waking dream' (Bion, 1962) in the analysis. In Bionian terms the waking dream/metaphor gathers up beta elements that are transformed by alpha function into dream elements for further thinking and dreaming.

There could be reasons to allow material to continue to evolve in derivative form, as well as times it could feel over-stimulating to make a direct link to the analytic couple. As I look back many years later, this comment has a feeling of rightness to me. The situation in the room was stimulating – a boy going through puberty and an older woman. I felt towards Frank as I might when attracted to a man, including some preoccupation with these feelings outside of sessions. Within the privacy of my sexual fantasy there were also elements of an older, more sexually experienced woman with a virile, but unexperienced young boy/man. I was also well aware that Frank was not actually a young man, but a boy. I believe that my ways of relating to him in the hours always kept this in mind, but that the transitions in him were stimulating to him and to me.

Soon after, Frank told me that his uncle asked: '(D)id your analyst propose yet?' Frank said, '(I)t's weird you want me to come so much, since most people go once or twice a week'. I said: '(S)ometimes people are un-comfortable with positive feelings, but I imagine you felt confused about whose ideas to be loyal to'. Frank nodded. He seemed to register that sharing and understanding his loving and sexual feelings could be helpful to him. I think that my effort to bear with my erotic feelings towards Frank, despite these accusations and my own discomfort, helped Frank to tolerate and integrate his own sexual and romantic feelings more fully.

Discussion

My comments to Frank were intended to have an open-ended 'un-saturated' (Bion, 1962) quality, in order to allow Frank's feelings, thoughts and experiences to develop further. New bodily sensations and related emotions can feel like a taboo area to both patient and analyst. An analyst has to be willing to brave this territory if she expects her patient to be able to. While it is often useful to proceed in an unsaturated manner, it is especially true in relation to the physical changes of adolescence. The bodily changes and sensations of adolescence are so big that they can only be taken in gradually.

When helping an adolescent to name erotic feelings, we are also indirectly implying certain attitudes towards sexuality – that sexuality is part of us, that even very intense feelings can be shared. When I look back at this material it seems right that I did not interpret Frank's story about the teacher in relation to incestuous feelings towards his mother, (while of course there would be an element of truth to this). Such a genetic interpretation would have been avoidant of the erotic feelings in the room and could have signaled to Frank my unwillingness to be close to his feelings.

An analyst might not directly interpret derivative material in some situations. The 'perverse' children described by Alvarez (2012: 122) might take such an interpretation in an addictive direction and be unable to use it to think. Sexually over-stimulated or abused adolescents might be better served by discussing sexuality in more derivative form, as they have too often been victim to sexuality crashing through. Over-concrete children, such as those on the Autism Spectrum, would be unlikely to use an explicit transference interpretation fluidly, rendering such comments useless or confusing. Also, a therapist must consider how much preparatory groundwork there is in a treatment that might allow intense feelings to be taken on with more confidence. Frank had already been in analysis for two years and we had weathered some other storms.

It is my impression that interpreting this material to Frank explicitly was useful. Leaving these feelings unspecified could imply that they were too catastrophic to identify. Instead, very loaded feelings were named and the boundaries and purposes of our work remained in place.

Retrospectively, the erotic transference-countertransference with Frank emerged at a specific time in the treatment and was more in the background subsequently. Shortly after my patient's erotic transference to me reached a height (now 13-years-old), he started a romantic relationship with a girl his age which continued over the next two years. I was impressed with Frank's growing ability to talk directly with her about his feelings.

I believe that the erotic transference experienced with an emotionally available but safe object became a launching ground for Frank's own erotic life. His experience of having a single object who was paying attention to him, and to whom he was paying attention, allowed for a deepening capacity for intimacy. His mother's depression likely made 'the potentiating capacity of eroticism' (Elise, 2017: 35) more important in the analytic relationship than it might have been had these feelings been more available in his family.

Adolescents frequently present with bravado, which masks their developmental unreadiness for some experiences. The period of erotic transference-countertransference allowed Frank a trying-on of feelings and fantasies, as well as some room to verbalize these experiences. Adolescent treatment often has this quality – a dress rehearsal[8] is allowed for issues that feel unsafe – either for reasons of conflict, or developmental unreadiness. Adolescents often experience first love with an unavailable object, but important growth is happening meanwhile.

My experience of Frank's erotic transference is much as Searles described in his 1958 paper, 'Oedipal love in the countertransference'. That is, that the child accepts the unrealizability of his oedipal strivings not mainly through fear of and identification with the forbidding rival parent, but:

> ...through the ego strengthening experience of finding that the beloved parent reciprocates his love – responds to him, that is, as being a worthwhile and lovable individual, as being, indeed a conceivably desirable love partner – and renounces him only with an accompanying sense of loss on the parent's own part.... This child emerges ... with his ego strengthened out of the knowledge that his love however unrealizable, is reciprocated.
>
> (Searles, 1958: 188)

Emotional dulling can occur if the 'beloved parent had to repress his or her reciprocal desire for the child, chiefly through the mechanism of unconscious denial of the child's importance to the parent' (Searles, 1958: 189).

Davies, an American Relational analyst, suggests that erotic transference can be infantilized and seen only in pre-oedipal or oedipal dimensions. She suggests that as inhibitions or symptoms caused by infantile conflicts are understood, 'the rich efflorescence, not the disappearance of passionate desire in the analytic relationship' often ensues. Within the 'relatively safe confines of the analytic space' 'there is a freedom to experience those aspects of sexual desire and erotic fantasy that are part of emergent self-experiences' (1998: 752).

Davies relates a riveting moment from her own family life, which informed her understanding of emergent adolescent sexuality. Davies and her husband were engrossed in conversation when their daughters (who had been playing dress up) ran by. The 12-year-old:

> ...had piled her long dark hair on top of her head and had put on a clingy black jersey, slit up the side. The outfit was completed with black fishnet stockings, patent-leader high heels and a red garter. I was astounded, but her father let slip an almost imperceptive but still subliminally audible gasp – a gasp heard loud and clear by his very vulnerable daughter woman and her then immobilized but horrified mother. In a series of microseconds, meaningful looks of danger and confusion ricocheted spitfire

40   *Mary T. Brady*

around this now palpable triangle, and my daughter, crying hysterically, ran from the room.

(1998: 759)

Gathering himself, Davies' husband went to talk to his daughter. Later, equilibrium apparently restored, Davies asked what he had said to accomplish this:

'I told her the truth', he said, 'that I had never seen her looking so beautiful before … in such a grown up way … that it had taken my breath away … that I liked it … but that it was something I was going to have to get used to'. 'Did she say anything?' I asked. 'No', 'but she smiled the most beautiful smile'. And then he smiled.

(1998: 760)

Davies suggests that her husband's honest acknowledgement allows a 'beginning recognition' of adolescent emergent sexual subjectivity and of parental capacity to recognize it and deal with his or her own response to it in a thoughtful manner. An adolescent can experience being the object of another's sexual response in a reasonably titrated manner when that response is both forthright and contained. I was struck by the pauses in the husband's speech, which Davies represented three times by '…' These pauses seem to me a helpful communication in addition to the words themselves. The pauses imply one can stop to think when in the midst of tumultuous feelings.

The analyst of an adolescent must be able to withstand a series of anxieties in relation to sexuality – e.g., 'Is what we're talking about too exciting?' 'Is my interest too voyeuristic?' – in order to help the adolescent tolerate her or his own excitements and anxieties. This willingness to tread in an anxiety-provoking and taboo area can hopefully lend what I call an 'erotic sufficiency' to our work with adolescents. Davies sees analysts' ability to reflectively contain their own desire as similar to parents' acceptance of the incest prohibition. Such thoughtful containment allows the patient's subjectivity to develop.

Lombardi (2017) comments: '(A)dolescence involves confrontation with a *choice* that becomes decisive for all subsequent development: this choice consists of either facing up to adolescent turbulence or mobilizing all possible strategies to avoid it' (2017: 113). This period of treatment felt turbulent to me as well as, I imagine, to Frank. While I do not feel I was at any point inappropriate or flirtatious in the sessions, outside of the hours I thought I must have been losing my mind to have strong feelings of attractions to a 12-year-old. In retrospect, I think that Frank and I were able to sustain turbulence without closing it down too quickly, yielding an 'erotic sufficiency'.

Erotic field

My work with Frank took place a decade and a half ago when I was still a candidate in child analysis. As I reflect on it now, I am struck that my experience with Frank was of a 'bi-personal field' (Baranger and Baranger, 2008; Molinari, 2017), 'analytic third' (Ogden, 1994) or 'intermediate area of experience' (Winnicott, 1971), though the Freudian supervision I was in at the time did not employ this language. My experience was of a continuous exchange of emotional elements that through dreams and narratives (such as the 12-year-old impregnating his 36-year-old teacher) 'find a way of expressing and narrating what is going on in the depths of the relational exchange' (Ferro, 1999: 158).

Shared meanings and feelings could be elaborated with Frank in a way that did not have to be too pinned down. Meanings could continually take shape from a shared (though not directly expressed on my part) experience of erotic and romantic longings. These longings could also come into contact with a reality of limits in the relationship and the allowance that these longings be transformed for other purposes, such as Frank's assumption of his romantic and erotic life. It is interesting that while coming from a Freudian view that emphasized the intra-psychic, my supervisor seemed entirely comfortable with this way of working.

The supervision[9] I was in was instrumental in helping me not to inhibit erotic feelings in my relationship with Frank. The use of a consultant may be particularly important in an erotic field to help (as Bion says) to think while feeling and feel while thinking. In the context of the above clinical moment I recall my supervisor saying that it was good that I liked males, implying that Frank did not have to be deprived of the subtle ways this would come across in my interactions with him. I am reminded of Elise's comment:

> …what of the analyst's libidinal investment in that unique patient, in that analysis. An analysis cannot rest on the patient's libidinal energies alone. We might think of erotic energy as circulating in multiple directions in the intersubjective field of an analysis – a libidinally alive matrix…. A clinical situation of vibrancy can foster patients' increased libidinal investment in *themselves*.
>
> (2017: 49)[10]

It is interesting to consider how the work with Frank might have been different with a heterosexual male analyst or a gay or lesbian analyst. It is important for analysts to be fluid and imaginative in experiencing ourselves as male or female, father or mother, or in a homosexual or heterosexual role with a patient. Still, it seems to me there are times that the specific genders of the pair are important, and perhaps especially so at puberty. Some early adolescent girls relate to me as if I may be able to help figure out the mysteries that are befalling them – after all, I have gone through similar bodily changes. In the current clinical material, the constellation of a heterosexual boy in early

42   *Mary T. Brady*

adolescence and a heterosexual female analyst may have allowed a particularly intense version of feelings that surely would have also been present in some form with this patient and a different analyst.

The terms 'erotic transference' and 'erotic countertransference' seem to me too static to capture the fluidity, subtlety or complexity that is better conveyed in the dynamic concept of an 'erotic field'. Hartmann (2017) in a memorial paper for Muriel Dimen highlights her complex use of field theory. He says, '(B)etter to speak to/in the erotic field than to codify it as the patient's "erotic transference"'. To reify the transference is to forget that 'recursively, to reflect on desire and to contain it, enhance each other' (Dimen, 2011: 59; Hartmann, 2017: 133).

When I think back to the period in my work with Frank when erotic feelings were in the forefront, it feels almost impossible to say, 'whose feeling is it?' Frank experienced my recommendation of frequent sessions as a possible seduction. His looking at my body was stimulating to me. I think of the complexity of any single moment such as when Frank traced the veins on his forearm and I felt attracted to him as I might to an adult, masculine man. These were my feelings, located in me and unspoken. But, Frank's subtle and un-self-conscious action, might also represent a new sensuality and budding awareness of his body, which I was also reacting to.

At times there are feelings that might belong mainly to one member of the analytic couple. Frank felt frustrated that I did not let him in on my private life. But even such an experience (that was mainly his) includes a whole history of familial boundary experiences for both patient and analyst. Such personal experience of boundaries would become in some way part of the erotic field.

Conclusion

Analytic work with adolescents brings to mind words like 'visceral', 'intense', 'in motion' and 'palpable'. At times adolescents have been considered poorly suited for analytic treatment[11] (Freud, 1958). The changing body of the adolescent patient presents particular challenges to containment and pressures towards enactment in the treatment of adolescents. Lombardi (2016), commenting on Ferrari, notes: 'a lack of experience with the adult world establishes the necessity for the adolescent to "act in order to know" (Ferrari, 2004)' (2016: 4). When analysis can help an adolescent to understand and contain their bodily and familial changes, the bodily based psychopathologies (eating disorders, cutting, substance abuse), which are characteristic disturbances of adolescence (Anderson, 2004; Brady, 2016) may be prevented or mitigated.

As I complete this chapter, I think about its title. Is it 'entering the erotic field with the adolescent patient or some other verb: what about 'surviving' or 'tolerating' or 'enjoying' or 'playing in' or 'braving?' As I mull over these verbs, they all have some element of truth, but 'braving' is perhaps the most fitting – and thus the title changes … I end this chapter with Alvarez's reminder that:

Erotic field 43

Sometimes the positive transference is harder to take and stay with than the negative; and when it is sexual, too, it demands much courage, honesty and respect from us in our countertransference responses.

(2012: 129; this volume, Chapter 1)

Notes

1 A search of Pep-Web resulted in 1,785 references for 'erotic transference', 592 references for 'erotic countertransference', 15 references for 'erotic transference, adolescence' and only 3 references for 'erotic countertransference, adolescence'. For a recent welcome exception to this neglect see *Journal of Child Psychotherapy*, 2017, Volume 43(1) is devoted to adolescent treatment, and 'opens with three papers which tackle the reality of sexual and erotic transference, and the handling of this, within the psychotherapies of adolescent patients. As each author remarks, the literature on the topic has historically been somewhat slender' (Stratton and Russell, 2017).

2 For an exception to this generalization see Alvarez's description of 'perverse sexuality' (2012: 122) in a seven-year-old child.

3 It would be interesting to study the responses of adolescents to the use of the couch. In my experience some adolescents find the use of the couch sexually stimulating and others find it a refuge that helps them to talk about sexual feelings without having to look at the analyst, or these may both be true at different times.

4 Person's (1985) paper on erotic transference in adults contends that male patients are more resistant to the awareness of the erotic transference and that female patients are more resistant to the resolution of the erotic transference in the cross-gendered treatments she studied. It would be interesting to study this question in adolescent treatments. In adolescence, particularly at puberty, the gender of the pair may matter more than at any other age.

5 In contrast to a classical view of countertransference as a hindrance, espoused by Reich (1951).

6 It is interesting to note the different but perhaps related issues that led this teen and his mother to accept a recommendation for more intensive work. Frank's acceptance of the recommendation followed his recognition of newfound vigor as he began to use his mind to separate himself from his mother's sunken depression. His mother's not unrealistic concern that Frank would get in trouble with his risk-taking friends involved the dangers of separation.

7 Atkinson and Gabbard (1995) note that voyeuristic looking precedes genital sexuality in the ordinary sexual development of boys. Lena comments on a 16-year-old boy's gaze 'to penetrate into my eyes or to stare at my body. I felt very uncomfortable, embarrassed, intruded upon, at times repulsed by him' (2017: 47). The intrusive quality of that boy's gaze was later understood as related to intrusion he had suffered. Frank's gaze seemed more as Atkinson and Gabbard describe.

8 See Laufer (1968: 115) re masturbation and masturbation fantasies in adolescence as 'trial action' sometimes leading to developmental progression and sometimes to deadlock. My emphasis here is on the emergence of erotic feelings within the analytic work.

9 It is noteworthy that in the few articles I could find on working with the erotic transference with adolescents, supervision was frequently mentioned: e.g., Lena: 'Supervision represented a vital 'third' that enabled me to think about the dangers of focusing only on the maternal and infantile aspects while avoiding talking about sexuality…' (2017: 53).

10 Clearly Elise recognizes that 'the analyst's creative energies are not to be a substitute for the absence of such energies in the patient; rather, they are best seen as an enlivening

44 *Mary T. Brady*

contribution to the analytic encounter, even if, paradoxically, they are used to narrate deadness and devitalization' (2017: 51).

11 A. Freud (1958) thought that adolescents separating from their objects were not able to sufficiently 'transfer' or attach to a new object, which made them difficult or impossible to treat. She felt that help might instead be aimed at their parents. Though many analysts did not share her view, if did seem to have a chilling effect on attitudes towards the intensive treatment of adolescents for some time. A panel discussion at the American Psychoanalytic Association on analysis of adolescents, summarized by Sklansky (1972), concluded 'few contemporary adolescent patients are analyzable … once in analysis a variety of parameters of technique far beyond those used in the classical analysis of adults are necessary' (1972: 134). The one dissenting panellist was Adatto, who commented that certain adolescents with 'sufficient ego capacities and transference readiness can catapult an analysis into intensive productive work, rarely observed in adults' (1972: 138). More recent literature has emerged which differs from this concern regarding adolescent analyzability (Laufer, 1997; Paz and Olmoz de Paz, 1992).

References

Alvarez, A. (2012). Types of sexual transference and countertransference in work with children and adolescents. *The Thinking Heart: Three Levels of Psychoanalytic Therapy with Disturbed Children.* Hove, East Sussex, UK and New York, NY: Routledge.

Anderson, R. (2004). Adolescence and the body ego: The re-encountering of primitive mental functioning in adolescent development. Unpublished paper presented at the 16th Annual Melanie Klein Memorial Lectureship, January 8, 2005, Los Angeles.

Atkinson, S., & Gabbard, G. (1995). Erotic transference in the male adolescent-female analyst dyad. *Psychoanalytic Study of the Child, 50,* 171–186.

Baranger, M., & Baranger, W. (2008). The analytic situation as a dynamic field. *International Journal of Psychoanalysis, 89,* 795–826.

Bion, W.R. (1962). *Learning from Experience.* London: Heinemann.

Blum, H.P. (1973). The concept of erotized transference. *Journal of the American Psychoanalytic Association,* 21, 61–76.

Blos Sr., P. (1967). The second individuation process of adolescence. *Psychoanalytic Study of the Child, 22,* 162–186.

Brady, M.T. (2016). *The Body in Adolescence: Psychic Isolation and Physical Symptoms.* New York, NY: Routledge.

Davies, J.M. (1998). Between the disclosure and foreclosure of erotic transference and countertransference: Can psychoanalysis find a place for adult sexuality? *Psychoanalytic Dialogues, 8,* 747–766.

Dimen, M. (2011). *Lapsus linguae,* or a slip of the tongue: A sexual boundary violation in an analytic treatment and its personal and theoretical aftermath. *Contemporary Psychoanalysis,* 47, 35–79.

Elise, D. (2017). Moving from within the maternal: The choreography of analyticeroticism, *Journal of the American Psychoanalytic Association.* 65, 33–60.

Ferrari, A.B. (2004). *From the Eclipse of the Body to the Dawn of Thought.* London: Free Association Books.

Ferro, A. (1999). *The Bi-Personal Field: Experiences in Child Analysis.* London: Routledge.

Freud, A. (1958). Adolescence. *Psychoanalytic Study of the Child, 13,* 55–278.

Freud, S. (1915). Observations on transference love. In Strachey, J. (Ed. & Trans.), *The Standard Edition of the Complete Works of Sigmund Freud, Vol. 12,* 159–171. London: Hogarth Press.

Greenberg, J., & Mitchell, S. (1983). *Object Relations in Psychoanalytic Theory*. Cambridge, MA: Harvard University Press.

Hartmann, S. (2017). Muriel Dimen, field theorist. *Studies in Gender and Sexuality*, *18*, 132–135.

Holtzman, D., & Kulish, N. (1997). *Nevermore: The Hymen and the Loss of Virginity*. Northvale, NJ: Jason Aronson Inc.

Jackson, E. (2017). Too close for comfort: The challenges of engaging with sexuality in work with adolescents. *Journal of Child Psychotherapy*, *43*(1), 6–22.

Katan, A. (1951). The role of "displacement" in agoraphobia. *International Journal of Psychoanalysis*, *32*, 42–50.

Kristeva, J. (2014). Reliance, or maternal eroticism. *Journal of the American Psychoanalytic Association*, *62*, 69–85.

Kulish, N. (1998). First loves and prime adventures: Adolescent expressions in adult analyses. *Psychoanalytic Quarterly*, *67*(4), 539–565.

Langs, R. (1981). *The Therapeutic Experience and Its Setting*. New York, NY: Jason Aronson.

Laufer, M. (1968). The body image, the function of masturbation, and adolescence – Problems of the ownership of the body. *Psychoanalytic Study of the Child*, *23*, 114–137.

Laufer, M. (1997). Developmental breakdown in adolescence: Problems of understanding and helping. In Laufer, M. (Ed.), *Adolescent Breakdown and Beyond*. Madison: Indiana University Press.

Lena, F.E. (2017). Working with and "seeing through": Sexual transference in the psychotherapy of an adolescent boy. *Journal of Child Psychotherapy*, *43*(1), 40–54.

Little, M. (1951). Counter-transference and the patient's response to it. *International Journal of Psychoanalysis*, *32*, 32–40.

Lombardi, R. (2016). Entering one's own life as a goal of clinical analysis. Unpublished paper presented at the Scientific Meeting, November 14, 2016, San Francisco Center for Psychoanalysis, San Francisco, California.

Lombardi, R. (2017). Body and mind in adolescence. In *Body-Mind Dissociation in Psychoanalysis: Developments after Bion*. Abingdon/New York: Routledge.

Molinari, E. (2017). *Field Theory in Child and Adolescent Psychoanalysis: Understanding and Reacting to Unexpected Developments*. Abingdon/New York: Routledge.

Ogden, T.H. (1994). The analytic third: Working with intersubjective clinical facts. *International Journal of Psychoanalysis*, *75*, 3–19.

Ogden, T.H. (1995). Analyzing forms of aliveness and deadness of the transference-countertransference. *International Journal of Psychoanalysis*, *76*, 695–709.

Ogden, T.H. (1997). *Reverie and interpretation*. Northvale, NJ: Jason Aronson.

Paton, I. (2017). Within or without: negotiating psychic space with an adolescent at risk of developing a narcissistic personality structure. *Journal of Child Psychotherapy*, *43*(1), 23–39.

Paz, C., & Olmoz de Paz, T. (1992). Adolescence and borderline pathology: Characteristics of the relevant psychoanalytic process. *International Journal of Psychoanalysis*, *73*(4), 739–755.

Person, E. (1985). The erotic transference in women and in men: Differences and consequences. *Journal of the American Academy of Psychoanalysis and Psychiatry*, *13*, 159–180.

Racker, H. (1953). A contribution to the problem of counter-transference. *International Journal of Psychoanalysis*, *34*, 313–324.

Racker, H. (1957). The meanings and uses of countertransference. *Psychoanalytic Quarterly*, *41*, 303–357.

46 Mary T. Brady

Reich, A. (1951). On countertransference. *International Journal of Psychoanalysis, 32*, 25–31.

Samuels, A. (2000). The erotic leader. *Psychoanalytic Dialogues, 10,* 277–280.

Searles, H. (1958). Oedipal love in the countertransference. *International Journal of Psychoanalysis, 40,* 180–190.

Sklansky, M. (1972). Indications and contraindications for the psychoanalysis of the adolescent. *Journal of the American Psychoanalytic Association, 20*(1), 134–144.

Stratton, K., & Russell, J. (2017). Editorial. *Journal of Child Psychotherapy, 43*(1), 1–5.

Winnicott, D.W. (1949). Hate in the countertransference. *International Journal of Psychoanalysis, 30,* 69–74.

Winnicott, D.W. (1971). *Playing and Reality.* London: Tavistock Publications.

Editor's Introduction to:
Traversing challenging terrain: discussion of Mary Brady's 'Braving the Erotic Field'

Dianne Elise's trailblazing writing assists clinicians to develop a theoretical and ethical container to rely on in working with embodied emotion. It is an honor to have her discuss my preceding chapter.

Like Alvarez in Chapter 1, she emphasizes that the therapist not just contains, but stimulates and elaborates the patient's process of growth. Elise emphasizes moreover that the analyst's erotic energy and creativity is also engaged in the endeavor.

Elise points here to the salience of seeing the erotic in its 'less polite' forms in work with children and adolescents than is generally the case with adults. She underlines the value for adult treatment of seeing the erotic infant, erotic child and erotic adolescent in the adult.

Elise emphasizes that sexuality has receded as a focus in psychoanalysis and sets out to redress that balance. My own experience is that I have not so much set out to remind clinicians of the erotic, but just that it is there in ourselves and in our patients as well as between oneself and one's patient if we are not afraid to see it.

DOI: 10.4324/9781003266303-5

3 Traversing challenging terrain: discussion of Mary Brady's 'Braving the Erotic Field'

Dianne Elise

I am especially pleased to discuss this ground-breaking contribution in which Mary Brady tackles not only the challenging topic of eroticism in the analytic dyad but specifically in work with adolescents where many additional factors have the potential to intensify anxieties in clinicians. In reviewing the literature on erotic transference and countertransference with adult patients, Brady notes that literature still remains sparse regarding work with adolescents; erotic feeling can feel especially taboo and may lead to avoidance on the part of the clinician.

Bringing her expertise in work with adolescents to the forefront, Brady's emphasis on erotic embodiment – that which is palpably visceral in both the body of the patient and of the clinician – is especially cutting edge. She writes: 'Erotic transference and countertransference can be particularly fraught because of the intensity of emergent bodily sensations' leading to, as she says, 'a challenge for analysts to talk about feelings the adolescent may have barely begun to name. Indeed, budding sexuality and the memories and feelings it stirs in us of our own sexual beginnings are no small things to metabolize'.

Truly, it is very hard to directly discuss erotic feeling and especially when the embodied reality of erotic feelings is present *in the analyst*, not solely in the patient, whether adolescent or adult. The immediacy of erotic embodiment takes us as clinicians into terrain we have little training to navigate: to our bodies and our sexuality in relation to work with a patient. We are used to relying on our intellects to approach difficult issues *in our patients,* and analysts have a long history of using intellectualization as defensive avoidance of our own embodied experience.

Our own unfolding histories of sexuality, including from our own adolescent lives, can influence us in a subterranean manner of which we often do not have full awareness. In the past two decades, especially within the Relational School, this topic of erotic life in the consulting room has been taken up more courageously in journal articles, but in our offices, we are often still falling far short of having the desired facility with actual clinical engagement in this realm. Thus, Brady's scholarly work is a particularly significant contribution, including both of her books: first, in 2015, *The Body in Adolescence: Psychic Isolation and Physical Symptoms* and more recently, *Analytic*

DOI: 10.4324/9781003266303-6

Engagements with Adolescents: Sex, Gender and Subversion (2018). We are fortunate as a professional community to have one of our colleagues taking up the challenge of contributing her theorizing on erotic embodiment to the analytic conversation that the analytic literature constitutes.

Brady's clinical vignettes are compellingly poignant, such as when a growing boy asks: '(H)ave you always been that short?' Another touches her leg with a pick-up stick, comments that her stockings are 'shiny' and later asks, '(A)re they stockings?' Or a girl, making out with her boyfriend in his car for the first time, saying: 'I found myself tracing your initials in the steam on the window'. I want to underscore that while our adult patients are typically more guarded about sharing such undefended vulnerability with us, they too are similarly preoccupied – with wedding rings, clothing, our embodied physicality, with impressions gleaned as we meet them in the waiting room, eye contact, walking down hallways, physical proximity in passing by one another, etc. I want to stress that what Brady writes about braving the erotic field absolutely needs to be applied to our work with adults. Many nuanced responses to such embodied interactions – especially when erotic – typically go unvoiced if we as clinicians do not facilitate this level of expression (Elise, 2019).

Brady moves right into the transference relationship: when this 16-year-old girl in analysis, 'spoke about being on the verge of having intercourse with her boyfriend,' Brady asked her, '(D)o you think having sex will change anything inside you or between us?' That question, impressively direct, epitomizes how an analytic approach can so deepen and enrich not only the content of the material but the quality of dyadic engagement about sexuality within the analytic field.

Brady also attends to the specific impact of the use of the couch, noting that her patient Evelyn 'asked to use the couch in order to talk about sexuality. My agreement for her to lie down evoked intimate and erotic feelings in her towards me'. I have often found in my own practice that when patients move to the couch, erotic revelations start to unfold (Elise, 2002). A number of articles in the literature focused on adult treatment explicate the erotic meanings use of the couch can have, as well as the increased likelihood that more forbidden expressions of erotic longing may be expressed by the patient. But analysts are *behind the couch* and may themselves be hiding from not only the patient, but from their own feelings of vulnerable exposure of seemingly taboo erotic feeling.

Brady takes up such countertransference angst: 'Frank was tracing the veins in his forearm with his finger. I was struck by … [noticing that] – his forearm had changed from that of a boy to that of a man. At this moment I felt attracted to him in the same way as I might toward an adult, masculine man … I had to struggle to sort out my own feelings of attraction to Frank to keep myself from withdrawing from him due to anxiety about my erotic countertransference'.

She goes on to underline an important theoretical point, suggesting that 'the very terms "erotic transference" and "erotic countertransference" can feel

50   *Dianne Elise*

defensively remote and antiseptic …. (p.) [and] do not fully capture the intensely interactional nature of these experiences (p.) … seem[ing] to me too static to capture the fluidity, subtlety or complexity that is better conveyed in the dynamic concept of an "erotic field"' (Chapter 2). I could not agree more fully!

As I have written (Elise, 2017), the vitalization of the clinical situation, viewed as a libidinal force field, constitutes 'an expanded meaning of erotic transference-countertransference, where both patient and analyst engage their erotic energies and where this engagement is not specific to (though it may include) erotic desire for the other' (p. 45). Such feeling moves through, as Brady says, a continuous exchange of emotional elements in the dreams and unfolding narrative elaborations of the analytic field. In her depiction of the erotic field, Brady locates her thinking about clinical expressions of erotic life within an analytic field theory based in the Barangers concept of a bi-personal field, Ferro's and Civitarese's Bionian formulation of the field, Ogden's analytic third and in Winnicott's focus on an intermediate area of experience.

As she delineates, current conceptualizations of the analyst's role stress that an analyst is a co-participant in the creative unfolding of a dyadic conversation meant to further the development of the patient's capacities of mind towards increasing elaboration of personal meaning. The analytic field is viewed as encompassing the subjectivities of both patient and analyst, where each is implicated in its formation *and formed by it*.

As Ogden, Ferro and Civitarese each compellingly illustrate throughout their work, the creative capacities of the analytic pair to imaginatively co-construct an aesthetic form gives shape and meaning to personal experience. As Brady underscores, expansion of the entire personality is facilitated by an analytic process that integrates bodily components of experience, rooted in erotic vitality, with creative elaborations of emotional truth. Like Brady, I emphasize that this analytic process is not solely to *contain*, as in the modulation and tolerance of affect, but to *elaborate* the symbolic capacities of the patient's mind that in the analytic setting will most often unfold in a narrative building process (Elise, 2019).

I am especially glad to see Brady including Winnicott in a paper on erotic life in the analytic field. In his uniquely nuanced attention to the importance to an individual of creative vitality in living, Winnicott has much to offer analytic field theory (Elise, 2018). I have suggested that erotic energy and creativity are mutually reinforcing – captured in Winnicott's term: a 'vital spark'. Winnicott underscored that access to this quality of aliveness is just as crucial for the analyst as it is for the patient. The analyst's emotionally enlivened presence offers to a patient an object relationship with potential, a potential space where the patient might risk coming to life. As Brady states, excessive timidity on the part of the analyst can foreclose a growing capacity for both engagement and containment of sexual feelings, yielding what she aptly terms 'erotic insufficiency' in our work. This phrasing is felicitous as it captures so much in the pairing of just two words and, hopefully, will be

Traversing challenging terrain 51

available to keep in mind as we all go forward in our efforts to further develop our clinical abilities within an erotic field.

In my 2019 book, *Creativity and the Erotic Dimensions of the Analytic Field,* I put forth the premise that psychoanalysis is an erotic project. I suggest that a creative aesthetic can provide a clinical container for the engagement and exploration of erotic life within the analytic field of each treatment. An atmosphere of libidinal energy can be seen as a crucial aspect in enlivening the intersubjective field – the erotic dimensions of the psyche and of the psychoanalytic process. When fully articulated as an energy potential in both participants, what I term *analytic eroticism* can offer libidinal engagement within an ethical frame as a stimulus to emotionally embodied thinking that can lead to transformations in many dimensions, including the erotic. The analyst holds, contains *and stimulates*; each of these capacities is mobilized in the service of the patient's growth. An intertwining of the erotic and the creative in the embodied, affective interaction of the analytic dyad allows for deepening contact with an authentic sense of being.

As Brady emphasizes in her explication of Samuels, the erotic includes more than sex itself. We are challenged to consider what is actually meant by 'erotic'? The word 'erotic' with its specific connotation of a sensuous sexuality elicits both excitement and uneasiness, as if we're entering the arena of 'soft' porn. Ironically, given our Freudian beginnings, this uneasiness is especially prevalent within psychoanalysis. As many have noted, sexuality has receded as a focus, the profession de-sexualized in the object relational emphasis on a maternal matrix that is itself presumed to be asexual.

Slavin (2016) recently wrote: 'Something funny happened to psychoanalysis on the way to the 21st century. Sexuality, as the centerpiece of our understanding of human motivation and conflicts – indeed as one of the central discoveries of Freud's psychoanalytic endeavors – got somewhat lost. Whereas psychoanalytic thinkers in the first 50 years of the 20th century were passionately … engaged in discussions of the vicissitudes of the libido … such discussions were virtually nonexistent in the latter part of the 20th century … therapists often know little or nothing about their patients' sexual lives … this subject is studiously, even prudishly, avoided' (p. 2). Interestingly, analysts and people more generally, seem to be more comfortable with the term Eros, understood to mean a generalized life force even though bearing the name of the Greek god of sexual love. Yet, even that term may cause disquiet in certain configurations: Noelle Oxenhandler, author of the 2001 book, *The Eros of Parenthood,* reported that her title was frequently misunderstood as *The Errors of Parenthood.*

When thinking analytically about erotic life, we are broadening the concept of sexuality beyond the specifically genital to an understanding of how libidinal energies enliven the entire personality and shape the mind. Quoting Slavin (2016) again: 'Freud consistently emphasized … an expansive understanding of sexuality, of sexual drive, of libido … in extending sexuality from circumscribed genital connotations to the erogeneity of the body as a whole, and thence to the mind itself (p. 3). In a similar vein, a very astute article by Moya and Larrain (2016) compared the aligned theoretical conceptualizations of Freud and Merleau-Ponty, highlighting that what was original to Freud's thinking on sexuality was his expanded formulation of libido deriving from, but going beyond genitality. Sexuality is a dimension, an atmosphere present within us that involves the totality of the person, and a 'vital force' – an embodied energy that circulates bringing us into contact with other persons and with the world.

Developmental eroticism

I want now to touch briefly on some of the earliest developmental layers of erotic life that precede and set the stage for what Brady has so poignantly described in adolescent development. Thomson-Salo & Paul in their 2017 article titled, *Understanding the sexuality of infants within care-giving relationships in the first year,* recently offered a compelling account of infant-parent eroticism in joyful, reciprocal interaction. Drawing from infant observation, neuro-physiology research and infant-parent clinical work, they sensuously detail parent-infant erotic life, noting that the sexuality of infants has not been given enough recognition. They emphasize: 'Acknowledging the baby as a person with his or her own body, sensuality and sexuality, is vitally important' (p. 320). They give example after example of the 'intensely pleasurable excited gratification' (p. 321) that is mutually engaged by parents and infants and that is needed 'to start the baby off well as a person' (p. 325). We see that attachment and sexuality are intertwined beginning with earliest object relations rather than theorizing a pre-oedipal attachment that is then sequentially followed by a sexual development seen entirely as oedipal.

As development proceeds towards more explicit oedipal strivings, it is crucial, as emphasized in Brady's explication, for the oedipal child to experience that the parent can see him or her as a future desirable love partner (Searles, 1958), as a physically appealing and 'erotically viable creature' (Samuels, 2000: 277), someone who can delight the parents and make their 'eyes light up' (Alvarez, 2012: 126; Chapter 1, this volume).

Concentrating on the stimulus to the development of the child's libidinal self by being enveloped in an embodied, erotic relation with each of the parents brings our focus to the *healthy* contribution of parental eroticism to the child's development, with pathology resulting from *deficiencies* in the parental erotic matrix. Attention is to the advantages of ample maternal and paternal eroticism and to the problems stemming from a deficit – a deficit that cannot conceptually be reduced to a uniform expression but that must be understood to take form in an extensive range of manifestations that undermine the vitality of the child. Just as we regularly encounter failures in holding and containing, so too can parental eroticism go awry in a number of directions. Similarly, analytic eroticism can be used productively or, alternatively, fall prey to destructive dynamics (Elise, 2019).

Traversing challenging terrain   53

In parallel to what I have been noting regarding avoidance/erotic devitalization in parents, Brady's term 'erotic insufficiency' describes a falling back from the challenges of engaging the erotic within the clinical interchange: the dangers of too little erotic engagement often come about in reaction to a fear of too much erotic intensity, yet avoidance only increases the likelihood that erotic elements can get out of control. Brady emphasizes this point, citing Jackson (2017) who writes: 'we should not underestimate our propensity to avoid, negate and defend ourselves against these dynamics, even when we are conscious of them' (p. 6) rationalizing as safe and containing that which is 'essentially evasive and defensive on the part of the therapist' (p. 12, Chapter 10, this volume).

Readers will recall Jackson's example of feeling powerfully jealous when his 18-year-old female patient tells him of kissing a boy and evokes in Jackson a startling 'sense of outrage as if she had actually been unfaithful to me' (p. 18). Although Searles (1965) is rightly cited for his courageous theorizing about oedipal complementarity – the analyst's appreciative desire for a developing patient in parallel to that of a parent for an oedipal child – he too lost erotic ground at times. For example, Searles writes about the treatment of a young man whom Searles started to feel was 'dearer to me than anyone, including my wife'. Searles soon found himself agreeing that it made excellent sense for the patient to move to another part of the country! Clinicians can be quite unsettled by the intensity of our own embodied erotic responses and reach defensively for the rigid control of our intellectual understandings. But what about the other side of the coin, when ethical erotic boundaries are not maintained in clinical work? As Brady stresses, intense feelings in the analyst, when not eliciting alarm and reactively avoided, can be prone to some form of acting out.

Negotiating the boundaries in erotic engagement

It is crucial to see that narcissistic difficulties in a clinician are an intrinsic part of sexual boundary violations; it's not just about sex. A sense of narcissistic deprivation can intensify hunger for forms of erotic gratification that may undermine the integrity of an analysis and harm a patient. Narcissistic currents exert their force within the analytic field of a treatment until a vulnerable clinician succumbs to an ethical lapse, whether overt or undetected.

I have proposed the metaphor of a riptide (Elise, 2015a) as more apt than the familiar 'slippery slope' image in describing the strong currents of the explicitly erotic in our clinical work. Imagery of the ocean much more captures what analysis is truly about: a swim in the unconscious, where little can be seen, only felt, and where dangers are not very predictable, nor easy to avoid. One cannot do analysis from 'the shore', yet getting in the water means submitting oneself to all sorts of currents; even a strong, careful swimmer is potentially challenged to the maximum of ability in encountering a truly threatening situation. One must contend with the experience of being out of

54　*Dianne Elise*

control, in danger of drowning. This metaphor emphasizes the importance of advance awareness of the potential for being swept away by erotic feeling within the consulting room. Here is where our theorizing and clinical material offered in our evolving literature can prepare us to expect the unexpected.

I have offered my conceptualization of analytic eroticism as a theory of technique that centers on the analyst as a libidinal being who has the potential to use erotic energies aesthetically, with clinical integrity. Brady illustrates this capacity exceedingly well in the clinical work that she shares with us. Attention to, rather than avoidance of, the erotic can further develop our clinical ability to engage, negotiate and creatively channel these potent forces and to help our patients to do the same. This creative engagement with the erotic can provide an aesthetic container that opens space for erotic life within the analytic field without undue sense of threat or loss of appropriate boundaries.

Clinicians can themselves be confused about what containing the erotic truly means. As Brady emphasizes, the clinical aim should be to enlarge our capacity to hold a creative space for erotic elements that historically, both within our profession and in life more generally, have been under-contained and, unmanageable, have overflowed into boundary violations. We have not paid *enough* attention to eroticism in the analytic field. As a consequence, individual clinicians do not have a *theoretical* container to rely on in working with this realm of embodied energy and emotion. One then enters an area in the analytic field of a treatment that is not sufficiently 'mapped' by our training. Brady's work in the erotic field is a significant contribution to that mapping effort that needs to be ongoing within our literature and brought into our sessions.

Many patients, adult as well as adolescent, need help from the clinician in locating their creative spontaneity and their erotic vitality. The analyst has to actively generate an atmosphere that facilitates, even brings to life, a patient's own libidinal energies. This task requires the clinician's libidinal investment, an investing that needs to be palpable to the patient as an alive aspect of the analytic field where the analysis becomes 'a joint creation of two inter-communicating worlds. It's like sharing a space of virtual reality or a dream space, or entering into a kind of dance' (Civitarese, 2012: 172). The dance between Frank and his analyst that Brady shares with us is so touching.

Conclusion

As Brady writes, clinicians can fear encountering, let alone utilizing, the erotic in the clinical situation, especially when it escapes the bounds of the more familiar oedipal transferences. Understanding our role in terms of attachment has been much more palatable, allowing for distance from the enormity of passions experienced in embodied sexuality. To recognize that psychoanalysis has an erotic nature – that patient and analyst are libidinally, bodily engaged – can be troubling. Passion can destabilize one's sense of self, both in a clinician

Traversing challenging terrain 55

as well as in a patient. Yet, we cannot 'put out' the fires of erotic life, nor should we want to eliminate this powerful fuel to creative living, in spite of its combustible nature. We hope for an opening of the self to aliveness, richness of experience and meaning as we saw developing in young Frank.

The handling of eroticism within the analytic field of the clinical dyad is deeply influenced by how the profession as a whole holds, or does not hold, the erotic. The long history of sexual boundary violations within analytic practice does not seem to have improved, suggesting that, indeed, the erotic is *not* well contained by the profession (Elise, 2015b). We are in need of direct, nuanced attention both clinically and within theory building to many facets of the erotic. Brady has contributed beautifully to this effort with her theorizing and rich clinical material. Ideally, a skillful, fluent and creative inhabiting of what I conceptualize as *analytic eroticism* such as we see in her clinical exchanges, will expand the clinical container for the erotic as both a subject of analytic theorizing and as an experience within the treatment dyad. I reiterate: the analyst holds, contains *and stimulates the patient's process of growth*; each of these capacities is mobilized in the service of the analytic goals as Brady shows in her work with Frank. As she states: 'I believe that the erotic transference experienced with an emotionally available but safe object became a launching ground for Frank's own erotic life...' allowing for a deepening of a capacity for intimacy. Leaving these feelings unnamed could imply that they were too catastrophic to identify. Instead, very loaded feelings were named and the boundaries and purposes of our work remained in place' (Chapter 2, this volume)

Brady's courage is evident in her work with Frank: she bravely reveals: 'I thought I must have been losing my mind to have strong feelings of at-tractions to a twelve-year-old'. 'I felt towards Frank as I might when attracted to a man, including some preoccupation with these feelings outside of ses-sions'. But she doesn't flee from these feelings; instead she makes good use of a supervisor, a third, to negotiate this territory in order to help her patient to do likewise. She emphasizes the importance of the use of a consultant to provide balance. I agree that this step is absolutely crucial. However, it is unfortunately the case that anxiety over erotic countertransference often leads to an avoid-ance of seeking *even that guidance*. The tendency to turn in and isolate is quite powerful; when clinicians have come to me to consult about erotic feeling towards a patient, they often state how much time they deliberated about whether or not to talk *with anyone* about this particular clinical situation. Embarrassment and guilt is typically quite intense and fear of censure acute.

Hopefully, as we continue to evolve as a profession, clinicians will feel less inhibited in bringing up concerns related to erotic transference and counter-transference, and to erotic life within the analytic field more generally, such that sexuality – the original cornerstone of psychoanalysis – will no longer be a silent taboo in our professional lives. We may then consider the fullness of being – including the vitality of the erotic – that can be brought to the practice of psychoanalysis.

References

Alvarez, A. (2012). *The Thinking Heart: Three Levels of Psychoanalytic Therapy with Disturbed Children*. Hove, East Sussex, UK and New York, NY: Routledge.

Brady, M.T. (2015). *The Body in Adolescence: Psychic Isolation and Physical Symptoms*. New York, NY: Routledge.

Brady, M.T. (2018). *Analytic Engagements with Adolescents: Sex, Gender and Subversion*. New York: Routledge.

Civitarese, G. (2012). *The Violence of Emotions: Bionian and Post-Bionian Psychoanalysis*. London: Routledge.

Elise, D. (2002). Blocked creativity and inhibited erotic transference. *Studies in Gender and Sexuality*, *3*, 161–195.

Elise, D. (2015a). Reclaiming lost loves: Transcending unrequited desires. Discussion of Davies' "Oedipal Complexity". *Psychoanalytic Dialogues*, *25*, 284–294.

Elise, D. (2015b). Psychic riptides: Swimming sideways: Reply to Dimen, Gabbard, and Harris. *Psychoanalytic Dialogues*, *25*(5), 593–599.

Elise, D. (2017). Moving from within the maternal: The choreography of analytic eroticism. *Journal of the American Psychoanalytic Association*, *65*, 33–60.

Elise, D. (2018). A Winnicottian field theory: Creativity and the erotic dimension of the analytic field. *Fort da*, *24* (1), 22–38.

Elise, D. (2019). *Creativity and the Erotic Dimensions of the Analytic Field*. London: Routledge.

Jackson, E. (2017). Too close for comfort: The challenges of engaging with sexuality in work with adolescents. *Journal of Child Psychotherapy*, *43*(1), 6–22.

Moya, P., & Larrain, M.E. (2016). Sexuality and meaning in Freud and Merleau-Ponty. *International Journal of Psychoanalysis*, *97*(3), 737–757.

Oxenhandler, N. (2001). *The Eros of Parenthood: Explorations in Light and Dark*. New York, NY: St. Martin's Press.

Samuels, A. (2000). The erotic leader. *Psychoanalytic Dialogues*, *10*, 277–280.

Searles, H. (1958). Oedipal love in the countertransference. *International Journal of Psychoanalysis*, *40*, 180–190.

Searles, H. (1965). Oedipal love in the countertransference. In Searles, H. (Ed.), *Collected Papers on Schizophrenia and Related Subjects*, pp. 284–303. New York, NY: International University Press.

Slavin, J.H. (2016). "I have been trying to get them to respond to me": Sexuality and agency in psychoanalysis. *Contemporary Psychoanalysis*, *52*(1), 1–20.

Thomson-Salo, F., & Paul, C. (2017). Understanding the sexuality of infants within caregiving relationships in the first year. *Psychoanalytic Dialogues*, *27*, 320–337.

Editor's Introduction to:
On the new semantics
of transference love

Reformulating the concept of transference love from a contemporary Field Theory perspective, Giuseppe Civitarese makes a groundbreaking contribution to this collection. First, he argues that love, including transference love, is the deepest possible way of knowing someone. Second, he suggests that in contemporary psychoanalysis, the 'logic' of love takes the place of the logic of the intellect and is at the heart of analysis. Civitarese employs Hegel, as extending a model of how a logic of love (Freud's '*Liebe*') can only be obtained on the level of a relationship of symmetry, regardless of whether it is between an analyst and adult, child or adolescent patient. Further, the asymmetrical relationship of therapy only makes sense if it succeeds in establishing a mutual affective recognition, a 'we'. This 'we' in Bion's terms is reflected in the concept of 'at-one-ment' or mutual recognition. Civitarese suggests that if we see mutual recognition (the opposite of Hegel's description of the Master/ Slave relationship) as the heart of the healing process, then we must remove the obstacles that prevent a genuine affective bond.

Civitarese suggests that distinctions between 'erotic transference' (read acceptable) or 'eroticized transference' (read unacceptable) are pair specific, rather than simply manifestations of the patient. Further, he sees terms such as 'eroticized' as reproaches of the patient that generate excessively superegoic functioning in the pair. Civitarese, to my view, rightly asserts that '*If one adopts the concept of an erotic field then whatever happens in the session is not yours or mine, but ours*' or in other terms, '*the dream we both dreamt*'.

This introduction to Civitarese's ideas cannot do justice to another aspect of this chapter and one that is intrinsic to Italian Field Theory (and to Civitarese's version of it) – that is, the rich imagistic use of metaphor. Civitarese is immersed in literature, as well as film, employing images and narratives ranging from Greek mythology to South Korean film.

Field Theory eschews saturated interpretations in favor of the growth of the mind through the elaboration of waking dreaming and narrative. I would argue (and I think Civitarese would agree) that while child analysis can sometimes seem as something on the edge of psychoanalysis, that it actually prefigures Bionian and post-Bionian Field Theory developments. Bion's second analyst, Melanie Klein's major theoretical innovations were based

DOI: 10.4324/9781003266303-7

58   *Giuseppe Civitarese*

especially on the play of the very young children she analyzed. The 'play' of play therapy allows for the development of images and narratives that are at the heart of the development of alpha function and the growth of the mind.

As I suggested in the Introduction, we must examine all theories in terms of what they help us with and what troubles they leave us with. It is a premise of my work in this volume that thinking in the bi-personal field allows a fluidity and minimizes a defensive distance from our patients as we negotiate erotic territory. Civitarese suggests the metaphor of the drama, co-written by the pair. For some patients, this could feel *as if* – I could imagine a feeling response of – what is more real than love? While I understand that Civitarese rightly sees the dream, or the waking dream of a particular drama, to be the essence of psychic reality, I imagine that this is not simple clinically. As I discussed in Chapter 2, the rightful dangers of analytic seduction have outweighed a concern for 'erotic insufficiency'. What of erotic insufficiency in this theoretical model by treating our passionate response to the budding erotic and sexual feelings of a patient as dream or drama? I return to Searles (whom I discussed in the Introduction and in Chapter 2) choosing his tie for his hospitalized patient – this is a waking dream and yet one so fully felt that it is as real as anything in life. I would suggest that our shared dreaming of love, or here, at-one-ment, must have a vitality and immediacy to it. The self who is in love with a patient, is not the predominant self who lives one's life in the world, but it is a self and a self that not just the patient has to relinquish (to live his/her own life in the world), but a self that we also have to relinquish (with regret) to live other aspects of ourselves in the world.

4 On the new semantics of transference love

Giuseppe Civitarese

In a poem entitled *Semantica dell'amore* (semantics of love), Carlo Carabba writes that in English the word 'love' can refer to many things, while in Italian 'amore' would always have only one meaning and, he adds, 'painful'. Taking inspiration from his exquisite lines of poetry, from which I also drew the title of my contribution, I have structured my text in four 'stanzas' (in Italian not only the name of the parts in which a poem is divided, but also a room in the house).

In the first I discuss the Freudian concept of transference love[1] as theorized in the classic 1915 paper and emphasize the role that some ideological issues play in it. In Freud the concept of so-called transference love has always lived in an area of ambiguity. It is false and true at the same time. It is the repetition of something ancient, linked to the patient's childhood neurosis, and as such is interpreted as a phenomenon of resistance; but it is also the engine of the cure and the experience of a new and meaningful relationship. In contemporary psychoanalysis the attitude of suspicion towards transference love is increasingly giving way to the idea that it is in fact not a manner of avoiding suffering and thinking, but of knowing the other in the deepest possible way and as a quest for acceptance.

In the second 'stanza' I analyze the structure of recognition (*Anerkennung*) according to Hegel, as the most convincing model we have of how we become human – basically, the way we acquire self-awareness. The general paradigm of psychoanalysis has changed: one could say, with a slogan: no longer the experience of transference love as a support for interpretation and intellectual knowledge, but theory and technique as tools to achieve a new relational experience. In essence, the logic of *love* (Freud's '*Liebe*') tends to take the place of the logic of intellect as abstract understanding. The asymmetrical relationship of therapy makes sense only if it succeeds in establishing mutual affective recognition. By definition this can only be achieved in a dimension of equality. It happens when from the *I/you* division patient and analyst rediscover, so to say, the *we-ness*, that is, how they *both* unconsciously contribute to writing the tales of the session.

I start with Hegel, as his thinking represents the most convincing theorization of how a logic of *Liebe* can only be obtained on the level of a

DOI: 10.4324/9781003266303-8

60   *Giuseppe Civitarese*

relationship of symmetry, regardless of whether it is between adults, children, or adolescents. This does not mean that for everything else there cannot be (and in therapy there *must* be) different skills and maturity. Dealing here with Hegel's concept of recognition also gives me a chance to point out that, although it has inspired much psychoanalysis, it is often misunderstood as *conscious* recognition, a paradox, given the discipline's nature of 'science' of the unconscious.

In the third 'stanza' I illustrate how in Bion's thought Hegel's 'recognition' translates into the concept of emotional tuning or *at-one-ment*. My belief, indeed, is that what we learn in this area from speculative thinking can make our own concepts clearer; if only, because they are formulated with other languages and from other angles. Basically, even if Hegel does not use this term, we owe him the first real theory of the intersubjective constitution of the subject, and I would say also 'aesthetic', given the role that emotions and sensations play in the process.

Finally, in the last 'stanza' I draw what seems to me to be the logical consequences of what has been said so far and I present, precisely, a new semantics of transference love, that is, a different way from the traditional one of assigning it a meaning within the analytic relationship.

In fact, I look at the distinction between erotic and eroticized transference within the framework of analytic field theory and make some clinical observations. I do not think that discriminating between perverse and nonperverse forms of erotic transference is useful within the analytic space. To my eyes it reflects an attitude of diffidence towards the patient that easily can become ideological and hinder mutual recognition.

Finally, I would like to point out that I see the new semantics of TL which I try to illustrate here as always valid, regardless of the severity of pathology, or even age of the patient – as what is at play is the 'molecular' processes of thinking. Generally speaking, I do not see any essential difference between child or adolescent psychoanalysis and adult psychoanalysis. On the contrary, I think that the theoretical and technical renewal of adult psychoanalysis is derived precisely from that which, because of the prevalence of the epistemological model, has long been considered 'not really' psychoanalysis.

Ferrum and ignis

In 1955 the *Rivista di Psicoanalisi* republished the Italian translation of Freud's (1915) essay *Observations on Transference Love*. In an introductory note the editor explains, among other things, that: a) the purpose of the initiative is not to remind analysts of the rules of ethics; b) but that the article has an 'instructive value' for non-analysts; c) that 'the acute aspects' of TL that it describes 'are much less frequent', since the conversion hysterias in which 'the most explosive manifestations' occur have diminished; d) finally, that by now it would be possible to have a partial dissolution of the transference before it becomes too 'difficult to manage'.

On the new semantics of transference love 61

Read today, these lines make us smile. In fact, the pathology of transgression of deontological rules is wide (Gabbard and Lester, 2002; Celenza, 2011); it is not at all true that acute (or chronic) aspects have decreased in frequency; nor is it true that, when they do occur, these situations are easier to handle; it remains quite indefinite what the 'instructive value' of the paper is for non-analysts. On the whole, the note seems to reflect the climate of the time, which we may imagine to be much less permissive than today and seems to have the purpose of reassuring the public about the risks of treatment.

These risks were well evident to Freud, much less fearful than many of his followers and less in need of easy reassurance. His essay still leaves us admiring his style and content. Freud is extremely balanced and avoids any absolute position. He examines the various aspects of the problem; he calls a spade a spade. He makes observations that go beyond a technical paper and that integrate all that he has written in the course of his work on the meaning of human love.

I review the text paying attention, especially, to the metaphors with which it is interwoven. Apparently marginal, if compared to the theoretical framework, they contribute powerfully to its expressive effectiveness and conceptual strength. Striking, for example, is Freud's reference to tragicomedy, a theatrical composition in which serious and painful events are mixed, as in tragedy, and happy ending and other elements typical of comedy. Theatre is the prevailing analogy in the text. TL is a 'theatrical' love. It always is, even when the image of the classic patient with conversion hysteria is not at stake. 'Theatrical' is used to allude to something contrived, exaggerated, aiming for effect. TL is thus born from the beginning under the sign of fiction. The 'comic' part of the tragi-comedy essentially concerns this aspect. The image of theatre is reassuring. On stage you just pretend to die, except, of course, if the theatre is on fire. In fact, later in the essay the tragic part appears with this highly dramatic image. It may happen, Freud implies, that with TL one easily passes from comedy to tragedy. You think you are watching *A Midsummer Night's Dream* and suddenly you find yourself in *Othello*.

Before re-reading Freud's essay, the idea had settled in me that TL is equivalent to resistance. But the issue is not really in these terms (or not only). In fact, Freud writes that TL is a phenomenon that has its own consistency, and that if anything it is exploited by the resistance to pursue its own goals. TL in itself is true love but it would be used for other purposes: 'Nor is the genuineness of the phenomenon disproved by the resistance [...] transference-love seems to be second to none [...] being in love in ordinary life, outside analysis, is also more similar to abnormal than to normal mental phenomena' (1915: 167–168). Freud's move is subtle and actually leaves the possibility of framing TL within a mobile interplay of multiple factors.

Another image that is also 'theatrical', is when Freud resembles the analyst to the magician who evokes a spirit from the underworld with arcane formulas. He would be a very poor magician if he were immediately frightened and sent the spirit back down without questioning him.

62 *Giuseppe Civitarese*

After all, even the metaphor of the shipwreck[2] ('If the patient's advances were returned it would be a great triumph for her, but a complete defeat [*Niederlage*] for the treatment' (Freud 1915: 166); but in the Italian translation 'defeat' is 'shipwreck' [*naufragio*]) has its own theatricality. From Lucretius' *On the Nature of Things* onwards, with the addition in the scene of the figure of the spectator watching from the beach, the shipwreck is one of the key images of our collective imaginary.

Last, no less apt than those of fire and shipwreck to evoke danger is the figure of the chemist handling explosive materials.

In Freud's characterization the patient comes across as the image of a woman easily prey to passions, fickle, capricious, untamed and untamable. Such a character is indeed from Greek tragedy, like Medea, Antigone or Electra; but also, from vaudeville: she tries in every way to test the analyst, to seduce him, except later to reprimand him. The patient is capable of any ruse, even of pretending to be cured. 'No matter how amenable she has been up till then', Freud says, 'she suddenly loses all understanding of the treatment and all interest in it, and will not speak or hear about anything but her love, which she demands to have returned. She gives up her symptoms or pays no attention to them; indeed, she declares that she is well' (1915: 162).

So 'she' is a serial lover, which is quite frustrating for the narcissism of the doctor, but also reassuring, as it reminds him that for the drive the object is interchangeable. Like the Sphinx, she is stubbornly committed to confronting the analyst with the same dilemma between compromising the cure and re-ciprocating love. And then, depending on the moment, impetuous, defiant, unreasonable, disdainful, selfish and undisciplined.

With such an irrational and untrustworthy character, the therapist is the one who must keep his nerves steady, must not delude himself (since it is a false love, he must not be too proud for the conquest), must never fail in his ob-ligation of discretion, must not think as a moralist. He must not lie, he must not frighten himself, he must know how to deal with the agent provocateur of resistance. He must not dare to express affectionate feelings for the patient (abstinence is not only about physical deprivation), but he must also remember that here ethics and technique go hand in hand; he must realize that, while he has experience and knowledge, with TL he is moving in uncharted waters.

In short, he must not deceive himself on several points and above all he must not give in. Like a good soldier, but without adhering to any form of fanaticism, he must engage simultaneously in three fields of battle: counter-acting his own desire, containing the patient's desire (and the strength that sexual life has taken in her) and finally disproving the profane who have a false image of the method of treatment as dangerous and morally dubious.

From the point of view of critical theory, feminism and deconstruction, it would be easy to see some well-known cultural and ideological stereotypes at work here. The play that Freud writes for the theatre of analysis – we have said – is a tragicomedy (in the end, as life is) in which we have a *she* and a *he* characterized in very different ways. If we had to summarize it in a slogan, we

On the new semantics of transference love 63

could say: the feminine, that is 'unreason', and the masculine, that is 'reason' or, in Kantian fashion, the categorical imperative (all those 'must, must...'). On stage, however, there are also other male characters. They mostly play second-rate parts: the priest, the magician, the insurer, the chemist, the gynecologist, Tolstoy, the agent provocateur and, lastly, the surgeon who uses 'the *"ferrum"* and the *"ignis"'* (Freud, 1915: 171)[3]: the cohort of men in an amphitheatre comes to mind, as in André Brouillet's famous 1887 painting *A Clinical Lesson at the Salpêtrière*, which depicts the great Charcot, all bent over the mystery of women and their bodies.

The joke of the priest and the insurer, on the other hand, serves to warn the analyst against believing that he can heal by matching the patient's TL. The patient (the insurer) would not change her position one iota, even if she were 'dying'; instead, he (the priest) would be manipulated into taking out a new insurance policy. Today we would read the little story as a way of reinforcing distrust for woman and as a subliminal suggestion addressed to the analyst to arm himself with a solid malpractice insurance if he is contemplating some risky move.

Finally, Freud provides the rather crude story of the dog race. The dogs in this case would be the patients (thus, 'bitches'), who should not be misled into accepting a precarious and uncertain solution ('the sausage'–penis), and instead led to the ability to eat *many* sausages. The sexual symbolism is evident and confirms a rather devaluing vision of sexuality and of women.

Between the lines we can glimpse the fear that men have of female sexuality (the 'dark continent'; Freud, 1925: 244) and in general of the subversive aspect inherent in sexuality tout court. An analysis of the text from the perspective adopted by Foucault (1976) in *The History of Sexuality* would easily highlight an essential ambiguity. This seems to be one of the places where, in *Observations*, as in *Civilization and its Discontents*, wanting to liberate sexuality, Freud denounces that it is repressed.

On the other hand, it is also a place where this same repression is reaffirmed through the proliferation of *discourse* on sexuality that Foucault sees as now inserted within devices of power. It must be said that even Foucault is ambiguous with Freud. He does not completely agree with him, but sometimes he does; for example, when he writes that psychoanalysis has the merit of having kept open the dialogue with madness, instead of contributing to locking it up in asylums.

Now, the main result to which our brief analysis of some metaphors of *Observations* has led us is to highlight the attitude of suspicion and mistrust that Freud somehow suggests (or prescribes) to the analyst, and the ideological traces of which it is an expression. If we were to characterize in a general manner what has changed in our way of conceiving TL, perhaps we could indicate precisely this aspect. The question to be posed is the same as Freud's: 'can we truly say that the state of being in love which becomes manifest in analytic treatment is not a real one?' We know what the courageous answer is: TL has 'the character of a "genuine" love' (Freud, 1915: 168). Nonetheless, it

64 *Giuseppe Civitarese*

is as if Freud immediately let this disturbing truth slip away by making the concept of 'resistance' shine in the firmament of psychoanalytic theory and technique. But immediately another question arises: what happens then if psychoanalysis no longer relies on resistance to get an idea of how the therapeutic relationship is going? What happens is that TL takes back the truth that was being obscured by the light pollution produced by the notion of resistance?

Recognition

The panorama of psychoanalysis changes at the beginning of 1960s and with the emergence of Winnicott, Bion and later with Kohut and the revaluation of Ferenczi's work, and with the so-called relational psychoanalysis. What happens? These authors revise the very parameters of treatment. They reinterpret the concepts of unconscious, dream and emotion. The subjectivity of the analyst is increasingly considered, and therefore his role in determining the significant events of the session. The main therapeutic factor is no longer knowledge of unconscious psychic processes and the reconstruction of the patient's past, but rather psychic growth in the here and now and the increased capacity to think, acquired through the therapeutic relationship. A gradual shift takes place from an epistemological to an ontological psychoanalysis (Ogden, 2019). This involves developing a new theory of thinking. We came to theorize in a radical (i.e., coherent and rigorous) way that it takes another mind to make a mind.

The model of the development of mind is the mother-*infant*[4] relationship; that is, the relationship between a mother who has the ability to speak and a child who at birth does not have such a channel available to communicate yet. Winnicott's concepts of primary maternal concern and Bion's concepts of capacity for reverie become pivotal. Asked at a seminar to say how the mother loves her child, Bion replies that the mother loves the child with her capacity for reverie. At the 'molecular' level, a mind is made whenever a situation of being one or at-one-ment is realized. In essence, this concept establishes that the logic of love is now fully at the center of the psychoanalytic theory of therapeutic factors and that we must therefore see TL in an entirely new light. As Elise (2019, emphasis added) writes, 'Psychoanalysis *is* an erotic project'.

As we know, the word at-one-ment indicates the instant when mother and child or patient and analyst are on the same wavelength. It is roughly equivalent to the concepts of 'dyadic expansion of consciousness' (Tronick, 1998), 'moment of meeting' (Stern, 2004), empathy, etc. Bion says that when such moments occur, a fragment of truth is generated; and that this truth is the food that nourishes the mind. We realize at once that it cannot be an intellectual content, except to a limited and inevitably superficial extent; that it necessarily results from the concurrence of both mind and body; that it is conceivable as the birth of an element of order in the chaotically disordered situation of the real in which the newborn is immersed. It is as if mother and child, but then any two human beings, were already predisposed by the fact that they have, like the elements of chemistry, certain valences that can act as devices of contact/communication with others. Another image could be that of the encounter between antigen and antibody or between the molecule of neurotransmitter and its receptor. In all of these cases something 'clicks'.

Essentially what happens is that in the right conditions human beings recognize each other. At-one-ment describes at a high level of resolution how mutual recognition works. It is the mechanism that Hegel places at the basis of the process that leads to the acquisition of self-consciousness. Indeed, this is one of the cases in which speculative thinking and psychoanalysis can function as a kind of binocular vision that gives depth and thickness to a concept that is key for both. Therefore, I now succinctly mention Hegel's theory as it illustrates with exemplary clarity how at the heart of recognition there is the logic of *Liebe* or, to use Freud's expression, the 'experience of being loved [*Liebeserfahrung*]' (1930: 130).

To define the characteristics of the relationship from which recognition arises, in *The Phenomenology of Spirit,* Hegel (1807) describes various types of alienated relationships: between Antigone and Creon in Sophocles' drama; between Rameau's nephew and Bertin, in Diderot's novel of the same title; or in general between master and servant. The key principle is that you are in a relationship of alienation when, instead of being on a plane of equality or parity, you remain on a plane of inequality or domination.

Let us dwell on the relationship between master and servant. Both derive material benefits from the relationship. However, both live in false consciousness. The former because he deludes himself that he has the affection and gratitude of the latter, who is necessary to him as a workforce; the latter because he knows that he is only a servant and therefore lives in a sort of split consciousness and is forced to speak the language of dissimulation. At this stage, they do not recognize each other. The master is arrogant, the servant in bad faith. Basically, hate predominates, and not love, *but without love it is not possible to feel really alive in existence*. If things go well, only a divided existence is possible. In the field of art, an extreme example of this condition is the male protagonist of Kim Ki-Duk's (2012) film *Pieta*.

In the therapeutic relationship the same thing applies. A relationship mainly grounded on knowledge, or in Bion's 'K', is ultimately an instrumental relationship. I may know an object but not love it, or I can take advantage of the knowledge about myself that another transmits to me, but I will not *necessarily* love him/her. But what do we mean when we say that what ultimately heals in analysis is the new relational experience?

It means that there is no information or instruction that succeeds in providing a sense of basic trust in the other. There is no education that can give an affective and relational competence. In fact, it is not just a matter of rationally knowing how to behave, but also of *feeling* and knowing through the body, without being able to say *how*. It is correct to think that all theories of mind, of psychic development and of psychoanalytic technique are ultimately aimed at

66   Giuseppe Civitarese

enabling a new 'experience of love'; that in essence they have no other function than indirectly to ensure that little by little bonds are created – the main vehicle being, if seen from the point of view of metapsychology, mutual projective identification.

In the master–servant relationship, I repeat, both subjects live in alienation. The master deludes himself that he is in control of himself, but he is not, because his existence depends on the other, and the love of the other cannot be commanded. Before he can discover that he really can become the 'master of himself', in the sense of being vital and possessing a full feeling of agency, he must go through the painful experience of a moment of vertigo. That moment consists in acquiring the conscience that he can become himself only through the other. In other words, he must accept that he is inhabited by *otherness* or by the negativity of the unconscious.

This acceptance implies an act of confession to yourself and forgiveness for the arrogance of thinking you can be an absolute singularity. Simultaneously, the confession and the request for forgiveness also concern the concrete other, with respect to whom the subject admits his dependence (with Lacan, 1966: 268, his desire for the Other's desire, i.e., a wish for recognition).

So 'confession' and 'forgiveness' are to be thought of as simultaneous and reciprocal. I repeat, confession consists in the master admitting, if he wants to be not only a master but a human being (i.e., loved/recognized), that he needs the servant's love; and that, in this, master and servant are equal, they have the same dignity. On the servant's side, it means to confess that he lived in falsehood and that in order to exist he too needs not only the master's pay but also his affection. Forgiveness consists on the part of the master in forgiving the falsehood of the servant, and on the part of the servant in forgiving the arrogance of the master. In fact, what they mutually confess and forgive is *difference*. Difference (what ultimately generates fear and hatred) is not completely cancelled out by recognition, but is nevertheless balanced by a comfortable area of identity.

In the same way, in their relationship, in terms of the value they attribute to themselves, patient and analyst depend on each other's recognition and *necessarily outside any relationship of asymmetry or domination*. The situation of equal dignity is due, so that recognition is not vitiated by instrumental interests; that is, it is not inauthentic. It is important to realize that at the heart of the process of analysis is the logic of *Liebe*. If the analyst is aware of that, he avoids giving too much weight to the cognitive aspect – which in itself represents a problem only if separated from the sphere of affectivity. Besides, he would avoid, as Freud already recommends in *Observations*, all *furor sanandi* (the Latin expression used by Freud (1915: 171) is much stronger than 'zeal' or, as it has been translated in the *SE*, 'passion' to cure; actually 'furor' means 'insanity' or 'madness'). On a more theoretical level, recognition means to abandon the idea that you can rely on *will* to empathize or to love, something which is notoriously impossible.

On the new semantics of transference love 67

Now, conscious recognition, as Hegel's concept is often equivocated when imported into psychoanalysis, is not capable by itself of guaranteeing such a relationship of equality. Only the logic of *Liebe* can do so, and only to this logic can be referred the power to heal the wound of non-recognition from which the cruel Superego, and the defense of splitting that causes psychic suffering, were born.

De facto, conscious recognition could still conceal an intimate split between intellect and reason – if by 'reason' we mean a function of ideo-affective integration that expresses the intentionality of the non-divided subject. Instead, from the *I/you* of mere difference we should come to rediscover the *I (you)-you(I)* of identity, that is to say to rediscover the *we* (or *we-ness*) of linking.

We should try to have this aspect of symmetry in love very clear because it is the source of many misunderstandings. Between Tosca and Mario, who loves more? and between Romeo and Juliet? or between Hippolytus and Phaedra? and between mother and child? The answer is obvious: *love does not admit relationships of subordination and supremacy*. If there is a bond of love, by definition it is reciprocal and symmetrical. And if it is authentic, it means that it escapes conscience and will. It cannot be the result of any excess in empathic intention or in the register of sentiment (or *sentimentalism*). But then, if we think back to what we have said about *Observations*, does it not seem evident that Freud's 'scientific' and suspicious gaze does not fit well with the logic of *Liebe*?

Nowadays, this is the theoretical knot to untie if we want to re-invent the concept of TL. If we really see mutual recognition at the heart of the healing process, then, for consistency, we need to remove the obstacles that prevent its development. The process of any successful analysis would be to move from the initial relationship in which the patient is the needy 'servant' working for the analyst (providing him with a livelihood), and the analyst is the 'master' of the tools of knowledge, to a relationship in which a genuine affective bond is established.

According to the Freudian image of the chemist, it is as if all the analyst's expertise consisted in making two human substances come into contact for as long as necessary and under safe conditions, so that they could 'react' with each other and give rise to something new. This is what the analytical setting does. It creates a situation of proximity that favors the development of links by giving the opportunity to engage in a long 'conversation'.

We usually idealize the true self as a fragile and precious part of the personality forced to hide. In this way, however, we do not see the other, *monster-like* side that the true self represents in the eyes of others, but ultimately, by identification with the obstructive object (Bion, 1958), also in the subject's own eyes. True self is like the Beast waiting to find a Beauty who will kiss him and transform him into a handsome prince.

How? It is not very clear, Barthes (2007: 381) observes about this fairytale, but he puts forward a surprising hypothesis: 'Beauty, evidently, does not love the Beast; but, in the end, won over (it matters little by what, let us say: by the

68 *Giuseppe Civitarese*

conversations she had with the Beast), she tells it the magic (and requested) word: "I love you, Beast'". Barthes expresses our issue playfully. He writes that after all, one cannot know if in the end Beauty really did manage to fall in love with the *other*. Perhaps, if she did, it might have been by virtue of all the *conversations* they had. In short, psychoanalysis would be an *ars erotica* and not the *scientia sexualis* it claimed to be – not Krafft-Ebing but Ovid.[5]

At-one-ment

The issue is how to translate the insights discussed above (mutual recognition as the engine of the healing process and the removal of obstacles that prevent its development) into a practice of care. If I had to answer the same question in my turn, I would say that in post-Bionian field theory the fulcrum of therapy lies in the moment in which, (having embraced the concept of unconscious as a psychoanalytic function of the 'personality' *of the couple)*, the analyst goes beyond the *I/you* split and comes to the *we*. *Such a move makes it impossible for him to remain in an attitude of suspicion towards the patient.* In a flash, he regains a relationship of parity or equality. What the couple or the small group-of-two has unconsciously dreamed up can only be seen in principle as the *truth* of what *is* happening. Even if the couple were to deceive themselves, at the unconscious level this would not undermine their relationship of symmetry. The *we* then does represent the moment of at-one-ment.

In analysis, listening to sense and meaning of unconscious communication in terms not of the *I/you* separation but of the reconciliation expressed by the *we,* goes precisely in this direction. If there is curiosity to know the other, if this drive to individuate oneself in infinity is not inhibited, then perhaps any form of knowledge, even the most intellectual, may translate into a shared sentiment of intimate consonance. At the bottom of the 'cure' – of whatever presents itself as technique and knowledge – there is always the possibility of mutual recognition based on the logic of *Liebe*, one which is inhabited by the spectrality of the pairs guilt-repentance and confession-forgiveness.

In the analytic relationship, theories (and the corresponding technical devices) that promote the overcoming of the *I/you* split and make us rediscover the symmetric 'we' develop more effective antibodies to counteract the asymmetry – moreover, dialectically necessary – of the relationship. Transcending the *I/you* split (the sphere of mere relationship) is not possible if we do not also overcome the split between abstract rationality (intellect) and the erotic/affective body (sensibility). Finally, reconciliation should not be seen as an event that happens once and for all. Ideally it is always happening or *not* happening. Being born is an illusion, you never stop being born.

The subject's feeling of vitality needs to be continually nurtured. It coincides with the lifelong process of becoming a subject. It could be described as becoming both more *finite* (individuated, with a strengthened ego) and *infinite* (with a larger and more tolerant soul, with more perspectives on things, richer

On the new semantics of transference love   69

in humanity). If things go well, that is, if the individual is not confronted with an excess of 'difference' (in a more concrete sense, with an amount of traumatic stimuli), a balance is reached, and not a situation of absolute fusion with the other. Such an eventuality would not even be desirable, because it would be tantamount to completely zeroing out difference and therefore one of the two poles of the dialectics of identity.

For Bion at-one-ment corresponds to the intersubjective *truth* that is generated between mother and child (or between any two individuals) when a situation of emotional attunement takes place. This intersubjective truth is the food that allows psychic growth. The central idea seems to me to be that truth is no longer a static concept (a content) but a process, a becoming, a living. Being at one with the other (in unison) is a state of being that is inevitably lost and regained repeatedly. *It could not be otherwise*, because as you see yourself reflected by the other, and therefore you recognizes yourself, you see yourself as both the same and different, and reciprocally. The couple's mutual recognition and the feeling that corresponds to it, constitutes their truth. In this 'truth', which coincides with common essence, there is nothing fixed and predetermined, nor is there anything absolutely conscious/active or absolutely unconscious/passive.

This process, then, which we could define as the becoming-yourself or 'subjectivation', concerns not only the self-other dyad (my neighbor), but also the self-Other dyad. With the capital letter we mean the sociality that participates in it through the forms of pre-reflexive intersubjectivity of instincts and reflexive intersubjectivity of language. Seen from the polarity of intersubjectivity (Civitarese, in press), which together with that of subjectivity 'constitutes' the subject, the becoming subject of the individual and the becoming social subject of the group proceed simultaneously.

At-one-ment or 'truth' or 'value' or 'bond' or 'linking' is then nothing more than the happy result of a negotiating process – which runs consciously, but mostly unconsciously. In fact, Antigone (having buried her brother Polynices against Creon's will) declares that she *does not know* where the (eternal) laws that drive her to do what she does come from. The norms of this social space, which is therefore to be understood as an 'ethical' space, that is, a space in which everyone is engaged in discourse that per se is a giving reasons for their actions and an assuming obligations (Brandom, 2019). This negotiation, *which also involves emotions and feelings*, actually consists in a living, in a form of living, which is ultimately a 'second nature'.

In the dialectic of intersubjective recognition, what is at stake is the value as a person that each ascribes to himself as a reflection in the eyes of the other. If I confess to myself that I am sensitive to the value the other person ascribes to me, I make myself vulnerable to the mortification of discovering that I may not have any. Like Diderot's Bertin, I would see the abyss of abjection open wide before me. At the same time, if I am interested in the value that the other assigns to me, it is because I attribute a value to him, otherwise what he thinks would be completely indifferent to me. The risk of mortification forces me to realize that we are on a plane of equality. Consequently, I can differentiate myself as a subject only if I am not indifferent to the other, only if I appear 'different' to him, that is, not as a thing among things, and vice versa the other to me. The value that I have for the other and that the other has for me constitutes *our* truth and at the same time *my* truth. What is true for me can only be true if it is also true for the other. This value of truth derives precisely from being in common with both of us, something with respect to which neither of us is not touched.

The true meaning of analytic cure is to initiate a process that over time makes one less and less indifferent to the other; said otherwise, that leads to the constitution of a baggage of truth, or to a mutual feeling of worth in each other's eyes. 'Value', 'truth' and 'bond' are thus terms that account for the degree of falsity or authenticity of the self as well as freedom. That is, freedom understood as not being linked in a relationship of mere domination-indifference. Bion would say: freedom from a relationship under the banner of mere intellectual knowledge of the other (in minus-K; where K stands for 'knowledge') and not under the banner of experience (in O) – since K (not preceded by the minus sign) is to be reserved for curiosity that may eventually lead to O (Civitarese, 2019a, 2019b).

At-one-ment corresponds to the creation of a third, 'objective', 'universal', 'impersonal' point of view that brings each of the subjects out of their absolute point of view and thus allows them to resolve the conflict of different points of view. The *social* construction of this point of view (which, I repeat, is also a point of 'feeling'), truth, table of values, is what we call the process of sub-jectivation. Settling difference implies engaging in a relationship in which each one describes and re-describes the other from his own point of view, while also incorporating aspects that are foreign to himself until some form of re-conciliation is achieved. It is the activity of coordinating. The bond is the union of two distinct points of view to constitute a common (coordinated) point of view. Each link realizes the difference of the common viewpoint about what is true, authoritative, worthy of value, as opposed to all subjective viewpoints. The common point of view is primarily a sensible concept, which then also acquires a properly intellectual content. Unification concerns both cognitive (abstract) and evaluative (emotions) points of view. In fact, emotion is an 'affective' point of view on things and as such expresses an evaluation.

Again, at-one-ment comes from atonement, which means expiation, re-conciliation and redemption. It is an act of reparation; even if, unlike Bion, Klein (to whom we owe this concept), does not theorize its reciprocity, that is, the fact that paradoxically it is also the mother who must 'repair' the damage done in phantasy to the child (and by analogy to the patient, or any subject to an object with whom he has a bond). It has to do with healing a wrong by confessing the guilt and obtaining forgiveness. The injustice is done to God, where 'God' is the name we give to the infinite and symmetrical dimension of community. At root, any wrongdoing comes from arrogance, that is, from considering oneself different (superior) to the other. In other words, it is *difference* pure and simple; the original sin of the very fact of existing, that is, of *ek-sistere* in the double meaning of 'coming out of oneself' through giving hospitality to the other and at the same time coming out of a state of absolute indifferentiation.

As in Sophocles, the condition of existing is inherently tragic, since hubris emanates from something that, already in its mode of being alone, the subject *had* to do or *could not avoid doing*. Otherwise, tragedy and life (any life) would not be inherently noble. The 'tragedy', from a certain angle, is that the various egos are all both 'obliged' and legitimized *to be*, to differentiate themselves, which really represents the zero degree of arrogance. But in so doing they distance themselves from the 'God' of their communal substance, which is also essential to the harmony of life. Sin is thus always a sin of hubris, and yet a *necessary* one.

In normal social practices, the individual is continually required to 'suppress' himself as such in order to assume the point of view of the community. Simultaneously, the more he identifies with everyone's values, the more he is validated, the more he asserts himself as an individual by 'suppressing' the community. Self-consciousness is a 'self-image' (the 'story' of oneself), and the description/image one gives of oneself expresses what values are at stake in being oneself. Each person thinks of himself ('tells' his own story) as a particular 'type', that is, as a person who typically does certain things and who in this way differentiates himself from other types; better still, an 'individual' distinct from the mass of other individuals, and whose uniqueness does not fit into any *pre-determined* type. At birth, the ego in itself is 'empty', it is only 'pure consciousness'. It can find itself or its identity only outside itself, in what others think it is. It is for this reason we say that the ego is constitutively alienated, estranged.

However, there is a big difference between the physiological and constitutive alienation of the ego and the alienation that generates anxiety and disease. In the second case, what is corrupted is the dialectical play between subjectivity and intersubjectivity. This happens when, on the push of anxiety (or, better, fright), one of the two terms (subjectivity and intersubjectivity) assumes dominance over the other. It is then that arrogance/*hubris* is triggered (Civitarese, 2020a, 2020b). Having a heightened sensitivity to such phenomena, that do not yet present themselves as *overtly* pathological, helps us to diagnose the split in both individual and collective forms of unhappiness.

Erotic transference and theory of the analytical field

Bion writes that 'In psychoanalysis, when we approach the unconscious – that is, what we do not know – we, patient and analyst, are certain to be disturbed. It is inevitable for both patient and analyst to be upset. In every consulting-room, there ought to be two rather frightened people: the patient and the psychoanalyst. If they are not both frightened, one wonders why they are bothering to find out what everybody knows' (Bion, 2005: 104).

72 *Giuseppe Civitarese*

The distinction between erotic and eroticized transference is an artificial one and has always seemed to me to be a way (assuming the point of view of the doctor making the diagnosis), of defending oneself from the kind of fright Bion is alluding to in this passage. To my eyes, then the adjectives ('normal'/'erotic'/'eroticized'/'perverse') in the end are simply synonymous with less/more intense, containable/un-containable: therefore, not an absolute but pair-specific index. That is why, in the end, I use almost indifferently the terms erotic or transference love. When the analyst repeatedly interprets the eroticized ('bad') transference, the underlying text is a reproach addressed to the patient for wanting to persist in cultivating a sentiment that was crossed out at the beginning. If she (usually is a 'she') knows that, why does she insist? She is mad at me because she knows that I am not an option for her. She gets sad when I am away. And the analyst doesn't think that there is 'away' and 'away'; that the patient's sadness could come from lack of presence *now* in the room, not *then* and outside. Interpretation easily ends up inducing guilt because it contains an exhortation to change – and in so doing bolsters the Superego – even if 'some' love can be expressed through passion for knowledge.

The distinctions between different kinds of TL may make sense from a perspective of studying psychopathology but not in an authentic dimension of treatment. From certain entomologist descriptions, the patient comes out as Kafka's cockroach. One forgets that it is the gaze (precisely, Krafft-Ebing style) of others that makes him so. The discourse of sexuality is objectified as a concrete aspect of the patient's life and psychology. But this implies a dramatic deafness to the unconscious meaning of words and actions. TL is distinguished from erotic transference, as if there were the sex of angels and the sex of animals and nothing in between. The analyst arrogates to himself the role of judging between good and bad TL and many times this is precisely what is resented by the patient as an 'abuse'. He does not see, for example, that even the disgust aroused by certain expressions of TL that are very sexualized could have something to do, not with perversion per se, but with the dynamics illustrated by Kristeva (1980) in regard to separation from the maternal body. In some cases, it could be the way in which the couple depicts the need to escape the danger represented by an excess of closeness. Let us not forget that there is 'perversity' already in language, which in fact functions according to a principle of substitution or sublimation of 'normal' instinctual gratification (Kristeva, 2005).

There are authors who have recognized the positive values of transference love as an index of vitality, who also underline, if anything, the concept of 'erotic deficit' or 'erotic insufficiency' (see Brady, Chapter 2), and who are not inclined to use simplistic dichotomies between good and bad TL, etc. (Searles, 1958; Ogden, 2007; Elise, 2017). However, the question remains as to what the best technique is to handle this material. Indeed, TL remains lavic because the issue of recognition, (which is always in play even as we exchange opinions about what the weather will be), comes to the forefront in a way that cannot be evaded. I agree with Searles when he says that the patient's ego is

On the new semantics of transference love 73

strengthened by the fact of knowing that, although unrealizable, his love is reciprocated (1958). The issue, however, is technique. For example, what if a sexual sensation on the part of the analyst were treated as somatic reverie? If one adopts the concept of erotic field, then it means by definition that whatever happens in the session is not yours or mine but ours. As Brady puts it rightly, the real point is 'whose feeling is it?' By the way, this is *not* the idea of field that interpersonalists have, or the Barangers, which is much closer to the concept of enactment.

From a field or radically intersubjective angle, the erotic/eroticized transference are addressed as narrative genres unconsciously selected by the 'common' mind of analyst-and-patient-as-a group to make sense of the emotional experience lived in the here and now. If the analyst allows himself to be the critic of a story of which he has the ability to forget *who* wrote it – adopting in this way a true phenomenological stance – and if he concentrates on the truth it contains, whether it is hate or love, *he will not be frightened anymore*. In fact, he will focus on the unconscious *emotional function* inherent to *any* discourse – 'unconscious' in the proper sense or in the sense that, even if 'known', was attributed only to one or the other of the members of the analytic couple. Listening to virtually *anything* from this 'third' intersubjective vertex helps him on the one hand to keep the temperature of the relationship under control, and on the other hand to get in touch with the patient without demeaning her feeling.

S. arrives at the session always dressed in an elegantly seductive way. The analyst senses her charm. Oddly enough, he notices that more and more he thinks with pleasure of when he will meet her. S. sometimes verbalizes explicit sexual fantasies about him. In turn, the analyst makes erotic fantasies about the patient and feels stings of jealousy when she describes her many relationships with other men. From a classical point of view we would talk about resistance, manipulation, eroticization of transference or countertransference, etc. From a relational perspective we would pay attention to the possibility of enactment. For example, the analyst might come to discover that he or she has been recruited to enact a play. In this play the phantasy of transgression would be a repetition of the vaguely 'incestuous' climate of the relationship with her father with which S. had saved herself from being sucked into her psychotic mother's depression. What these readings have in common is that they explain the text of the session with the biography of the 'author' – or the presumed author, that is, S.

There is, however, another way of framing things. S. and the analyst together could be seen as the authors who unconsciously staged this drama – so, not really 'unknown', but only put between parenthesis as singularities. If we focus on the drama itself as the text of the session, and no longer on what it reflects of just one of the author's past or current life, we can more easily intuit what is *truly* expressed in the actuality of the encounter. The 'trick' that can be used in order to avoid collapsing on reality – which then is *dead* – is to think that it is the story of a dream. Why 'trick'? Because it is the way we remind

74　*Giuseppe Civitarese*

ourselves that analysis is about psychic reality, and that only by modifying psychic reality can we hope to influence material reality. In fact, *reality needs to be interpreted, not dreams.*

But that's not enough. Indeed, in the traditional interpretation what is missing is not the search for the unconscious meaning of the phenomenon, but the capacity to grasp its truth without setting the theatre on fire or without 'humiliating' the patient. We must also 'pretend' that it is the dream *we* both dreamt, otherwise we fall back into the quicksand of the *I/you* split and therefore of distancing and distrustful listening. The tentative story would be: we had a dream (or wrote a novel together). In this dream/novel there was a patient named S. who was very seductive with her analyst; in his turn the analyst felt an increasingly intense desire for S., but of course they could not satisfy concretely their desire without falling into unethical behavior. What in this case would the emotional climate of the session be? A mixture of desire and frustration. The next issue would be: is it likely that this narrative reflects a certain reciprocal 'absence' or lack of responsivity?

A possible critic of this drama, who would try, so to speak, to extract from it the grain of truth that it contains, would think that unconsciously S. and the analyst as authors represented a situation like at the beginning of Romeo and Juliet, of strong sensuality and mutual attraction, which will become an impossible love. If after some time we have a new scene, of Judith and Holofernes (Civitarese, 2012), in which we actually discover that seduction is not an expression of mutual attraction or love but of hatred and manipulation, it would mean that the device of treatment has not been able to contain the explosiveness of the Romeo and Juliet bond. Things took a regressive and not a progressive turn (Civitarese, in press, 2021). It would *not* mean that since the beginning Romeo was not Romeo but Holofernes in disguise, and that Juliet was not Juliet but Judith in disguise. If we thought in this way, we would be looking for an ultimate truth in the name of the Freudian principle of 'distortion'. Instead, on the basis of the Bionian principle of 'transformation' (Civitarese, 2018), it would mean that the Romeo-and-Juliet situation has become a Judith-and-Holofernes situation because there has been a lack of recognition – perhaps as a result of essentially guilt-ridden interpretations (on eroticization, etc.).

The key point from both a theoretical and technical perspective, even in the Judith-and-Holofernes mode of emotional linking, would be to not think that the patient *alone* wrote the play, but that *patient and analyst* wrote it together. Post-Bionian field theory makes Bion's principle of negative capability an effective tool precisely by adopting the fiction of the 'unknown' author (as separate individual). In any case, it is up to the analyst to interpret the succession of the various scenes (or, to monitor the various climatic changes) and to ensure that they are a source of aesthetic, that is, mind-feeding experience, and not a source of vital danger to the patient and to himself. This is when the asymmetry of the subjective poles of the pair as individuals resurfaces. Of course, in a same relationship, asymmetry in knowledge or maturity and

On the new semantics of transference love   75

symmetry in love is perfectly possible, while asymmetry in love is not love, is unhappiness or obsession. Dante claims that, 'Love, that exempts no one beloved from loving',[6] means not only that, in a psychological sense, those who love cannot stand not being reciprocated, but also, in a theoretical sense, that we can speak of love only when it *is* reciprocated.

There are cases in which erotic transference takes on a psychotic quality. I was stalked for a long time by patient, A., who was not mine, but a colleague's. She had developed a powerful erotic transference towards me. If I had been the colleague, I would have thought that a 'stalking emotional function' ('function' means that both were unconsciously acting in the same way) had taken possession of the field – perhaps because a dramatic absence of the object as a bonding function had arisen. The fact that A. really persecuted me, who did not know who she was, can always be thought of, not as acting out and lateral transference, but as a scene that belonged to the field of the patient's analysis. Not only as a way (for the couple) to write the play entitled *Who is Afraid of Erotic Transference?* but, to make it more intense, by miming or acting it out in the only theatre that was available. By the way, using the metaphor of 'field' without implying that an 'indistinct third mind' is born would be theoretically 'empty'. At most, it would correspond to the use some 'relational' models make of it. Indeed, the concept of 'co-creation' should not simply imply that two separate subjects participate consciously and unconsciously in determining a certain event. It should mean that we renounce linking it to one member or the other of the analytic dyad.

We can see, I hope, how it is misleading to think that the field of analysis ends with the spatiotemporal boundaries of the material setting. At one point, after receiving some email threats from S., I had to contact the colleague, thus giving him the opportunity to reintegrate a split aspect of their relationship. Again, the dream would be: 'Once upon a time there was a patient who had an erotic transference toward a colleague of her analyst to whom she was completely unknown'. We would think of the simultaneous need of the system/couple both to represent an *unrequited* love and maybe also the need to preserve the bond – to not subject it to a stress test that it might not withstand – and, at the same time, looking for another mind that could absorb and contain the emotional turmoil.[7] Could there be a better play to stage the drama of an analysis where there is a mutual and deep unconscious feeling of rejection than inventing a situation in which one member of a couple aiming at *Liebeserfahrung* does not literally know who the object of his love is?

The case was dramatic, but also comical: as if the patient were saying to her analyst: mine is so little a transference (in the sense of mistaken, equivocal) on you that … I do it on another therapist (an imaginary 'other', myself as a character); and, at the same time: we can only express the passion that binds us by staging a drama of jealousy; or 'we are so unable to see each other that *our love does not exist*, as it would be if I (or you) were addressing it to a *de facto* non-existing figure. So, the core emotional meaning of the *pièce* that pervades

76 *Giuseppe Civitarese*

the relationship, like so often in Beckett, is the painful feeling of absurdity: according to the etymology of the word, a condition of 'being out of tune' or discordance.

It is possible that at a certain stage this could be precisely the truth of their analysis, an excruciating and unconsciously shared doubt about the other's love. It is as if, in erotic transference, they were both in A.'s position and in mine as the unsuspecting actor of the play in the role of the (by definition) rejector. In such cases, having interpreted the emotion that is behind the complex narrative, the analyst may wonder how to contain this tormenting feeling, how to be more welcoming or receptive. For example, one way to consider the less manageable manifestations of TL in session could be to ask why at a certain point there seems to be a need to let the body speak, or rather intercorporeity (Civitarese, 2019c), instead of words, which are also actions. This, in general, could be true when TL becomes eroticized, as if to signal the limits of interpretation and the need to focus more on non-verbal communication. But, as always, the true answer is in the question itself. This way of interrogating the intersubjective unconscious third mind that comes to life in any analysis *represents, in itself, an invaluable moment of recognition.*

If the analyst is courageous enough to detach himself from factual reality, that is, if he interprets the unconscious common texture of what in discourse is presented even in terms of concrete stuff, he can indeed be the chemist who delicately handles virtually explosive emotions, because this move allows him to find a proper distance, not too close and not too far away. The delicacy lies in not meta-communicating to the patient that she is crazy, omnipotent, capricious, manipulative, etc.; rather, that what she (they) feels is true but must be interpreted in the context of the fiction of analysis. In this way, the analyst both obeys the logic of *Liebe* and avoids the masochistic and destructive slope (Margolis, 2012) of giving in to incestuous relationships – as it is more likely to happen if he remains entangled in a discourse of mere reality.

In short, technically, explicit declarations of love, or true feeling of love, or even sexual excitement in analysis, are all 'theatrical', that is, 'true' but always to be considered from the perspective of the fiction that allows us access to psychic reality. This in no way would be an intellectualization; quite the opposite, precisely because, meant as 'true' and 'shared', it would be impossible for the analyst not to embody this knowledge (as Flaubert remarked of his famous character, *Madame Bovary c'est moi!*).

Conclusion

I don't think at all that sexuality has disappeared from psychoanalysis. What *is* disappearing is the idea of a direct causal link between sexuality and symptom seen from a positivistic or ultimate truth perspective: just the kind of view that 'generates' interpretations of the patient's perversion. A possible and fair response to the patient's direct offers of love should not stand on the realistic plane of acceptance or rejection – as it would in 'normal' life. Nor should it consist of rejection disguised as interpretation of defense or resistance. Rather, the analyst should, on the one hand, acknowledge the truth of the feeling expressed by the patient (i.e., interpret it as 'their' own feeling), while interpreting it as *a mutual need for recognition* and as a desire to be *existed* by the other. On the other hand, he should interpret this need as a truth expressed unconsciously through the narrative of the so-called 'transference love' by the field or 'third' constituted by both. The first approach is (should be) our ABC, 'look for the unconscious meaning', but the second is no less crucial if we want to shed some new light on TL.

Notes

1 From now on I use the acronym TL for 'transference love'.
2 In the Italian translation: 'naufragio'; but in English is 'defeat'.
3 It refers to the Latin version in which the last of Hippocrates' Aphorisms was more widely known: 'What medicine does not heal, iron heals; what iron does not heal, fire heals; but what fire does not heal, it must be considered incurable'. In this context, it is hard not to see this as the unintentional evocation of Sadian spectres.
4 In Lat. *infans* refers to the child that is not yet able to speak: *in-* privative prefix + *fans*, present participle of *fari*, which means 'to speak'.
5 Richard Freiherr von Krafft-Ebing is the German psychiatrist who in 1886 published the *Psychopathia Sexualis: eine Klinisch-Forensische Studie* (Sexual Psychopathy: A Clinical-Forensic Study), a kind of encyclopedia of all possible perversities. Ovid is the classic Roman poet who wrote the *Ars Amatoria* (The Art of Love) and the *Amores* (The Loves).
6 This is the H. W. Longfellow translation (1867) of Dante's famous line 103 of the Canto V of *The Divine Comedy*: 'Amor, ch'a nullo amato amar perdona' (Alighieri, 2003). See A. Aciman's (2013) interesting note on alternative translations in English.
7 See Bion (1961: 125): 'the group can no longer contain the emotional situation, which thereupon spreads with explosive violence to other groups until enough groups have been drawn in to absorb the reaction'.

References

Aciman, A. (2013). Recapping Dante: Canto 5, or a note on the translation. *The Paris Review*, 4. https://www.theparisreview.org/blog/2013/11/04/recapping-dante-canto-5-or-a-note-on-the-translation/

Alighieri, D. (2003). *The Inferno*. Transl. by H.W. Longfellow, New York: Barnes & Noble Classics.

Barthes, R. (2007). *Il discorso amoroso. Seminario a l'École Pratique des Hautes Études 1974–1776, seguito da Frammenti di un discorso amoroso (inediti)*, cit., p. 381.

Bion, W.R. (1958). On arrogance. *International Journal of Psychoanalysis*, *39*, 144–146. Reprinted in Bion, W.R. (1967). *Second Thoughts*, pp. 86–92. London: Karnac, 2007.

Bion, W.R. (1961). *Experiences in Groups: And Other Papers*. London: Tavistock.

Bion, W.R. (2005). *The Tavistock Seminars*. London: Routledge.

Brady, M.T. (2022). *Braving the Erotic Field in the Treatment of Adolescents*. London: Routledge.

Brandom, R. (2019). *A Spirit of Trust: A Reading of Hegel's Phenomenology*. Cambridge, MA: Harvard University Press.

78 Giuseppe Civitarese

Carabba, C. (2008). *Gli anni della pioggia.* Ancona: Pequod.

Celenza, A. (2011). *Sexual Boundary Violations: Therapeutic, Supervisory, and Academic Contexts.* Lanham, MD: Jason Aronson.

Civitarese, G. (2012). Losing your head. *Abjection, Aesthetic Conflict, and Psychoanalytic Criticism.* Lanham, MD: Roman & Littlefield.

Civitarese, G. (2018). Traduire l'expérience: Le concept de transformation dans Bion et la théorie du champ analytique. *Revue Française de Psychanalyse,* LXXXII(5), 1327–1386.

Civitarese, G. (2019a). On Bion's concepts of negative capability and faith. *The Psychoanalytic Quarterly, 88,* 751–783.

Civitarese, G. (2019b). Bion's O and his pseudo-mystical path. *Psychoanalytic Dialogues, 29,* 388–403.

Civitarese, G. (2019c). The birth of the psyche and intercorporeity. *Fort Da, XXV,* 6–25.

Civitarese, G. (2020a). The limits of interpretation: A reading of Bion's "On Arrogance". *International Journal of Psychoanalysis.* DOI: 10.1080/00207578.2020.1827954.

Civitarese, G. (2020b). Regression in the analytic field. *Romanian Journal of Psychoanalysis, 13,* 17–41.

Civitarese G. (2021). Bion's graph of "in search of existence". *The American Journal of Psychoanalysis, 81,* 326–350.

Civitarese, G. (in press). Intersubjectivity and analytic field. *Journal of the American Psychoanalytic Association,* in press.

Elise, D. (2017). Moving from within the maternal: The choreography of analytic eroticism. *Journal of the American Psychoanalytic Association, 65,* 33–60.

Elise, D. (2019). *Creativity and the Erotic Dimensions of the Analytic Field.* London: Routledge.

Foucault, M. (1976). *The History of Sexuality, Vol. 1: An Introduction.* New York: Vintage.

Freud, S. (1915). Observations on transference-love. *SE, XII,* 157–171.

Freud, S. (1925). Some psychical consequences of the anatomical distinction between the sexes. *SE, XIX,* 241–258.

Freud, S. (1930). Civilization and its discontents. *SE, XXII,* 57–146

Gabbard G.O., & Lester E.P. (2002). *Boundaries and Boundary Violations in Psychoanalysis.* Arlington, VA: American Psychiatric Association.

Hegel, G.W. (1807) *The Phenomenology of Spirit.* Cambridge, UK: Cambridge University Press.

Ki-Duk, K., Director (2012), *Pieta.* South Korea.

Kristeva, J. (1980). *Powers of Horror an Essay on Abjection.* New York, NY: Columbia University Press.

Kristeva, J. (2005). L'impudence d'énoncer: La langue maternelle. *Revue Française de Psychanalyse, 69,* 1655–1667.

Lacan, J. (1966). *Écrits: The First Complete Edition in English.* New York, NY: W W Norton & Co Inc.

Margolis, M. (2012). Analysts who have sexual relations with their patients: The central role of masochism. In Holtzman, D. & Kulish, N., *The Clinical Problem of Masochism,* pp. 187–195. London: Roman & Littlefield.

Ogden, T.H. (2007). Reading Harold Searles. *International Journal of Psychoanalysis, 88,* 353–369.

Ogden, T.H. (2019). Ontological psychoanalysis or "what do you want to be when you grow up?". *Psychoanalytic Quarterly, 88*(4), 661–684.

Pinkard, T. (1994). *Hegel's Phenomenology: The Sociality of Reason.* Cambridge, UK: Cambridge University Press.

Searles, H. (1958). Oedipal love in the countertransference. *International Journal of Psychoanalysis, 40*, 180–190.

Stern, D.N. (2004). *The Present Moment in Psychotherapy and Everyday Life.* New York, NY: W.W. Norton & Company.

Tronick, E.Z. (1998). Dyadically expanded states of consciousness and the process of therapeutic change. *Infant Mental Health Journal, 19*, 290–299.

Editor's Introduction to:
Child, parents and psychoanalyst: binocular vision in the erotic field

Writing the introductions to these chapters is a labour of love, and absolutely is the case with this chapter. The pleasure of offering Molinari's chapter to the readers reminds me of the way growing our capacities for the sexual erotic goes into the relational erotic goes into the intellectual erotic. And back again.

The erotic field in this chapter is different in certain ways from the erotic field between myself and my patient in Chapter 2 or between Jackson and his patient in Chapter 10, where the field is more obviously centered on the feelings in the pair (while of course always involving the unconscious group relations of the family and the larger culture). Here the erotic field is a group the analyst has become a part of in working with a young girl and her parents. Child work is particularly complex because the analyst has relationships with the actual parent or parents, as well as to the couple if there is one, as well as to the child. In this way the field is different than in individual work with an adult (albeit where spouse/parent/child(ren) of one's patient or larger cultural systems are always *psychically* present).

I could say child work *in itself* requires a sort of 'braving' in the complexity it presents to/with the analyst. Here, Molinari needs to lend herself imaginatively to the erotic life of the parental couple, to a marital crisis she feels implicated in between the parents, to the serious losses each parent has suffered, and to how all of this unconsciously impacts the child. Ferro's (1999: 150) view that a child is often the carrier of a family's illness, which may have been latent and emerges thanks to the child's symptom is relevant here, as is my Bionian approach to parent work (1999) emphasizing the need for constant attention to intrapsychic and intrafamilial processes (Molinari describes that here as binocular vision). The inter-generational aspect of a child's symptom (here compulsive masturbation) is prominent in this chapter, as it is in Kohen-Abdala's work in Chapter 11. As Molinari eloquently comments here, a family's problem, not infrequently produces a symptom in 'a' particularly sensitive subject whose psychic immaturity creates the availability of being a container of a malaise that is not only the child's 'own'. In fact, in this chapter Molinari intuits that the work with the parents is most pivotal in helping to resolve a problem that has been projected into the child.

DOI: 10.4324/9781003266303-9

In the Introduction to the prior chapter, also by an Italian Field Theorist, I commented that child analysis has much to offer adult analysis, rather than being some lesser version of it. In Molinari's hands, and in general, child analysis informs adult analysis through its greater emphasis on shapes and forms, which yield the beginnings of representability. Molinari offers a wonderful application of her use of visual images (so resonant for the child analyst) in her work with the little girl's parents, after hearing them describe the girl's symptom. She conveys her association to them of the way the hands painted by Egon Schiele convey a mixture of eroticism and pain.

Another creative element of this chapter is Molinari's description of the Greek god Eros (the only Greek god depicted as a child), who of course is depicted with a quiver of arrows, which can be shot to make the subject fall in love. Molinari describes the child's symptom as a kind of arrow, or in Bion's terms, 'wild thought' which the family group needs to begin to dream with the analyst. Molinari braved offering her own visual association to the parents, which they were able to use to begin to imagine the pain and the erotic in their family.

References

Brady, M.T. (2011). The individual in the group: An application of Bion's group theory to parent work in child analysis and child psychotherapy. *Contemporary Psychoanalysis*, *47*, 420–437.

Ferro, A. (1999). *The Bi-Personal Field: Experiences in Child Analysis*. London: Routledge.

5 Child, parents and psychoanalyst: binocular vision in the erotic field

Elena Molinari

Preface

In Draft M to Fliess on 25 May 1897, Freud, after having abandoned the seduction hypothesis as the origin of neuroses, proposes the associative process of traumatic experience (as he is portraying it at that point in his reflections). Contained in this text are important intuitions regarding the transgenerational, for example, that the symptoms of sons and daughters are often replays and interpretations of the conflicts belonging to their parents or to other relatives who came before them.[1] Each member of a family has internal representations of the other members that are a composition of what he or she experiences in the present and, for parents, what they have experienced with their own families of origin. Such representations are therefore interwoven out of hidden feelings and desires, fantasies, stories and illusions that initially are not shared. It is against this intricate background of different stories, which Freud (1909) called the *family romance,* that the parents' request for help for their children takes shape. Indeed, it happens not infrequently that the family entrusts to the child, through a symptom, the role of spokesperson of conflictual dynamics. At times parents establish a way of relating with a son or a daughter, that itself becomes an intersubjective location of the little group of family members' unconscious.[2]

At the present time, an awareness that the child is part of a relational and fantasmatic system has led all child analysts, though belonging to different schools of thought, to agree on the necessity of establishing a therapeutic alliance with the parents. Over time various techniques for involving the family have been developed, moving from occasional meetings with parents as an adjunct to individual therapy with the child, to participatory sessions with one or both parents, to treatment of the family as a whole (Novick and Novick, 2013; Whitefield and Midgley, 2015; Salomonsson, 2015; Goodman, 2017; Barish, 2018; Alvarez and Peltz, 2018).

Whichever setting is considered most appropriate for each situation, the child analyst must acquire the capacity to oscillate between individual therapy with the child and group therapy with the family, coming to a way of observing that Bion (1962) defines as *binocular vision.* This arrangement allows for

DOI: 10.4324/9781003266303-10

Child, parents and psychoanalyst 83

confrontation of the upset and its possible focalization in the family's treatment, in which each of the subjects is exposed to a catastrophic experience of transformation that contains, anticipates and catalyzes what isn't yet there. I will call this type of upset *psychoanalytic seeing*, borrowing the term from astronomy.[3] In fact, if every analysis can be a play, the treatment of a family is an amplified play since the analyst finds him-/herself at the crossroads of '*many forces which appear in the field under many disguises*' (Bion 1997: 645), as happens also in group therapy.

The experience of these difficulties has often already occurred in the initial meetings with the parents, in which the analyst can make of the experience something that intervenes between the story of the child's ailment and the fact that the center of the problem lies elsewhere. The possibility of picking up a trace of this undercover experience, which Bion (by analogy with radio) calls *interference* (1974: 72–73), can be the beginning of a chance to transform aspects not yet accessible to meaning – in an image, an intuition, a memory that allows an early focus in common through words. This early experience, in addition, gives evidence of how the problem that analyst and parents propose to analyze together (manifested in the child) may not be something that belongs to the past, but is still in existence in the moment in which it is brought to light for study (Bion 1957). Far from Freud's archaeological model in which it was possible to excavate buried objects in a relatively calm situation, interference manifests as a phenomenon closer to that described by Winnicott (1974) in 'Fear of Breakdown', in which what was in the past is again found in the present with the same incandescence.

Interference, then, at first a weak signal of group suffering, can be perceived if the analyst utilizes binocular vision – that is, the possibility of listening both to the conscious mind and the unconscious, permitting the analyst's internal gaze to focus in an oscillating way on both the subject and the group. Paradoxically, the child's suffering, (which seems to be the more accessible part of the family's malaise), can become one of the ways that the group unconsciously mobilizes obstacles to oscillation among the various perspectives, with the aim of avoiding mental pain that is not yet bearable.[4] If the analyst's binocular vision manages to remove itself from this focus on the child's symptom, it is then possible for it to be transformed from an obstacle into a resource.

As the group's passive subject – that is, as the subject that hosts suffering – the child can actively contribute to promoting the transformation of all the subjects of the group through movement, play and drawing. Moreover, the valorization of the child as a key element in the process of meaning–making (through his or her primary receptivity of bodily and aesthetic elements) limits the analyst being perceived as the repository of knowing, protecting the therapeutic relationship, at least in part, from the parents' normal ambivalence. Finally, it is necessary to add a brief introductory consideration of the various possibilities for considering and dealing with erotic aspects that can permeate the relational field.

84 *Elena Molinari*

Today, in comparison to the time when Freud described it for the first time, childhood sexuality is an accepted fact that can be thought and managed by the analyst with sufficient mastery; but if one considers the child as a member of the family group and undertakes an extended treatment with the whole family, it can happen that erotic elements at first confined to the child are also manifested in the parents – in forms that involve the therapist in an emotional realm of turbulence and distortion of the possibility of observation (Grinberg, 1985; Harris, 2011; Salomonsson, 2012; Hinshelwood, 2016).

The theoretical perspective of the relational field allows one not only to consider erotic aspects as a psychophysical manifestation of sexual desire, but also to remain vigilant about the aim of involvement and of mental coupling that these erotic aspects activate.[5] The presence of erotic elements, due to the high emotional temperature they generate, can push the analyst toward defensive enactments, or simply accentuate primitive feelings of love, hate or curiosity (Billow, 2000, 2003; Migliozzi, 2016).

The word *passion* (Bion, 1963) seems appropriate to describe the push toward coupling in a broader sense, both physical and mental. Passion is thus a function of the field connected to the possibility of utilizing primitive feelings without violence. In this sense, it is connected to reverie, which is simultaneously an effect and a way of expressing love.[6]

One can hypothesize that when it is present, passion – which can include metabolized erotic elements – represents a connection that reinforces the capacity to understand one another and promotes transformation of beta elements (raw sensory data) into alpha elements (units of meaningful experience).

Self-portrait with crossed hands[7]

The parents of Adele, age four, ask for a consultation following an urgent request by the teachers at her preschool because Adele masturbates compulsively. The parents have difficulty using the word *masturbation*. They relate that Adele has rubbed her genitals since the age of six months, using the narrow band of her highchair which is placed between her legs to keep her from slipping out, and later rocking on whatever supportive object stimulates her genitally. At about two years of age, she began to use her hands, and the parents had tried many strategies to make her stop: dissuasion, threats, punishment – but all to no avail.

The parents' story produces a cinematographic effect in me: imaginatively, I picture Adele drawing, playing, acting capriciously and then the visual field shrinks to her small hands (which her parents obsessively monitor) – as though I am seeing the special effects of a wide-angle lens alternating with a telephoto lens.[8]

In the second meeting, the parents start to shift responsibility between each other for some of their educational choices, creating a climate of light emotional tension. The father begins to bite his fingernails, at first furtively and

Child, parents and psychoanalyst   85

then in an almost embarrassing way. His teeth seem to inspect each finger, tearing away the little cuticles at the edge of each nail; the fingers enter the oral cavity and then come out accompanied by a small sigh of satisfaction. I find that something unusual is happening; rarely in the first few meetings do patients allow private gestures to emerge, free of inhibitions. Only at the end of the session – perhaps giving voice to some of my own nonverbal expressions of astonishment and discomfort – does the mother state explicitly that her husband's nail-biting is a gesture that he cannot seem to control, and for some months Adele, too, has begun to imitate him.

We adults agree to continue meeting for a while before initiating a formal observation of Adele. In subsequent sessions, I learn that the mother works as a physical therapist in a different city from where they live, and not only does she do the domestic chores and dinner, but she also looks after her husband's grandmother, a very elderly woman who lives with them. She presents a very detailed account of all this caregiving to unburden herself of the sense of guilt she harbors at not having much time to devote to Adele. So, her hands take care of many persons; they are concretely occupied both with the pain that inhabits the bodies of her patients, and the needs of her family members. But it is as though this pain is something that has to do with her own stifled needs; the pain continues to stick to her fingers.

Without being totally aware of it, when I review the meetings with these parents in my mind, I think of some of the images of Egon Schiele,[9] in which the hands are a central element, often in the foreground. These are gnarled hands, entangled, not infrequently of disproportionate dimensions to the body, and capable of expressing a deep pain more than other details – such as posture or facial expressions – are able to do. In many self-portraits, furthermore, Schiele depicts his own hand with the fingers artificially separated, almost as though he wants to express, in consonance with the cultural movements of the early 1900s and with Freud's revolutionary ideas, the non-solidarity or non-unity of the ego.

After some meetings during which, together, we question ourselves about Adele's need to re-create a pleasurable situation even in apparently calm moments, I mention a possible link between pleasure and pain:

> *Analyst:* I don't know if you have happened to see this, but a painter of the early 1900s, Egon Schiele, mixed eroticism and pain in his paintings. For example, you have told me that sometimes Adele has difficulty waiting for dinner to be ready, even if she is watching an animated cartoon that she likes. In short, sometimes the things that we like and we don't like get mixed together, and it's possible that Adele uses her hand to try to make pleasure predominate. We see this more when she masturbates, while what she doesn't like stays hidden.

This simple reference to pain has the effect of breaking open a dam that has held back not so much Adele's pain, but pain that has inhabited her parents' lives. The mother is familiar with Schiele and seizes the opportunity to tell me about the similarity in appearance between one of the painter's models and a friend of hers, who died in a road accident at the age of 20. Her description of her friend seems to be that of an alter ego. Even though eight years have passed, the pain of this loss is very alive, and the grieving process has not even begun. She cries as she recalls this and says that even now, she is not capable of going to the cemetery. Hence during the session, I again reflect on the rupture of the self portrayed in Schiele's paintings by the separated fingers.

The contorted bodies that Schiele puts forward not only communicate his own pain, but also, according to a recent interpretation, are a partial reproduction of the figures of hysterical women photographed by Salpetrier.[10] These women somatized a pain that was private, but it was also connected to their social situation of marginalization and denial of access to recognition as subjects in their own right.

I think of this mother as a carrier of personal pain, but also divided within herself between the effort to be recognized as a mother and as a woman. She is often oppressed by the tasks of caregiving and by the wish to maintain her own job; she wants to have the same rights as her husband, even as she takes his place in caring for his elderly grandmother. After my comment about the burden of caring for elderly persons who are not self-sufficient, the mother adds that for years she has also been caring for her mother-in-law (her husband's stepmother).

I ask how her husband came to lose his mother, and I am told of her terrible death in a bedroom fire when he was five years old. The account of the fire had the effect of transforming this big man seated beside me into a small child who was overflowing with guilt. Adele's mother tells me that, before going to sleep, her husband's mother had asked him to close the window to avoid allowing the curtain to be moved by a breeze that could bring it into contact with the heater. He had obeyed her, but then his father had reopened the window and gone out of the room, returning only when a blaze had erupted and there was no possibility of saving the wife.

Father's father remarried, and father grew up with this new step-mother whom Adele's mother describes as unaffectionate. Father's father became decisively violent – as in the worst of the Grimm Brothers' fairy tales – but without the happy ending. For father, the happy ending comes in with his meeting the companion to whom he has entrusted the care of his stepmother. Her hands allow him to preserve the image of himself as a good little boy, keeping him safe from expressing feelings of hatred or rage.

Notwithstanding the fact that husband and wife unconsciously use each other in order to keep intact the usefully defensive arrangements that guarantee a certain compactness of the self, they experience their marriage as essentially satisfying. They even plan to have a second child. First, however, they would like to resolve Adele's problem, fearful of the fact that a little rival could accentuate her obsession. At any rate, Adele's hands – just as in a picture by Schiele – are in the foreground, and they allow a glimpse both of erotic desire

Child, parents and psychoanalyst   87

(understood as a new birth and a better realization of the self) and of a body-mind that is painfully deformed by suffering.

As the treating therapist, I ask myself what my own analytic hands must do or not do. I think that a clear direction may be implicit in the parents' request to transform the masturbation. Transported into the analytic field, the masturbation appears to me as Adele's attempt to transform by herself a mixture of beta elements, a lump that instead needs at least one other mind in order to be thought. Thus, there is a clear warning for me as well: I must not be seduced by the pleasure of a way of caregiving that is nourished – like masturbation – more by fantasies than by a true meeting. It is a call to remain alert, one that necessitates observing this family's difficulties from different points of view and capturing in the field the passionate elements that promote mental coupling.

The parents' many stories alluding to death create a depressive vortex. Within a depressive vortex one loses sight of Eros, of the elements of beauty and pleasure that are indispensable for transformations to occur. The imaginative reference to Schiele seems to me to be a precious element to be preserved in my mind as something attached to an aesthetic and representative model of transformation.[11]

For now, Adele, the imagined new baby, and the parents themselves, so complementary to each other and clinging together, sketch out in my mind the picture of a young, middle-class family in a composition of love and death (or mortification of the self), as in Schiele's last painting.[12]

The houses: construction of side-by-side containers

After some sessions in which I observe Adele with her parents, the anti-COVID regulations relegate us to meeting on screen. The verbal conversation continues principally with the mother and with Adele, who stays in the room, playing partly on her own and partly interacting with her mother and me. The father, on the other hand, disappears temporarily from the therapy because of his work, connected to the health emergency, which takes him away from home for about two months. This distancing and the consequent loss of a certain family structure is echoed in the contents of sessions during this period.

The mother tells me of having received a turtle as a gift, but of being afraid that, in digging in the dirt, it might go into the neighbor's garden. There follows a lengthy account of the neighbor, who is a person with whom one feels uncomfortable, in contrast to the other neighbor, who is kind and affectionate with Adele. This fear suggests to Adele's mom that she shouldn't keep the turtle and should instead entrust to her own mother.

Together with Adele, I am shown pictures of their garden on a tablet, including the turtle, and then the tree in which they would like to build a treehouse for the little girl. Adele then builds a series of houses with Legos, which she juxtaposes on a little table to form a sort of city landscape. She assembles the Legos, breaks them apart and puts them together again, sometimes in an orderly way and at other times more chaotically.

88   *Elena Molinari*

I think about how the present uncertainty nourishes the desire for a secure shelter, a sort of hard shell adhering to her body, but such a shell cannot be considered sufficient because it is undermined by the use of the split, as a consequence the feeling of being persecuted. The treehouse is an attempt to construct another refuge, one for the child-self who feels attacked by the fantasma of ferocious animals – to which, however, it is difficult to give shapes and words beyond their location near home.

I search for a possible meaning in what Adele is doing, as though she, beyond being the '*porte-symptôme*' (Kaës, 1994) of the group, can also be seen as the subject capable of participating in the creation of symbolic transformations. This way she has of arranging houses, juxtaposing them and showing them off with pride to her mom and me, demonstrates her desire for closeness (added to by the absence of her dad), but it is also the representation of her wish and that of her parents for containment and nearness. I ask Adele to tell me who lives in the houses and if there are other children living there. Adele answers that there are other people, but now the houses are shut up and the people cannot be seen.

The motif of the house as an important sign of her relationship with her body and with her mother is noteworthy. In the symbolic development of the healthy child, the house rises up to overlap with the representation of the body and is almost always the first representation of something other than the self. In this sense, it could be considered a pictogram of the primary relationship, a memory repository of having been in unison: an experience that arouses the fantasy of being able to transcend the separating space necessary in order to draw, and the experience that allows containment of the anxiety that the child encounters when she begins to do so. The house is a graphic or plastic outline of the memory of having had a body and mind in common, but it expands and also graphically offers a space in which to work through early feelings of distance. Moreover, the house is the mental location that restores a feeling of belonging and of familial intersubjectivity, which provides a dwelling place for the desire for durable ties that guarantee continuation of the generations (Eiguer, 1994).

Adele's representation is like an oneiric image: a condensation of an individuation of the family's subjects that has taken place, but also of necessary reciprocal support to guard against collapse.[13] Such support, however, presupposes the closure of the houses and the invisibility of the life they contain. Adele's specifying this speaks to a containment function that cannot completely relate to difficult emotions – a representation that emphasizes more a defensive closure than the use of doors and windows as pathways of permeability.

In the closed and tightly overlapping houses, one can discern an attempt to dramatize, and thus to communicate through play, a feeling of 'uncanniness'[14] present in the analytic field that one glimpses in the chaotic juxtaposition of Lego blocks. From another point of view, however, the playtime construction with Legos makes me think of the necessity of the analytic task of constructing

Child, parents and psychoanalyst 89

or expanding the container through multiple experiences of connections, before unconscious contents can be confronted.

The fantasies, dreams, myths and artistic creations, and images introduced into the field by the child, are a basic, symbolically protected area for the psychic transformation of raw, undigested emotions and the growth of the mental container. In this sense, I also consider my associations to Schiele's work not only as my thoughts, but also as a further partial working through of the thoughts present in the group.[15]

> It could fall to a specific individual to have the capacity to formulate the thought or the idea. But I don't think that the actual germination of the idea is attributable to a specific individual. It is very difficult to localize the phenomenon.
>
> (Bion, 2005: 117)

In the attempt to catch hold of something in the lump of emotions that circulate in this little family group, I think of the houses painted by Schiele in the brief period between 1911 and 1913 in which he moves to Krumau, his mother's birthplace. In this part of Bohemia, the subjects of his paintings are primarily representations of houses without any people. As evidence of those who inhabit the houses, there are only clothes hung outside to dry.[16] These paintings of the Krumau houses allow me to see that sometimes loneliness can be juxtaposed without communicating. But in the detail of the clothes hung out to dry, I recover the hope of possibly revealing intimate emotional elements to the other, emotional elements that unite all human beings – just as laundry does. Furthermore, in the hanging clothes faith is present that warmth from outside can dry them.

I share Adele's play with her father, describing it in a Skype session in which both parents are present. In talking about the closed houses, we share the anguish of isolation that we are all experiencing and the loneliness it entails for Adele and for us all. The father underlines the non-tragic nature of a separation that will have an end, and by contrast he allows into our discussion the presence of a loneliness following the loss of a parent – the incredulity of abandonment and the rage that follows from it. This is an emotion known to his wife in relation to the loss of her friend, about whom she again speaks with great pain. Both parents try very hard to keep this suffering hidden, confined to memory, but it now resurfaces in connection with the forced separation.

I emphasize that in her play, Adele alternates moments of construction with those of relative destruction and difficulty in putting the Legos back together:

> *Analyst:* She, too, is having experiences of how difficult it is to put the pieces back together after having destroyed the houses. Her hands are not yet expert, and it might be that precisely in facing a similar experience, she might try to obtain pleasure for herself.

90 *Elena Molinari*

Both parents are moved by their daughter's difficulty and seem to better understand the her resort to masturbation. Toward the end of the session, they decide not to give away the turtle for which Adele seems to have developed an affection. In this session, through Adele's play, the parents gain access to a greater awareness of the losses, scarcely worked through, that both have suffered. In the decision not to get rid of the turtle, one sees an increased capacity to master the split, the withdrawal and the sense of persecution that accompany them.

Three women in one: the sister, the lover and the wife

Adele and her mother keep in daily contact with the father through Skype. Initially, the husband tells of all the pain he witnesses, and in particular the agonizing farewells of some of his patients who say goodbye to their loved ones before dying during a video call. This detail calls to my mind an interesting observation made by Resnik in an article entitled 'The Hands of Egon Schiele' (2000). Resnik examines a locomotive drawn by the painter at the age of ten, and in the smoke it emits, he identifies the trace of a hand. Schiele was the son of a station master, and according to Resnik's reconstruction, witnessed daily the separations between those who left and those who stayed, fixating on the painful gesture of the waving hand – and on something of his own difficulties with separation as well. Such difficulty was aggravated by the death of his father from syphilis when Egon was 15 years old, after some years of psychiatric disturbances due to the cerebral localization of the illness.

A somewhat surprising aspect of the evening conversations between husband and wife is that, after an initial phase marked by painful stories, the husband begins to get seductive, displaying his erotic desire in a completely new and explicit manner. It is not unusual that persons immersed in seriously traumatic and lethal situations cling to life through Eros, but initially the wife was scandalized by this and judged her husband severely. She talks to me about it in a session in which Adele is not present. I tell her:

> *Analyst:* It happens in a couple that each can be for the other a parent or a sibling, but discovering the lover in the other person is a healthy aspect, even if this emerges in an unusual way.

I say this thinking about how Schiele used his much-loved sister, Gertrude, as a model, portraying her in decisively erotic poses –until he met with 17-year-old Walburga Neuzil, known as Wally, who depicted a great many sexually explicit poses, including masturbation.[17]

Perhaps feeling some minor resistance on his wife's part, the husband's desire becomes ever more daring, until one evening he asks her to take off all her clothes and to become aroused by touching herself. Adele's mother is very annoyed by this and is consumed by fantasies that her husband may be attracted to another woman; certainly, she is not the lover whom her husband desires.

Child, parents and psychoanalyst 91

Categorically, she will not do certain things, and she feels wounded by being treated like a prostitute. Deep inside, her rage and displeasure grow at a dizzying rate – to the point that, for some days, she feels compelled not to answer calls from her husband on her cell phone or on Skype.

Thus, a very painful situation of loss of contact is created in both of them. The separation they suffer, at the moment not resolvable in a meeting, re-activates in each of them the echo of unresolved mourning. The husband sends a storm of messages to the wife in which he asks her forgiveness, pleading the innocence of his desires and expressing anger at her extreme reaction.

The wife seeks in me an alliance to sanction the 'pathology' of her husband's request so that she can use it in a possible petition for divorce. I think that she may also feel angry for having felt herself pushed by my words along this dangerous slope. Somewhat apprehensive about the unexpected direction toward which the situation seems to be heading, the only clear aspect seems to be the non-coincidence between the form of the father's erotic desire and Adele's compulsive symptom. But I am not yet capable of constructing a communicable narration about this assumed connection.

Holding a session with the couple together is scarcely do-able for practical reasons; furthermore, I vividly remember the father's embarrassment when the wife had verbalized his nail biting during our earlier sessions. The emergence of the erotic theme, narrated in an overly explicit way, risks producing a fracture.

Feeling somewhat responsible for not having been attuned to a register of tolerating the emotions at play, I think that my breakdown in providing effective psychic help may be located at the intersection of many levels in this familial group: the therapeutic one, the historical one and that in relation to Adele. Like me, the parents cannot have been capable of offering sufficient containment and emotional synchronization with Adele, who finds herself alone in managing an excessive quantity of pain through getting pleasure from masturbation.

I am also apprehensive about the emergence of an erotic turbulence that momentarily shores up the difficulty of getting through pain. I say to the mother:

> *Analyst:* I don't think that your husband had the intention of putting you in difficulty or dangerously exposing you. Sometimes exaggerating the wish to look hides the desire to be looked at.

After a silence, I add:

> *Analyst:* You had your friend with whom your feelings were truly mirrored. Maybe your husband seeks something similar in you.

As I speak these words, a possible connection is clarified for me between the two subjects that predominate in Schiele's work: the self-portrait and the erotic representation of his models' bodies. They can be seen as two sides of the same desire: looking and being looked at passionately. Outside the session, I reflect on the fact that to undertake a self-portrait, artists often make use of a mirror. Schiele, too, painted his by using – at least initially – the very mirror that had been given to him by his mother when he was 16, on the occasion of her departure for Vienna's Academy of Fine Arts in 1906. Having been orphaned the year prior to painting the self-portrait, Schiele clings to this mirror as though it could represent the maternal eyes in which he is reflected. This experience was mostly unknown to him as he was growing up because of his mother's difficulties in being with him during his early childhood and then again in adolescence, in that she herself was burdened by grief and difficulty related to her husband's illness. A 'dead' mother, psychically, is thus agonizingly sought after in a compulsion for self-portraiture.[18] The relation to eyes that gaze lovingly plays out for Schiele in the relationship with his sister, and then with other, subsequent models, in an increasing capacity for distancing from the familiar. The counterpoint between the events in Adele's family and Egon Schiele's work is obviously an arbitrary element, but a useful one for transforming emotional upsets into images.

The wife doesn't comment on my reference to the intimate confidentiality and mirroring with her friend, a relationship that seems to precede formation of the birth of the third, (understood as psychic space in the meeting with the other-than-the-self), toward which the husband is pushing her through the erotic relationship. She agrees, however, to an evening Skype call with her husband. Adele's mother gradually allows herself to be seduced in the dialogue with her husband – not to the point of concretely undressing, but liberating herself from inhibitions about speaking of the desire to get out of the suffocating role of caregiving to which her husband, too, contributes to incarcerating her.

After a little while, the husband comes home, and he, too, manages to open up about the pain and anger that he has held inside him for many years, never finding a means of expression except through his body, in the desire to tear off tiny pieces of skin from his fingernails. One can imagine that, beyond the normal young sexual impulse, the tragic events of life spurred Adele's father to seek pleasure and consolation in masturbation during his youth, more so than normally happens.

Schiele recalls in his diary how sexual passion 'burned him' during his childhood and how sexual impulses pushed and lifted him up. He relates that at the same time it was more a terrible torture than a pleasure.[19]

The forced separation resulting from the pandemic has brought back to the surface the old way of confronting first the mother's loss and the father's a little later, rendering the audacious request made to the wife a kind of waking dream in which there is both the pleasure of the body that comes from masturbation and the mental pleasure that comes from looking and being looked at by the mother. The computer screen employed during the video calls perhaps played a role in creating this mirroring effect and a distance/closeness that was useful in inducing greater freedom of thought and word.

Child, parents and psychoanalyst   93

Paradoxically, in a scenario where death seems to dominate, this couple finds the words with which to relate to each other more intimately, to transform distance into closeness, to invent for themselves a new pattern of intimacy. In parallel to a new framework for desire and for the exploration of pleasure in more adult ways by the parents, the problem of Adele's masturbation was attenuated, to the point that it appeared only occasionally and, in a way, more in keeping with her age.

Seeing and being seen

To see, which is also a tool for knowing, is a function that is physiologically quite deficient at birth. Binocular vision is a complex function that is refined in the first two years of life and fully established only at around the age of eight. This is a pivotal point in development because it permits one to focus on details, to be aware of a certain portion of space and of its depth and to utilize vision in the service of action. At the same time, it is an event that intersects with the development of knowledge, of awareness and of ideas.[20]

If we transfer this premise into the analytic relationship, what does *seeing* mean — seeing and focusing, being aware of what happens in a certain portion of space, and knowing how to use this information? How can we intuit and thus see the unconscious interweaving of relational connections and symptoms, and especially how can we share this in the family group?[21] The starting assumption is in family treatment, as in individual therapy, there is not a subject who thinks and one to whom the meaning of what is said or done is communicated (interpreted). From a Bionian perspective, thinking is not done inside the subject but is always, from the beginning, a relational piece of data. Just as seeing stereoscopically requires two eyes, thinking requires two subjects.

In the relationship with a very small child, beta elements — which constitute the initial legacy of the child's bodily sensations — become perceptions that have a meaning merely by passing through the alpha function of the other, which actually thinks them with him. In this early phase, if we want to set up a parallelism with the visual function, it is possible to say that mother and child are trying to learn how to put sensation and emotion together in order to capture simultaneous images. In biological vision, each eye sees an image, and in order to avoid doubling, it is necessary to learn a way of coordinating that guarantees the perfect superimposition (fusion) of what each eye sees. Analogously, one can say that every time mother and child understand each other emotionally, which successfully focuses their respective feelings/emotions in the here and now, the two of them reach an emotional unison that creates an affective pictogram (an alpha element). Over time, the production of many alpha elements allows the structuring of a function (the *contact barrier* — Bion, 1962: 100), which generates an early distinction between the conscious and the unconscious. At the beginning, everything is conscious; it is sensation and perception. The unconscious is created in the relationship of two subjects

94   *Elena Molinari*

who manage to focus on and share an emotion; the term *binocular vision* describes the rapport between these two parts of psychic functioning.

The possibility of having the experience of a group relationship, such as, for example, that of the family, can be an occasion to see in greater depth or clarity, something that is beyond normal perceptive capacity – a way to approach comprehension of parts of the self that are otherwise inaccessible.[22] These are proto-mental states, elements that get registered in a sensorial way and are not spontaneously directed toward signification – forms of procedural memory, implicit or not declared, early traumas that get deposited in the body, in a memory without recollection.

One could say that within a group therapeutic framework, the possibility of tridimensional vision is generated, a vision that is deeper and clearer. In biology, tridimensional vision is the result of a very complex integration imposed by the necessity of mastering the distance between the two eyes. This distance would generate perceptive distortions were there not an intervention from a system not so much acting as a corrective (as happens for the fusion of the images of the two eyes), but instead as a system that can learn to integrate different information that correlates memory with many associative areas of the cortex. Psychic learning, which permits tridimensional vision in a network of conscious and unconscious relationships, sometimes starts from a fracture in this network: the malaise of a group member. In a family, not infrequently, this malaise converges in a child's symptom, that of a particularly sensitive subject whose psychic immaturity creates the availability of being a container of a malaise that is not only the child's own.

The symptoms manifested by a child activate in the parents the desire and attempts to take care of the symptom, but also defensive emotional reactions, sometimes primitive ones, and wild thoughts (Bion, 1997; Bolognini, 1994).[23] Wild thoughts can be compared to the preconceptions of a small child – emotions, affective states, basic wishes that must be thought. In the case of the group, however, wild thoughts – unstructured ones, unconnected to other thoughts – are often uncomfortable, aggressive, shameful. Although called thoughts, they are not fully such because they take on a form in which the physical and the psychic exist in an undifferentiated state.[24] Such thoughts generate a sort of contagion among the group's components and continue to circulate until the collective alpha function renders them thinkable and thus speakable. In this situation, too, it is the *transindividual* who thinks, not the single mind. The possibility of focusing on a wider, tridimensional vision, which is generated in considering the relationship between the subject and the group, has been described by the term *binocular vision* – not by chance the same expression used to describe the conscious-unconscious relationship.

Just as the conscious and the unconscious become the products of a gradual differentiation carried out by alpha function, the group's components become fully formed subjects to the degree to which each becomes aware of and masters his or her own emotions. In the group analytic field, a valid paradox exists: the greater the emotional identity of each component, the healthier the

Child, parents and psychoanalyst   95

relational connection. In other words, the more the parents take possession of their own emotions, the more the child has the possibility of developing without the burden of undigested emotions that are not the child's own.

The analyst's role: a corrective lens

Which method can the analyst use in a family or group field to help each of the subjects focus on their own emotions and distinguish them from those of the others? In the past 50 years, various methods of treating the child's difficulty in relation to that of the parents have been developed (Salomonsson, 2014). Those methods, like differing corrective lenses, propose different areas of focus in the therapeutic process. Some authors particularly concentrate on the child's internal world and that of the parents, while others place emphasis on supporting the parental function. Almost all attribute a crucial role to the child, agreeing that use of the child's nonverbal communication can improve the process.

Such a common position, however, is newly opened in answering the question of whether the child is considered a subject who participates in the process (and in what way), or whether he or she is merely influenced by it. The answer implies a different theory of technique. One option is for the therapist to focus on the child's unconscious needs and to communicate directly with him or her (Norman, 2004; Salomonsson, 2007); a different option is to consider the child's suffering as a result of the mother's or father's unconscious conflict. In this case, the analyst does his or her best to put the unconscious traumatic memories of one of the parents into contact with the child's symptoms.[25]

A third possibility is to consider the family as a small group in which the child's symptom represents – in addition to a difficulty – a possibility for each subject to move toward a psychic transformation that allows him/her to approach a level of optimal subjectivization. This technique involves focusing not only on suffering located in the past, but also on its reproduction in the present, in the analytic situation. Considering the emotional interaction among subjects, it is possible that the analyst concentrates on grasping how an emotion may be shared among the group's subjects. Focusing on emotional unison reactivates, (to a certain degree and at a group level), the initial pattern of the mother–child relationship, when reverie allows the child to recognize his or her own emotions in identification with the mother's feelings. Such identification permit the birth of the psyche out of the body. In other words, this emphasizes an identification of feelings between two or more components of the group, as the place in which each subject's difference comes into being and is given shape.[26]

Recognizing the emotion present in the intersubjective field and correlating it to the events of the analysis is what Bion calls *being in unison with O* in the session. Since O cannot be grasped with the intellect, to be receptive to the intersubjective unconscious level involves not only an observation of

96 *Elena Molinari*

the interaction, but also listening to the unconscious. *Speculative imagination* is a faculty of the mind that can create a common field between the field of imagination and that of comprehension, two areas that Freud maintained are distinct, but that Bion places in relation to each other through identification of their common space.[27]

The role of the child as a subject of the little group (parents–analyst–child) is that of one who is more capable than the others of activating the imagination, especially through play, and of drawing attention to some of the sensorial and aesthetic elements. The child is thus able to support the upward surge of usable images from the imagination and then eventually to transform them into a communication. The embodied experience of the child's symptom, then, can be considered the beginning of a potential space between perceptive experience and reflective experience, for each member of the group.[28]

The child as an erotic resource

Eros, in its Greek root, has not only the connotation of sexual attraction, but is also understood as a force that contains different though united elements. Sometimes these elements conflict, but without reaching the point of being dissolved (Ubaldo, 2000). In the Greek pantheon, the god Eros is the only divinity represented as a child – first a young man and then a small child who has been provided with a bow and arrow with which he can strike the heart of whomever he wants to make fall in love. Transferring this representation to the analytic situation, it is possible to think that, within the family, children represent the subject capable of introducing into the field arrows of *wild thoughts* that must in some way be transformed, thereby pushing those around them toward new thoughts. Wild thoughts, neither structured nor connected to other thoughts, are often uncomfortable, aggressive and shameful.[29] They are wild because all ideas, before being thought, are a mixture of elements that no subject alone can handle. But, it is necessary for the group together to reach the point of thinking what none of the members is capable of doing alone.

During the treatment of a child with his or her family, it is possible to both concentrate on the particular relationship between the child and the parents, and to attend to the group dynamics that flow through the family and into which the therapist enters to take part. One could say that oscillation between an analytic vision centered on the here and now of the relationships among the various subjects of the family, on the one hand, and the family as a group, on the other, is possible only in an erotic field – a field pervaded, that is, by passion and coupling without destroying the existence of individual subjectivities.

Initially, a symptom appears in the child, and it is from here that the analyst can start out, allowing the malaise to remain placed within the body, until the germ of an idea is mature enough to be born.[30] The first stage of

Child, parents and psychoanalyst 97

transformation of the symptom often coincides with the upward surge of an image into the field that brings with it an early feeling of consistency in the chaos of emotions, sensations that become more frequent and more pronounced in group meetings. If one considers the emergence of the selected fact[31] and the aesthetic experience as aspects of a turning point in the process, one can hypothesize that, in a therapy, the child can play an active role in causing the emergence of an 'aesthetic selected' fact – one that is also understood in the etymological sense of being connected to the senses.[32]

When one can make use of an image – not necessarily a shared one – the symptom is no longer only a manifestation of discomfort, but also becomes the staging of a fantasy that inhabits it and transcends it. Furthermore, being able to consider the sexual fact in a broader imaginative context allows the passage from erotic desire to passion, a dimension more symbolic of the connection that permits 'a dream, freed from space and time to move between individualities and generations' (DeToffoli, 2014: 248). With this family, then, one can say that: 'Thinking is [has been] bearable only by its sensual component' (Bion, 1975: 159), and that the little girl's arrows played an important role in the transformation of her parents' pain.

Notes

1 Freud intuited that the existence of unworked – through traumatic experiences – can influence subsequent generations. The transfer of psychic torment into another person, in general an offspring, avoids the painful working through that a grandparent or parent is not capable of suffering through. This theme has been developed by many authors, such as Faimberg (1988), Eiguer et al. (1997) and Imbasciati (2004).
2 Kaës (2009) writes: 'The unconscious is not entirely contained within the borders of individual psychic space. The psychic space of the connection is another location of the unconscious'.
3 *Astronomical seeing* refers to the amount of apparent twinkling of astronomical objects, such as stars, due to turbulent mixing in the earth's atmosphere, causing variations of the optical refractive index. The visual conditions on a given night at a given location describe how much the earth's atmosphere disturbs the images of stars as seen through a telescope.
4 Bion calls this phenomenon of obstacles to comprehension of emotional truth *inversion of perspective*. López-Corvo (2002) observes that Bion himself relates inversion of perspective to binocular vision.
5 'Sex is a name, but none of us "sees" sex, though it is a word we often use' (Bion, 1977 reprinted in Bion 1991: 206).
6 'When the mother loves the infant, what does she do it with? … My impression is that her love will be expressed by reverie' (Bion, 1962: 35).
7 This title is inspired by some photographs of Egon Schiele from 1914.
8 Only in retrospect did I realize that this initial cinematographic effect could have influenced my reference to Egon Schiele's artistic work. Bonito Oliva (1984) writes: 'Schiele's positioning is the consequence of a visual emphasis that utilizes a sort of framing that seems to predict cinema, as artificial and unnatural – shooting from above, examination from below or from the side, the foreground, a three-quarters view'.
9 Schiele was an Austrian expressionist painter (Tulln an der Donau, June 12, 1890 – Vienna, October 31, 1918).

10 According to Klaus Albrecht Schröder (2000), Schiele had had access to see the photographic monographs of hysterics observed by Charcot.

11 L. Pistiner de Cortiñas (2009) maintains that art has the same function in the therapist's mind as a womb that progressively generates in the patient the capacity to contain and transform.

12 In his final painting, *The Family,* done shortly before his death, Schiele depicts a young pregnant wife (in her sixth month) and her own death that occurred three days later. The baby who was never born is thus only imagined by the painter; it is represented by an ambiguous pose between birth and the squatting position of an older child between the maternal legs. The painting's overall composition harkens back to being contained within the other, as though to express the wish of every human being, not only of the child, to be contained by the body and mind of another.

13 As defined by Kaës (2009), unconscious alliances permit a group's subjects to reinforce in each member some of the processes or functions or pathological structures from which s/he obtains something beneficial to his/her own psychic stability.

14 The word *uncanny* in Italian loses its connection with the house. From a semantic point of view, the German term, *umheimlich,* is the opposite of *heimlich* (from *heim,* house); *heimlich* means comfortable, trusted, intimate, belonging to the house. Thus, *unheimlich* means unusual, foreign, unfamiliar. Freud also uses the term *unheimlich* to mean 'confined to the house, hidden'. Uncanniness is born when, in either an object or a situation, characteristics of otherness and familiarity are combined into a sort of 'affective dualism' (Tricomi, 2001).

15 One could say that 'in thinking, we do not produce thoughts, but we grasp them' (G. Frege, 1918: 68).

16 Cresti and Nannini describe Schiele's representation of houses in Krumau as 'like a sterile mother, like a womb bereft of twentieth-century history still to come, an eroded womb from indifferent waters – ever more indifferent and cold'. In addition, in the painting *The Dead Mother,* Schiele represents even more explicitly the theme of a lack of maternal containment; here he depicts a small child wrapped in the black cloak of his dead mother, as understood by Green (1969).

17 In 1915, after the relationship with Wally had been ruptured, Schiele marries Edith Harms, with whom he shares his life and art until 1918, when both die of the Spanish flu a few days apart.

18 As a testament to Schiele's frenetic activity, Fischer (1996) brings up the fact that Rembrandt, himself passionate about the genre of self-portraiture, at the age of 28 had produced only half the number of self-portraits painted by Schiele.

19 A. Roessler, ed., cited by Comini, 2018: 42

20 The word *idea* has its roots in the Greek etymon *eide,* to know, which in turn is rooted in a past tense of the Greek verb *orao,* to see.

21 Psychoanalytic intuition concerns being 'able to "see" the meaning' (Bion, 1970: 223).

22 Bion (1961) postulates the existence of a third state of mind that defines *inaccessible.* He refers to proto-mental states as vestiges of physical events experienced by the fetus and in perinatal life – thalamic fears or sub-thalamic fears that have never had access to working through. The proto-mental system is represented as something in which the physical and the mental are located in a differentiated state.

23 *Wild thoughts* is a term which Bion uses to describe those thoughts that seem not to belong to us, that conflict with the rest of our personality and that in groups seem to be transmitted to us by the mind of an other, almost without filter and without special carriers. In reality, these thoughts await placement in a wider thinking apparatus that can contain them and contextualize them.

24 'I have postulated the existence of a proto-mental system in which physical and mental activity is undifferentiated' (Bion, 1952: 236).

Child, parents and psychoanalyst 99

25 Fraiberg's (1975) term for unconscious maternal conflict deposited into the child is a *fantasma of the nursery*.
26 Kaës (1998) notes that we find ourselves confronting a psychic reality without a subject that would acquire autonomy, inevitably coming into being between subjects (the psychic space of intersubjectivity) and through subjects (the psychic space of transobjectivity).
27 Freud employs the term *Fantazieren* to speak of imagining and of Bildung to indicate the work of constructing concepts.
28 The bodily is itself a psychic event, even though in a form unknown to us (Freud, 1940).
29 Bion (1980) writes that wild thoughts are in the air, but no one has the courage to think them because they fear that they will be asked, 'Why are you playing with that dirty idea?' (p. 201).
30 'Can we allow ourselves to seize the germ of an idea and plant it where it can be developed until it is mature enough to be born? We must not immediately expel the wild thought or the germ of an idea if we do not believe that it could survive if it were made public. When we make it public, it is then that we can give it a good look and decide whether to call it a memory or an intuition or a prediction or a prophetic statement, or even a sick germ' (Bion, 1980: 200–201).
31 Bion (1962) described how, within the chaos of emotions and sensations that suddenly enter the field fast and furiously, an emotion can become more clear – becoming, that is, a selected fact that permits a new feeling of coherence.
32 In *Transformations* (1965), Bion emphasized that when he thought of having captured the meaning of a symptom, it was often 'by virtue of an aesthetic rather than a scientific experience' (p. 52).

References

Alvarez, A., & Peltz, R. (2018). Conversations with clinicians. *Fort Da, 24*(1), 66–93.
Barish, K. (2018). Cycles of understanding and hope: Toward an integrative model of therapeutic change in child psychotherapy. *Journal of Infant, Child & Adolescent Psychotherapy, 17*(4), 232–242.
Billow, R.M. (2000). Bion's "Passion": The analyst's pain. *Contemporary Psychoanalysis, 36*, 411–426.
Billow, R.M. (2003). Relational variations of the "Container-Contained". *Contemporary Psychoanalysis, 39*(1), 27–50.
Bion, W. R. (1952) Group dynamics: A review. *The International Journal of Psychoanalysis, 49*, 235–247
Bion, W. R. (1957). The differentiation of the psychotic from the non-psychotic personalities, *International Journal of Psycho-Analysis, 38*, 266–281. [Reprinted in *Second Thoughts* (1967)].
Bion, W. R. (1961). *Experiences in Groups*. London: Tavistock.
Bion, W. R. (1962). *Learning from Experience*. London: Tavistock.
Bion, W. R. (1963). *Elements of Psycho-Analysis*. London: Heinemann.
Bion, W. R. (1965). *Transformations*. London: William Heinemann [Reprinted in London: Karnac Books 1984; Reprinted in *Seven Servants*, 1977].
Bion, W. R. (1970). *Attention and Interpretation*. London: Karnac.
Bion, W. R. (1974). *Brazilian Lectures*. Rio/São Paulo No 2. Río de Janeiro: Imago Editora.

100 Elena Molinari

Bion, W. R. (1975). *A Memoir of the Future, Book One: The Dream*. Rio de Janeiro: Imago.

Bion, W. R. (1977). *A Memoir of the Future, Book 2: The Past Presented*. Rio de Janeiro: Imago Editora [Reprinted in one volume with Books 1 and 3 and 'The Key' London: Karnac Books 1991].

Bion, W. R. (1980). In Bion Talamo, F. (Ed.) *Bion in New York and São Paulo*. Perthshire, Scotland: Clunie Press.

Bion, W. R. (1997). *A Memoir of the Future, Book Three: The Dawn of Oblivion*. Rio de Janeiro: Imago.

Bion, W. R. (2005).*The Tavistock Seminars*. Karnac Books, London.

Bolognini, S. (1994). Transference: Erotised, erotic, loving, affectionate. *The International Journal of Psychoanalysis*, *75*, 73–86.

Bonito Oliva, A. (1984). La crisi e le spoglie dell'arte [The Crisis and the Scrutiny of Art]. In *Klimt Kokoschka Schiele: Disegni e acquarelli [Designs and Watercolors]*. Torino: Mazzotta.

Comini, A. (2018). Dessin: La ligne de vie d'Egon Schiele. *Egon Schiele, Fondation Louis Vuitton*. Paris: Éditions Gallimard.

Cresti, R., & Nannini, N. (2010). *Passaggio a Krumau: Omaggio a Schiele [Journey to Krumau: Homage to Schiele]*. Catalogo della mostra personale (catalogue of the personal exhibit), Centroffset Reggio Emilia).

DeToffoli, C. (2014). *L'esperienza della psicoanalisi, a cura di B. Bonfiglio, 2014*, Milano: Franco Angeli.

Eiguer, A. (1994). *L'inconscient de la maison*. Paris: Dunod.

Eiguer, A., et al. (1997). *Le générationnel*. Paris: Dunod.

Faimberg, H. (1988/2005). *The Telescoping of Generations: Listening to the Narcissistic Links between Generations*. London: Routledge.

Fischer, W. G. (1996). *Egon Schiele, 1890–1918: Pantomina di lussuria, visioni di mortalità [Pantomime of Luxury, Visions of Mortality]*. Taschen: Koln.

Fraiberg, S., Adelson E, & Shapiro V. (1975). Ghosts in the nursery. A psychoanalytic approach to the problems of impaired infant–mother relationships. *Journal of the American Academy of Child & Adolescent Psychiatry*, *14*(3), 387–421.

Frege, G. (1918). *Ricerche logiche [Logical Investigations]*. Milano: Guerini e associati, 1988.

Freud, S. (1909). Family romances. *SE*, *9*, 235–242.

Freud, S. (1940). An outline of psychoanalysis. *SE*, *23*, 139–207.

Goodman, S. (2017). The balancing act: Concurrent parent–child work. *Journal of Infant, Child & Adolescent Psychotherapy*, *16*(4), 252–257.

Green, A. (1969/1983). Moral narcissime. In *Narcissisme de vie, narcissisme de mort*, pp. 177–206. Paris: Gallimard.

Grinberg, L.(1985). Bion's contribution to the understanding of the individual and the group. In Pines, M. (Ed.), *Bion and Group Psychotherapy*, pp. 176–191. London: Routledge & Kegan Paul.

Harris, A. (2011). Chapter Two: The individual in the group: On learning to work with the psychoanalytical method (1978). *The Tavistock Model: Papers on Child Development and Psychoanalytic Training*, pp. 25–43. London: Karnac.

Hinshelwood, R. (2016). Containing primitive emotional states: Approaching Bion's later perspectives on groups. In Levine, H., & Civitarese, G. (Eds) *The W.R. Bion Tradition: Lines of Development*, pp. 407–419. London: Karnac.

Imbasciati, A. (2004). A theoretical support for transgenerationality. *Psychoanalytic Psychology*, *21*, 83–98.

Child, parents and psychoanalyst 101

Kaës, R. (1994). La parole et le lien. *Les processus associatifs dans les groupes*. Paris: Dunod.

Kaës, R. (1998). L'intersubjectivité: Un fondement de la vie psychique. *Repères dans la pensée de Aulagnier Topique*, *64*, 45–73.

Kaës, R. (2009). *Les alliances incoscientes*. Paris: Dunod.

López-Corvo, R. E. (2002). *The Dictionary of the Work of W.R. Bion*. London: Routledge.

Migliozzi, A. (2016). Passion. In Levine H., & Civitarese, G. (Eds) *The W.R. Bion Tradition: Lines of Development*, pp. 407–419. London: Karnac. [2016, pp. 315–326].

Norman, J. (2004). Transformations of early infantile experiences: A 6-month-old in psychoanalysis. *The International Journal of Psychoanalysis*, *85*(5), 1103–1122.

Novick, K., & Novick, J. (2013). Concurrent work with parents of adolescent patients. *The Psychoanalytic Study of the Child*, *67*, 103–136.

Pistiner de Cortiñas, L. (2009). *The Aesthetic Dimension of the Mind: Variations on a Theme of Bion*. London: Karnac Books.

Resnik, S. (2000). The hands of Egon Schiele. *International Forum of Psychoanalysis*, *9*, 113–123.

Salomonsson, B. (2007). 'Talk to me baby, tell me what's the matter now' semiotic and developmental perspectives on communication in psychoanalytic infant treatment. *The International Journal of Psychoanalysis*, *88*(1), 127–146.

Salomonsson, B. (2012). Has infantile sexuality anything to do with infants?. *The International Journal of Psychoanalysis*, *93*(3), 631–647.

Salomonsson, B. (2014). Psychodynamic therapies with infants and parents: A critical review of treatment methods. *Psychodynamic Psychiatry*, *42*(2), 203–223.

Salomonsson, B. (2015). Therapeutic action in psychoanalytic therapy with toddlers and parents. *Journal of Child Psychotherapy*, *41*(2), 112–130.

Schröder, K. A. (2000). *Egon Schiele e la "finis Austriae."* Milano: Skira.

Tricomi, F. (2001). *Estetica e psicoanalisi [Aesthetics and Psychoanalysis]*. Catanzaro: Rubbettino.

Ubaldo, N. (2000). *Atlante illustrato di filosofia*. Firenze: Giunti Editore.

Whitefield, C, & Midgley, N. (2015). 'And when you were a child?': How therapists working with parents alongside individual child psychotherapy bring the past into their work. *Journal of Child Psychotherapy*, *41*(3), 272–292.

Winnicott, D. W. (1974). Fear of breakdown. *International Review of Psycho-Analysis*, *1*(1–2), 103–107.

Translation by Gina Atkinson, M.A.

Editor's Introduction to:
Elsa's sexual fantasies in a narcissistic and erotic transference

In this chapter the reader will notice a change from the Field Theory perspective of the prior two chapters to Christine Anzieu-Premmereur's 'combined relational and structural theory approach'. Anzieu-Premmereur asks the question 'is infantile sexuality still a common notion for psychoanalysts?' It certainly is for her, as 'the core of the intra-psychic life of the child, as well as the adult, and as the founding organizer of fantasmatic activities'. In considering what a theory offers us and what it might miss, it is clear that here the psycho-sexual development, disturbance and psycho-sexual 'process' are in the forefront.

In Chapter 5 we met 'Adele', a four-year-old with compulsive masturbation. Here we meet 'Elsa', first seen at age two in dyadic therapy with her mother and then in child analysis at age four. Elsa initially presented with encopresis, then a sleep disturbance and then compulsive masturbation (like Adele). The child analyst is quickly reminded of how commonly small children express disturbances through their bodies, or here the sexualization of a traumatic experience.

I would like to point the reader to the naturalness with which Anzieu-Premmereur speaks with her small patient about sexuality. As an expert in infant–parent work and the treatment of small children, Anzieu-Premmereur is adept at engagement with the body/mind concerns of small children.

In several chapters in this book, there are nodal or pivotal moments when the erotic is present in bodily form with a child or adolescent (here Elsa's physical requests of her analyst, or in Chapter 11 when Kohen–Abdala's little patient asks her to turn her back so that he can masturbate; or when Tyminski's patient 'rolls over' his forearm). These moments generate thinking and feeling, sometimes emotional upheaval in the analyst, and choices to be made in the moment. The nodal moment in this material is when Elsa points at her analyst's breasts and says, 'I want you', then points at her analyst's legs and asks her to 'show her my sex'. Elsa then asks to go to the bathroom to masturbate. I had the sense that Anzieu-Premmereur was very little thrown by these developments. We could wonder if both her immersion in the body/minds of young children as well as her psycho-sexual theory creates comfort and familiarity in her with children's sexuality.

DOI: 10.4324/9781003266303-11

6 Elsa's sexual fantasies in a narcissistic and erotic transference

Christine Anzieu-Premmereur

Is infantile sexuality still a common notion for psychoanalysts? Freud viewed it as the core of the intra-psychic life of the child as well the adult and as the founding organizer of fantasmatic activity. If the model in psychoanalytical theory is still the dream and the child's infantile sexual theory, psychoanalysis sets the dreamer off on the work of transformation: by restoring the part of the person that can be creative, whatever the early environment was, or despite how the real parents were, by working with the child's reinvention of them.

'Elsa', a developmentally mature two-year-old child in dyadic therapy with her detached mother, illustrates the role of infantile sexuality and the use of manic defenses against primitive depressive reactions to her parents' unavailability. My later psychoanalytic treatment of Elsa, age four, revealed erotic transference towards me as a narcissistic double and as a maternal figure. Infantile sexual fantasies were played and acted in imaginary scenarios for the next two years until the child gained a secure sense of self and identity, leading to a more Oedipal configuration. My work with the parents conveys how their own conflicts with erotic feelings and sexuality interfered with Elsa's moods and fantasies.

I first give a short view of some formulations of psychosexuality that combine relational and structural theory approaches. Then I describe the psychoanalytic treatment of Elsa at age two when she came for a consultation. She was refusing to move her bowels. I report my understanding of how the parents' fantasies interplayed with the child's sexuality in process.

Sexuality

The hegemony of sexuality in psychoanalysis is closely linked to the primacy of the pleasure–unpleasure principle. Psychoanalysis broadens the conception of sexuality by recognizing a part of the sexual outside the manifestations of sexuality. In introducing the notion of pregenital sexuality, psychoanalysis also separates sexuality from sex itself, recognizing a 'normal' sexual character to areas of the body other than the 'properly' genital areas.

The psychoanalytic conception of sex and sexuality cannot, therefore, be understood without reference to the recognition of unconscious issues of

DOI: 10.4324/9781003266303-12

psychic life. Sexuality is a particular behavior, an 'observable' behavior, but the sexual relates to an intrapsychic dimension; it is internal, internalized sexuality, it is an unconscious fantasy. By introducing the notion of libidinal co-excitation (1914a, 1914b) and that of sexual co-excitation, Freud put forward the idea of a possible sexualization of a non-sexual experience, of a traumatic experience.

Freud thus introduces the idea of a function of sexualization in the narcissistic economy, even in the self-preservation economy. He gradually moves from an identification of the sexual as a form of internalization of infantile sexuality, to a process of sexualization or desexualization of content and psychic experiences: the sexual appears as a process brought to the fore in the service or to the detriment of psychic life. The sexual also 'metaphorizes' other psychic issues. Psychoanalytic work helps to create representations and metaphors for disorganizing psychic experiences.

Green (2018) allows for a subjective dimension to drives by suggesting that drives are 'the matrix of the subject'. He proposed the idea of 'an erotic chain': drives should not be seen simply as a motivating force contained within the id. Rather, Green suggests that sexuality unfolds through a series of 'formations'. Conscious and unconscious representations organize a chain of erotic signifiers. Instead of fixing a certain point in sexuality, the focus is on a dynamic movement in this sequence. Elsa's case shows how psychosexuality can be seen as a process.

Laplanche's (1997) theory is important in reconsidering the role of the mother in infantile sexuality. Laplanche introduced the idea of sexualisation of the infant's arousal by the mother. Ultimately it is the mother's unconscious 'seduction' of the infant, claims Laplanche, that converts primary instinctual excitement into an autoerotic moment. Laplanche considers that the infant is not ready to integrate this experience with other experiences of the mother. This could be because of the dynamically unconscious nature of the interaction, which leaves the infant with a sense of inaccessible meaning, or what Laplanche calls 'enigma'. The mystery may be rooted in the enigmatic quality of the mother's gestures, which initially colours the infant's experience of his excitement, but then serves to intensify the seduction, finally becoming its central feature.

This idea of sexuality's otherness highlights some divisions in the sphere of love. Splits between sexuality and attachment are often encountered in clinical practice, when erotic desire comes into conflict with the need for a safe and stable relationship, as we often see with young children. The baby's infantile sexuality reactivates the infantile sexuality of the mother. Her reactions, interpretations and answers, will support or block the child's integration of erotic experiences into a genital organization. As in the analytic setting, the awakening of infantile unconscious associations in the analyst will be displayed in the countertransference, or in blind spots, shaping the analyst's interpretations and reactions, and eventually the child's capacity for integration.

Analysis, therefore, is to recollect an early object experience. To remember not cognitively, but through intense affective experience, a relationship that was identified with those enigmatic meanings as with cumulative transformational experiences of the self. The analyst functions as an evocative mnemonic trace of that object. The analytic situation will either induce a patient's regressive recollection of this early object relation, or resistance to it, as in denial by sexualization. From this point of view, transference shows the reaction to this primary object relation and helps to see how the patient remembers his/her own experience of this early object situation.

When a young child is experiencing a kind of recovering of a 'true self', (a mix of unconscious discovery and integrative process), there is a moment of 'surprise' in the session, associated with recovering of a function that has been lost due to repression, trauma or disorganization. Infantile sexuality and phases of exhibitionism are in a process of integration during those analytic sessions full of arousing but contained erotic play.

There is an important integrative quality in autoeroticism when it is linked to appropriate protective shields from the mother. Autoeroticism, as the bearer of autonomy, insofar as it is favorably invested by the mother, will allow for continuity with transitional space and object. If a body which takes pleasure is accepted by the mother, then the transitional area is a privileged meeting place between the lived body, (source of the first representations linked to autoeroticism), and the narcissistic and object investment on the part of the mother.

I present the case of a young girl whose precocious sexual arousal and early conflicts were the presenting problems. Her parents were involved in their own problems regarding love and sex; they didn't know these troubles could be connected with their daughter's symptoms.

Anal phase

Elsa's presenting issue was anal retention, which made her mother panicky. This is an example of infantile and erotic issues reactivated in a parent. Aggressive aims dominate the libido during the anal phase, while eventually receptivity becomes libidinized.

When Elsa became aware of her bodily ability to produce something, her love for her anal productivity and the wish to control it brought her into conflict with her mother.

The mutuality of the oral phase is then disrupted. Narcissistic wishes come into conflict with the wish to please the mother. Because of the child's projection of her own aggression, the mother is experienced as controlling and restrictive.

As we will see in Elsa's early play, she fears that something has happened to the inside of her body, that its contents have fallen out. A certain level of excitation is necessary to counteract this fear.

Elsa's use of the psychoanalyst as an accomplice to her excitement was a narcissistic transference, exhibiting to the mother (who was present in the room), how mutuality had been damaged by their conflict and by mother's lack of receptivity (due to her own issues with the female body).

In general, the vaginal cavity does not have the aggressive cathexis which the anus has. As Oliner (1982) wrote, the more closely the two stages resemble each other, the more the inner genital phase will be influenced by the unresolved aggression stemming from the anal phase, and the more the inner genital will lack differentiation from the anal sphere and be regarded as more destructive.

For Elsa, separation from the mother and mastery over her own body marked the resolution of this crisis, allowing for receptivity.

There is an important evolution in the capacity to relate to objects, leading to the turning to the father as the third who creates some separation from the mother, and as a love object. In the countertransference, the analyst was to move from a narcissistic double to a more ambivalent figure containing aggression and supporting the wish for identification with a female figure able to seduce.

Elsa's back and forth between regression and further Oedipal issues shows how arousal through intense erotic transference had been a compromise formation.

The magical omnipotent control of feces was to keep the symbiosis with the maternal object; this was in conflict with a better integration of bisexuality in a more Oedipal development. Elsa's regression to exciting play with her analyst was a seduction to get back to a sense of sameness. Eroticism can be a way to grasp on the adult's infantile wishes that were asleep in the unconscious and which can be awakened by the child in session. The capacity for symbolization was an important integrative tool in this area.

'Elsa'

Elsa was two years and four months old when her parents came to discuss her symptoms. She refused to move her bowels. Six months earlier (which is quite early), she was toilet trained, but she now no longer wanted to go to the bathroom. She held it in. She asked for a diaper at night to urinate and defecate alone in her room. Her parents were very proud of her mature behavior, since she was talking, thinking and telling stories like an older child. They felt secure when they started the toilet training, they were sure that she understood. But she took this capacity to an extreme and held her feces in.

Elsa was the second child, with a teenage older sister who was already dating and claiming her love life. Both parents had very busy professional lives. They were not really available to Elsa, working long hours, traveling a lot and very involved in their own needs for narcissistic reassurance via their professional lives.

Elsa spent half day at a day care center and her beloved baby sitter came to pick her up for the rest of the day. The parents had asked the pediatrician for advice regarding their daughter's symptoms. He had told them she wasn't ill

Elsa's sexual fantasies   107

and that they should avoid forcing the child. But Elsa's impressive self-control was frightening for the mother. She had a fight with her daughter in the bathroom, screaming at Elsa when she didn't want to urinate. The mother was afraid she would strike her daughter. Elsa's anxiety was so high that she vomited. Suddenly the parents discovered how moved they were by Elsa's symptom and how frightened Elsa was.

At home, they had a ritual: Elsa asked for a diaper, went to her room, defecated in the diaper and threw it in the trash; she was the one who was in charge of the situation. When the parents left Elsa with her grandparents, she completely stopped urinating and defecating, upsetting the whole family.

The mother reported having been depressed during Elsa's first year but refused to elaborate. She said she was afraid I would ask her to be my patient. Even when I tried to show her the confusion between herself and her daughter regarding the relationship with me, she explained she didn't want to talk about her depression. I understood that her negative and sad feelings were difficult to contain. She would only say that she had breast-fed Elsa for four months and that she had become depressed after weaning her. At the same time, her own mother had been sick, and she had become overwhelmed with anxiety.

During her pregnancy, she was fighting with her husband who had had an affair. After the birth, she believed her husband was disappointed because he had wanted a boy. However, the father took time off to be with his baby: he worked only part time for a year, since at the time Elsa's mother was in a challenging position in her job and couldn't take time off.

Father was really close to his daughter. But he was obsessively preoccupied with dirt: he didn't want the baby to make a mess at the table. He didn't want Elsa to refuse any food he offered her; it was his way of loving her, and his daughter repeated his sentences about food and dirt by heart. He was asking her to love him, and she was seduced! But he was disgusted by his daughter's dribble and cleaned her mouth all the time. This revulsion towards mess could have been interpreted by Elsa as a rejection of her femaleness. I thought Elsa was confronted with a combination of intrusive paternal control and maternal neglect.

Both parents were very cooperative with me. I proposed mother–infant psychotherapy on a twice a week basis and the father joined us once a month.

The wolf game

Elsa was a pretty, precocious, smart toddler, giving an impression at the outset that she was in control of the adults. For the first session, she came with her blankie, grasping her mother's dress, upset at coming to see me since it was the first time her mother had picked her up at the day care center. I told her how important it was to have her mother for herself. She put her blankie down and asked me to play wolf with her.

Very carefully she opened the Russian nesting dolls, which were on my desk, took out the smallest one and said: 'This is the baby, we have to

108 *Christine Anzieu-Premmereur*

protect him from the wolf. The baby doesn't want to sleep, and the wolf wants to eat him up'. I was to play a wolf, so I started making wolf noises and said to the baby: 'I am going to eat you, I like you so much!' Elsa was very excited, between fear and pleasure, and asked me to do it again and again.

Then I stopped and reminded her that we had to protect the baby. She asked me to fight the wolf. I used a very strong voice to tell the wolf he had to stop right away, or he would be punished; and I mentioned all the forms of punishment Elsa was afraid of, which I had learned from the mother: staying in the dark, being locked in a room. Elsa added a punishment: getting shots at the doctor's! We were in a very hot transference.

Each time I met Elsa, she asked me to play the wolf game and to repeat the same lines. At the end of the sessions, she took care of the baby, put him to bed and told the wolf that she would spank him. Oral and anal sadistic fantasies were at play in each session. After a few sessions, Elsa told her mother that she would be the one to yell at the wolf, and the mother played the wolf with great pleasure. Elsa enjoyed being in control of her mother and listening to her mother yell at the nasty wolf.

One month later, Elsa changed the game. She said I had to be a doctor called to the emergency room to take care of a baby who wasn't sleeping. I was supposed to give the baby the most painful shot I could! And to do it again and again ... Each time, I gave the baby some explanation about the punishment: being too noisy, disturbing the parents' sleep, or worrying the parents too much, as Elsa had done with her symptoms. Elsa wasn't too excited, but she was very pleased by this. She then decided she would be the one to spank the baby and she did it sadistically.

Suddenly, she decided that the baby was dirty, that she had to clean him, and she screamed: 'Oh he pooped!' She took tissues, cleaned the very dirty baby and asked me if she could go to the bathroom to throw the dirty paper away. From then on, we started playing inside the bathroom every session. At the beginning, I pointed out how dirty the poop was, and how well she was doing cleaning it, reminding her how she had been afraid of dirt.

The father's obsessive worry about dirt had made Elsa herself very careful with her appearance; retaining her feces was a way to please him and to stay connected to him. He agreed to be more flexible with his daughter and associated to the way he had been raised himself by a very strict mother and a depressed father.

After a while, I started telling Elsa and her mother how beautiful the poop was: 'What a lovely poop!' And again, the mother played with me, enjoying the poop. I told Elsa that we shouldn't throw the poop away, because it was very precious. And we started collecting small pieces of paper in a doll's potty, pretending it was poop.

At home, Elsa started collecting pencil sharpeners, like the one she had discovered in my office and she expressed her interest in them as a means of creating waste. I was amazed by the pleasure the mother discovered in buying sharpeners for her daughter and helping her to organize her collection: she revealed her own interest in compulsive behavior.

The defecation symptom transformed. Elsa started to ask to go to the bathroom at the day care center every day, but at home she still wanted a diaper. After a few weeks, she completely stopped asking for a diaper and went to the bathroom at home as well.

Both parents were narcissistically vulnerable, very interested in mastery and control. They had separation anxiety that they denied (the marital crisis, and mother's depression at weaning). Elsa was a strong, over-precocious girl, brilliant in her parents' eyes, but possibly disappointing because she was a girl. In her wolf game, Elsa showed her ambivalent transference towards me and projected onto me her primary fantasy: to be eaten by a mother figure. It was her way of representing her own impulses, her oral greed through projection. The wolf was to represent me in a narcissistic and at the same time maternal transference, and the oral greed was projected on the wolf/me. It was also a way of asking me to set limits and decrease her feeling of guilt: the wolf had to be punished, as she was when she had temper tantrums at home.

The fantasy of oral impregnation

Elsa gave me an understanding of her sexual myth of oral impregnation playing with the baby who was inside the doll: a mother gets a baby by eating. The sadistic behavior towards the baby may have been a sign of her feelings during the mother's depression: retaliation and keeping control of the unavailable object. How could she have seduced her mother and received attention from such a sad figure? She had been powerless and had wanted to have complete control.

After the depression at weaning, Elsa's mother shifted her attention. She was occupied with clothes and make-up so she would be attractive to men. She disclosed that her own mother had suffered from a colon disease which was believed for a long time to be cancer. She told me that she was overwhelmed by visions of her mother dying and by fantasies of being hurt in her belly and in the anal area.

Elsa's rage at her mother was related to a fantasy she played out with me and which she finally clearly explained to me: she thought when her mother disappeared (while away to take care of her own mother or to have time with her husband), that mother was looking for another baby.

Elsa imagined she wasn't the right baby her mother had been looking for. In a powerful anal fantasy, Elsa's mother's belly was full of babies. Because of her envy and her rivalry, and through identification with her mother, Elsa imagined she was pregnant. She was then afraid of losing her precious contents, and fearful of her mother's revenge. When the mother asked her to go to the bathroom to defecate, Elsa projected on her mother her wish to steal the baby and the sadistic pleasure that was connected with the fantasy. To defecate was to risk feelings of emptiness, passivity and powerlessness.

110 *Christine Anzieu-Premmereur*

The bowel movement symbolized a baby within her and a penis: by developing bowel movement retention, Elsa became simultaneously a pregnant woman, her mother and the boy that her parents would love. Elsa's intestinal tract became the arena in which symbols and fantasies were constructed.

For the libido, the anal phase is the meeting point between narcissism and object relation. The anal sphincter is the place between inside and outside where passive and active eroticisms are playing together. Elsa used her playing as a way to deal with her negative feelings towards her father's intrusive interventions about dirt and her mother's absence. She said: 'No' to her parents and had the feeling of being herself. The mirroring function of the parents gives the child, during the anal phase, a model of how to deal with dependency. If the parents show tolerance towards frustration and flexibility regarding what is forbidden, the child will feel less injury when confronted with passivity. Her parents' severity made Elsa turn inward again.

The way parents play their role is very important at this time. The father, mother's partner or the one who plays the role of a third in front of the dyad, can be the one who forbids the child to transgress taboos, interfacing with the mother's capacity for giving him/her the right to intervene between herself and her child. The 'thirdness' helps for the basis of symbolization in the child. The more the child can use playing and symbolization, the more she can agree to wait for gratification through compromise. Both parents were very creative by playing with Elsa during sessions and realized how deeply they had been involved in the control of her body.

A phallic girl

When Elsa got older, her fantasy moved to a phallic representation. She told me the baby was afraid of being wounded by defecating, and she said a confused sentence about being a baby boy: 'this kid is going see his pee pee fall off'. I asked her if the baby was afraid of losing his pee pee. 'Of course', she said. Each session after that she asked me to talk about how afraid the baby was of losing his pee pee when going to the bathroom. It was a game inside the bathroom, far from the mother who had to stay in my office. The repetition of the same game was very important for her. She was very serious, asking me to say again in the same words, how a baby could be fearful of losing his pee pee.

Through the retention Elsa imagined she possessed a penis within her and was pregnant. During her first games with me, she became pregnant by drinking chocolate or eating food, and the baby came out of her anus. One year later, we played the same games, but the baby was born through her vagina. When she started to masturbate, she gave up bowel movement retention and had pleasure through genital rather than anal–intestinal stimulation.

The phallic phase is the time when the child has to move from the narcissistic illusion of being omnipotent to castration anxiety, in order to integrate all the infantile pregenital steps into a genital and object-seeking sexuality. Dealing with castration anxiety means accepting limits to narcissistic wishes, being able to bear separation, absence and, finally, death, introducing the capacity for mourning.

At that challenging time, Elsa was typically using manic defenses and phallic exhibitionism. Through her development and with psychotherapy, she became able to struggle with castration anxiety and separation anxiety at the same time.

Ego ideal and parents

The integration of the parents' narcissism is an important part of the anal phase. We can imagine that the mother's narcissism is conveyed to the child through primary emotional exchanges, and that later on paternal narcissism is a source of the child's self-esteem. During the anal and phallic phases, the child feels the way the parents deal with her conflicts. Parents look for self-worth by considering their child's development as a continuity of what they give to her and their own identification with their child. They still have the fantasy of the child being a part of their own narcissism. And the child receives this parental projection as a 'gift' for her narcissism, through a phallic fantasy: being the mirroring figure of the parents' phallic narcissistic pleasure. This experience depends on how the parents feel more or less threatened by castration anxiety or depression.

If a mother needs her child to be a narcissistic complement of herself and asks her child to stay dependent on her, she won't allow her child to play an Oedipal scenario with her. Elsa's mother was very proud of her daughter's performances but wished her to be a mirror of her self-esteem. She couldn't stand her daughter's problems since she felt they were a narcissistic injury to herself.

The father was delighted by his beautiful and smart girl but tried to have her as a cute part of himself rather than an independent person; for example, he asked her to give a kiss to his male colleagues to get narcissistic pleasure and ignored her complaints about not wanting to kiss men.

Separation anxiety and sexuality

Elsa's mother didn't bring her back after the summer break.

She called me six months later, asking if she could come back because Elsa wasn't sleeping anymore. I thought Elsa remembered our play with the baby who wanted to wake up the parents in order to control them! She was three and half years old and didn't have her anal symptoms to protect her against new anxieties. When I met her again, she was still very smart, talkative, in control of the adults. The bathroom syndrome was forgotten, but she didn't sleep at night anymore, staying quietly in her bed in the evening, and calling her mother in the middle of the night. Her separation anxiety and her ambivalent difficulty with any loss had been contained by the former symptom.

112   *Christine Anzieu-Premmereur*

I started psychotherapy with Elsa, three times a week for two months. Then, because of Elsa's new symptom and her deep involvement in the treatment, I proposed psychoanalysis four times a week and her parents accepted.

Retaining her stool was Elsa's first symptom, her second was the sleeping disorder, and then she started to masturbate compulsively. At first her mother reported her daughter masturbating in bed. During naptime at the day care center she stimulated her genitals by manual repetitive rubbing and squeezing her clitoris or by using her blanket. Once Elsa asked for privacy during a session when she was sad, in order to masturbate. I interpreted her need for reassurance.

I remembered she had been weaned off the bottle when she was one and that she had started toilet training six months later. At that time her mother was preoccupied with her older daughter's first date, her own mother's illness and her husband's withdrawal. Then both parents had a kind of 'new love affair together' telling their daughters that they had fallen in love again; and their first daughter talked every night about her desire to make love with her new boyfriend: Elsa's environment was 'hot' and involved her in sexual arousal.

Elsa's masturbation wasn't at all a subject her parents could talk to her about. Elsa didn't have specific words to talk about her genitals, and her mother realized during the treatment that she herself didn't have a lot of words to talk about her genitals; Pee pee was the only way to represent the genitals, as if there were no difference between boys' and girls' genitals.

Masturbation has roots in autoerotic activity, when the use of the hand serves to maintain a sense of continuity with the mother's body. Then it becomes associated with fantasies, at first of phallic capacity, then about primal scene. More compulsive than calming, Elsa's masturbation was at first associated with her controlling anality. I saw Elsa's masturbation as a source of a feeling of narcissistic completion and of independence, but I think it also served as a source of developing fantasies about bisexuality, and parental intercourse as sadistic. Elsa played out representations of aggressive intercourse between two parents whose genitals were undifferentiated and phallic.

As with most children, Elsa entered analytic work as an enthusiastic partner. A new game appeared, showing the beginning of Oedipal fantasies:

> Both parents were in their room, they had locked the door, and they were sharing a wonderful bottle of wine, which tasted exactly like the older sister's bubblegum: too spicy for a baby. The baby was alone in his bedroom, in a rage. He had only a small bottle of milk! Elsa asked me to play the parents, by hiding myself behind the curtain and making noises which showed their pleasure. At the same time, she played being the poor lonely baby who was very curious, looking behind the curtain and feeling guilty, afraid of being punished.

We were in an Oedipal scenario, with three characters and a primal scene. But Elsa got too excited; her sexual arousal and her agitation were too high. The

Elsa's sexual fantasies 113

game was repeated many times, she was never tired of it, and she was screaming, jumping. I tried to show her conflict, but she didn't want me to talk to her, she denied having any anxiety.

During one session, Elsa had a bowel movement, and messed herself up. Her mother was upset. Elsa's excitement had made her lose control. Her shameful anal pleasure at losing control was a sign of regression, from imaginary play to defecation and from dealing with Oedipal figures to the former conflict.

I interpreted her manic reaction as a defense against her sadness, and her feeling of loss and abandonment. During the next session, I played the baby as depressed, unhappy and crying. Elsa didn't like that and decided that the baby had to be punished because he wanted to steal the mother's shiny jewelry.

The regression to the former sadistic play was associated with oral regression. To quiet herself, Elsa had to give a bottle to a crocodile toy, telling me how dangerous he was, since he wanted to eat all the characters. I interpreted the denial of her sadness as being related to her envy of her parents. She said that I wasn't fun and that she didn't want to listen to me. But she calmed down.

Castration anxiety and love for the father

We then had many sessions with a new game: the baby had a gender, he was a boy, a dirty one, he was worthless and Elsa put him in the trash.

A bottle with a nipple was the representation of a phallic attribute that the crocodile wanted for himself. And Elsa put the bottle inside her underwear, saying that she was a boy. I told her she felt powerless because she didn't have breasts like her mother, or a penis like her father.

The reoccurrence of the fear of losing an object and the regression to oral and anal self-comforting measures, are a common reaction to castration anxiety. Confronted with Oedipal fantasies, Elsa reacted with sadness and moodiness. These reactions appeared to facilitate the erotic turn to her father as the new love object.

When her mother left for few days on a business trip, Elsa played at being left alone in a cold room. I told her she seemed sad when her mother was away, as she was when her grandmother was sick. She asked me to play hide-and-seek and she looked for me. I thought she was asking me to play being the dying grandmother or the mother who disappeared when she was travelling. I had to replace her loss.

Then she said she was angry that her mother had to go away for two days. She asked me for something to eat, took the baby's bottle and started to suck it. She decided to play at being an abandoned baby in the wintertime. She screamed for food; lying on the floor with the bottle and her blanket, she asked me to hug her. I did it 'as if' playing being a mother who cares for her baby.

She then continued to play pretending her leg was hurt. But she stopped the play and told me very seriously: 'I miss my Mom'. Immediately, she jumped

114 *Christine Anzieu-Premmereur*

off the floor and played being pregnant while eating the dolls. 'Do you know what I want the most?' she asked me. I thought, nurturance, babies, penis … I didn't say anything but pointed out her belly filled by a pillow. She laughed and said, 'I want you!' pointing at my breast. She grasped the pen on my desk and told me she would take it home. I said: 'Oh, you would like to get my breast as if I were your mother, and my pen as if I were your father'. 'How do you know?' she said. Then she pointed to my legs and said she wanted me to show her my sex. I told her she needed to know if a woman had a penis or not, and I told her that she had a vulva and a vagina like her mother and me. She was silent, smiling. She said: 'I would like to go to the bathroom' (which meant to masturbate).

It seemed to me that Elsa turned to sexuality as her way of dealing with loss. She was looking for a comforting connection with me when she was depressed and at the same time, she was playing with sexuality. I told her about the connection between being sad, missing her mother and her need to masturbate, and she didn't leave the room.

She reported that the night before she had to masturbate in order to go to sleep. She asked me where the baby was when the mother was pregnant, and I told her about the womb. She was silent for a while, and she said: 'Do you know what I feel?' I looked at her carefully, remembering her former sadness and her excitement … 'I would like to stay with you tonight … I know you don't have any husband nor children, since in your office there is no room for them … I will stay here'. I told her how needy she was to have somebody who loves her without sharing this love with anybody else, and how sad and empty she felt when she didn't find that. She played staying in my room and being asleep, sucking her thumb.

During the next sessions, she came back to the baby play: a lonely baby facing a primal scene. Each time, the baby was less upset and sad. The baby became a girl who dreamed of growing up and being a woman with beautiful breasts, pointed nipples like the bottle and a belly full of babies. By moving from her phallic envy to Oedipal conflicts, she was discovering new defenses. Before a break for holidays, she told me she wouldn't miss me anymore since she was leaving with her father for vacation: 'I love my Dad!' she said proudly. I thought she knew how much he loved her.

Then Elsa calmed down and slept at night.

Erotic transference

A loving transference was there from the beginning, making playfulness easy. But it transformed into a search for impulsive physical contact, and the capacity for symbolic play was stopped in the eroticized transference. This erotic level of acting is challenging, but at the same time quite touching as a signal of helplessness. My countertransference was at first challenged by Elsa's impulsive acting and raw eroticism. Playing with a young child in a room creates a space for intimacy that allows for those arousals that are associated with omnipotent

Elsa's sexual fantasies   115

manic defense and a need for knowledge. I understood her impulses as an imperious need to seduce me when dealing with a depressive feeling of abandonment.

Elsa's sexual material in our sessions, highlighted how sexualization helped her to maintain a tie to her mother and regulate her fear of loss. Her provocativeness was an attempt to regulate the over-stimulation from her parents and sister's behavior. Regardless of cause, Elsa insisted on enacting her sexual concerns. She pointed to my genitals, asking me to remove my clothes and 'make love'.

These sexual themes intensified around separation for a family break. Elsa asked me to undress in the last session before the trip. Upon her return, she had a male puppet lie on top of the female puppet, requesting with a very seducing smile that she and I play at kissing and getting married, taking our clothes off. In her desperate attempt to connect via sexualization, she was also identifying with her sexually overcharged mother's way of connecting with men.

Those interactive movements of transference and countertransference put the analyst in touch with primitive internal areas that aid identification with the patient.

I thought how important it is to offer the patient a specific space and receptivity to her infantile motions still in search for a container. Seduction by the infantile omnipotence of the analysand is sometimes a blind spot that works as a narcissistic defense that put the analytic pair at risk. There is a narcissistic jouissance in the identification with the other's infantile.

Elsa's hyper-activity in sessions diminished when she could express her more depressive mood through play. The erotized transference enabled her to maintain the relationship with the analyst, facing the conflict between her wish for a solid continuous bond and her fear of the analyst's repeating early failures in her relationship with a distant, but overstimulating mother. Her sexual arousal could have been 'offering' herself as an object of seduction. She may have interpreted my interest in her erotic play as my specific way to relate to her, and actualizing her wish to be an object of love as infants do when they make themselves the object of pleasure of their mother.

Bolognini (1994) offers an understanding of different erotic transferences: the 'erotic' as a confused demand for love in a positive transference that can be interpreted, as opposed to 'eroticized transference', when child patients are engaged in acting at seduction and physical contact. Children exposed to situations of overstimulation are easily disorganized and put the analytic process at risk.

Different types of transference appear in an analytic process. Since child sexuality is polymorphous – perverse, as Freud told us, they have specific dynamic and mobility. Maintaining the analytic frame, paying attention to the child's reaction when frustrated and keeping interpretation as the essential tool, help most of the time at containing the patient and keeping the analytic work and elaboration.

Bisexuality

Pregenital bisexuality has its origin in the introjections of the balance between activity–passivity during the time when the baby is interacting with the mother. For example, playing between getting pleasure from mother and giving her some pleasure while looking at her. Then, proceeding along psychosexual development, identification becomes more specifically sexual and helps to integrate genital sexuality.

For Elsa's mother, her daughter's excellent brain was a masculine quality inherited from her own father, in an incestuous fantasy.

Elsa played 'being a boy' for a few months when she was four, wearing pants and hats like her father. Then she moved to a very feminine and seductive girl, very interested in dresses, like her mother, but still using her desire to be in control as a boyish quality. She used the masculine form for herself when she was giving me orders. She complained a lot at that time about the smell of my perfume, as a feminine quality she didn't want to share with me. She wanted to be the only 'girl with girlish quality' and asked me to be a pipe smoker! Playing with bisexuality, Elsa started to maintain she was a girl who would be a woman in the future who would have love affairs with men, asserting her sexual identity.

Elsa then stopped playing games when she was five. Action was no longer a way to express herself and to display her fantasies. She moved to a new form of symbolization which was a sign of her using sublimation: she started telling stories I had to write down. The characters had a gender identity and different generations appeared. For example, a grandmother saved a poor child whose parents had abandoned her. The mother had been jealous of her beauty and had convinced her husband to abandon her. Or a young girl wished to leave home with the boy she loved, but the mother called the police to arrest her.

Elsa became a very feminine pretty girl, still powerful and in control of adults, learning how to read by herself when she was five, trying to use her mother's make up, very interested in dresses and jewelry. She was able to stay alone in her room, playing or sleeping. Her mother no longer mentioned her daughter's masturbation.

Before the end of her analysis, (when she was five and half years old), Elsa reported a dream. A princess was crying. She cried so long that her hair fell out. She had lost everything. Her parents were away, both riding the same horse. She was abandoned. The princess was sleeping and, in her dream, saw that she had boy's clothes on and a sword to protect her. When she woke up, somebody had sewed a beautiful dress for her wedding, and a prince was waiting for her.

This dream showed a condensing of separation and castration themes, connected with Oedipal wishes. Elsa's favorite books on princesses and fairies influenced the dream.

Having the capacity to stay alone and sleep, Elsa dreamed, elaborating her Oedipal conflict. She got the ability to mourn and reported being worried

Elsa's sexual fantasies   117

about her grandmother's aging. She was able to bear loss. Her strong fixation at the anal stage, her precocious development and her pleasure in collecting made her predisposed to an obsessive character.

Separation-individuation was a challenging time for Elsa, whose identification with her depressed mother had made her strongly attached to her. Her strong relationship with her father helped her to separate from her mother. Sexual arousal was a way to deal with depressive feelings and separation anxieties, and at the same time influenced her development from the anal to the genital stage.

Conclusion

Elsa's psychoanalytic process showed that frustration and separation activate erotic arousal. She first experienced oral greed, anal pleasure and control, then masturbation with phallic fantasies, showing the changes in both her narcissistic libido and object relations. Facing the lack of pleasurable maternal presence, she had developed premature erotic arousal.

As development proceeds, the fantasies involved in infantile autoerotism are less and less connected with direct parental satisfactions, especially those coming from the mother. The interest in intimate relations between the father and the mother accounts for the intensity of the autoerotic excitement. What the child observed is reinterpreted as representations of pleasure. Infantile sexual theories, such as 'where babies come from' or 'where do they come out of the body' are answers to questions coming from the child's experiences with the parents, but infiltrated by eroticism and unconscious desire.

Infantile sexuality is a hidden secret, and even if now we know a part of Elsa's erotic world, it is difficult to figure out her infantile fantasies. As she often told me: 'You are dumb, you don't know, I have my dreams'. At the end of her analysis, she asked me if I knew about a book she took from her teenage sister's bookshelf in which boys and girls can explore stories about sex, anatomy and reproduction. 'Do you know about the sexy pee pee? It's not for you, you cannot figure out what sexy means! I know how adults make babies: by touching their tongues while they kiss!' Infantile theory is very strong!

Seeking expressions of infantile sexuality in what the patient is saying is one of the fundamental aspects of psychoanalysis.

Widlocher (2002, p. 30) said: 'Psychoanalysts are trained to deal with love and aggression more than with infantile sexual fantasies. The transference dynamic is based on the affects, and psychoanalysts are involved in the patient's conflicts and questions that come from love and hatred. Of course, psychoanalysts will use their knowledge about infantile sexual fantasies; but it is easier to be seduced by a patient's love transference or by a child who is supposed to be innocent than to refer to his or her infantile sexual wishes. What is difficult to admit is not infantile sexuality, which is now well

118 *Christine Anzieu-Premmereur*

recognized, but its role in psychoanalytical transference. The psychoanalyst participates in the patient's free association and helps him/her to build new representations of infantile fantasies, and at the same time has to respect how the infantile origin is kept hidden as a secret; that's why ambiguity is often a part of the transference counter-transference process'.

The child's play represents the first activity of sublimation, by putting representations into action–play. Then sublimation will appear within an economy under the primacy of the pleasure principle. Analysis and erotic transference are construction-reconstruction of the relationship with an exciting-calming object source of representations and sublimations, inside the cultural field. In Elsa's analysis we have moved from hyper-excitability and hyper-sexualization to symbolization and sublimation.

The surge of Eros frightens: its power to contain and even transform destructiveness, is never acquired in a stable way. The strength of Eros can be scary, it carries the 'madness' of infantile sexuality. Eros makes the notion of 'life drives' a dynamic force, whose energy is that of drive motions, a force endowed with a very precise function, of establishing links through libidinal investment.

Multiple representations of love were present everywhere in Elsa's analytic journey – except in the 'beyond' of the pleasure principle governed by the compulsion to repeat. It seems to me this is precisely because Eros is the fundamental binding force that animates all life.

References

Bion, W.R. (1970). Attention and interpretation. *Seven Servants*. New York: Aronson.

Bolognini, S. (1994). Transference: Erotised, erotic, loving, affectionate. *The International Journal of Psychoanalysis*, 75 (Pt. 1), 73–86. PMID: 8005766.

Ferenczi, S. (1932). The confusion of tongues between the adult and the child. *The International Journal of Psychoanalysis*, 30, 219–230.

Freud, S. (1966/1895). Project for a scientific psychology. *SE*, *1*, 273–293.

Freud, S. (1905). Three essays on the theory of sexuality. *SE*, *7*, 123–246.

Freud, S. (1914a). Remembering, repeating and working through. *SE*, *12*, 145–156.

Freud, S. (1914b). Observations on transference-love. *SE*, *12*, 157–171.

Freud, S. (1918). From the history of an infantile neurosis. *SE*, *17*, 1–124.

Freud, S. (1920). Beyond the pleasure principle. *SE*, *18*, 14–17.

Gaddini, R. (1970). Transitional objects and the process of individuation: A study in three different social groups. *Journal of the American Academy of Child Psychiatry*, 2, 347–367.

Green, A. (1995). Has sexuality anything to do with psychoanalysis? *International Journal of Psycho-Analysis*, 76, 871–883.

Green, A. (2018). *The Chains of Eros: The Sexual in Psychoanalysis*. London: Routledge.

Laplanche, J. (1997). The theory of seduction and the problem of the other. *International Journal of Psycho-Analysis*, 78, 653–666.

Oliner, M. M. (1982). The anal phase. *Early Female Development*, pp. 25–60. Dordrecht: Springer.

Widlocher, D. (2002). *Infantile Sexuality and Attachment*. London: Routledge.

Elsa's sexual fantasies   119

Winnicott, D.W. (1947). 'Hate in counter-transference'. *Through Paediatrics to Psycho-Analysis*. London: Hogart Press-Institute of Psychoanalysis.

Winnicott, D.W. (1953). Transitional objects and transitional phenomena – A study of the first not-me possession. *The International Journal of Psychoanalysis, 34*, 89–97.

Winnicott, D.W. (1967). The location of cultural experience. *Playing and Reality*. London: Tavistock.

Winnicott, D.W. (2018). Mirror-role of mother and family in child development, In *Playing and Reality*, pp. 18–24. London: Routledge.

Editor's Introduction to:
The tears of a clown: dreaming the erotic in the service of integration

In this chapter Kimberly Boyd and Christopher Lovett set out to describe Boyd's treatment of 'Mason', from ages seven to 13. Mason was adopted at nine months from an institutionalized setting in a foreign land. Boyd and Lovett note that they have been in consultation for several years with Anne Alvarez and reference her comment (2012, and this Volume, Chapter 1) that 'the normal baby is attracted to his objects, and if they give him time to ponder and linger over his experience, this, in itself, is highly integrating' (2012: 117, this Volume, Chapter 1). Boyd and Lovett ask here: 'what of the erotic life of a child who has not had the benefit of stable caretaking in his early life?' Clearly Boyd, with the support of Lovett and Alvarez, intended to 'ponder and linger' over Mason's experience. As Boyd and Lovett are well aware, this isn't so easy. Boyd's wish to pause and linger meets up with Mason's fragmentation.

Mason goes fast, he tells stories and makes dramas, but they don't build. Or painfully for his analyst, they seem like they might build, but are dismantled. The authors suggest that his internal chaos could at times be 'fetishized and highly erotized in a perverse scenario'. In these difficult ways, Mason tells his analyst what it is like inside him. Touchingly, Boyd decides to take notes of Mason's stories that they later refer to together. This is rightly in the service of slowing down the action, but also indirectly a statement of 'you exist – in these notes – in my mind'. While reading of Mason's fragmentation, I associated to Frankenstein's monster, sewn together from body parts. How can a baby feel whole, when there is not a single gaze, but rather an ever-changing array of caretakers?

Boyd notes that 'Mason' starts to wear eyeliner and some of his dramatic stories are of same sex romances. It is not clear at this point in the treatment if the analyst has raised this directly. I imagined another chapter Boyd and Lovett might write at some point to tell us more, as happily this treatment is ongoing. A gay or gender fluid teen could feel like a freak, or not know how to as-semble him/herself if he/she is not seen in his/her own way. Noting these parts of Mason could make him feel he can be accepted as he is. (I am aware as I write that I am using the masculine pronoun, which may be in question.) Of course, it is different for an early teen who is far more integrated than Mason to begin to name his/her/their experiences of gender and sexuality. Mason's

DOI: 10.4324/9781003266303-13

analyst may be trying to knit together shards of gender and sexuality, which may get made into some whole and then dismantled.

As analysts of teens who are growing up in a very different time and culture from that which we grew up in, we have the at times unsettling opportunity to try on, 'what might my own gender or sexual experience be if I was growing up now?' More is allowed and more may be confusing. This openness to imagine oneself, may help us to imagine the young teens we are presented with – giving them a chance to be themselves without too much of a demand that they be what suits us.

7 The tears of a clown: dreaming the erotic in the service of integration

Kimberly Boyd and Christopher Lovett

Much of what we understand about children is connected to the intensity of emotion that is characteristic of their early experience, often ranging from joy, to intense frustration and anger, as well as states of frightened confusion and deep sadness. The erotic lives of children, including loving, even passionate, feelings that can emerge from the analytic field between patient and analyst, have not, however, been the subject of sustained and concentrated interest. This stands in sharp contrast with the importance afforded to the erotic in adult analysis, beginning with Freud's (1915) writings on 'transference-love', although even in that domain some have noted a relative reluctance to address the erotic and sexual aspects of the transferential relationship (Bonasia, 2001). In contrast, Etchegoyen (1999), for instance, considers that 'moments of falling in love' occur in every analysis and that this development is not only useful, but also a necessary element toward establishing a productive analytic process and successful outcome. The adult literature does indeed include many writings characterizing erotic transference, such as Bolognini's (1994) description of a spectrum of erotized, erotic, loving and affectionate transferences. Thus, when we use the term 'erotic' it includes a continuum of emotional experiences that range from the 'pleasurable' to the explicitly exciting and sexual.

The emergence of erotic experience in all of these various forms in the treatment of the pre-adolescent or adolescent patient, as well as in younger children, can present a challenge to any child analyst or therapist. It also offers an opportunity to the child to discover, as well as rediscover, a capacity for pleasure in the expanding experience of the body and sexuality in an intersubjective world of relations. In pursuing the subject through the lens of analytic field theory, the treatment then involves the capacity on the part of the analyst to 'dream the erotic' in relation to the patient's experience. For instance, if gender and object choice can be considered an intersubjective construction (Harris, 2009), or an 'implantation' (Laplanche, 1989), then in this framework it would follow that the development of the erotic in the therapeutic setting would also require another mind in order to enable the somatopsychic construction of the various elements of erotic life.

In this context it is useful to recall Freud's (1920) introduction in his work

DOI: 10.4324/9781003266303-14

Beyond the Pleasure Principle of the idea of an instinct, Eros, the libidinal aim of which is 'to establish ever-greater unities and to preserve them' (Freud, 1940, p. 149). As Abel-Hirsch (2001) has pointed out, while Eros in Freud's conceptualization represents a drive, or 'a force which "binds together" the elements of human existence', it is also viewed as contributing to an increased sense of aliveness and vitality. Freud included in this 'life instinct', sexuality and love, but in this reworking of his final theory of the instincts, Eros was also depicted as including an overriding aim, that is, to bind things together in a manner that provided the means to experience something alive, new and, growing into its own potential as a form of life, living in the world of others. At the same time, Freud downplayed what Green (1986) has called the role of passion that lies at the heart of the various manifestations of Eros, each of which features the essential 'madness' that is present in all transferences, though perhaps most recognizable in erotic transference. From Green's point of view, it is 'only when a subject's madness … enters into the transference situation that the analysis is really taking place' (p. 237). In keeping with this perspective, Abel-Hirsch (2001) suggests that a person cannot engage in the binding of the passions, and thus the experience of any sort of meaningful intercourse with others or with oneself, without having access to some form of love.

As considered in the light of analytic field theory (Ferro and Civitarese, 2015), the practice of child analysis, as that well as that of adults, has moved toward a theory of technique that utilizes a model of dreaming, specifically, waking dreaming, as the most effective method for metabolizing the interactions between the patent and analyst. The most important therapeutic factor in this framework is seen as the search for emotional attunement with the patient, or what Bion (1970) referred to as 'at-one-ment'. Elaborating on the work of Bion (1962), the analytic session is viewed as an exercise in joint dreaming and playing. Playing is viewed as close to dreaming in its access to the primitive parts of the psyche, and in this sense is considered a form of 'waking dreaming' (Molinari, 2018). While the experiences of 'unison' between the analyst and the patient are seen as crucial to the therapeutic process, this does not mean that 'difference' is ignored or undervalued. A developing capacity for differentiation is essential to the process of achieving an increasing sense of unique subjectivity in the child. Abel-Hirsch (2001), in fact, points out that there is a paradox that characterizes the essential nature of Eros, and emphasizes that, once difference is recognized, there arises the possibility of intercourse and the generation of new life in the sexual, emotional and imaginative realms.

In a similar fashion, the analytic field, first described by Baranger and Baranger (1961–62), is conceived as located in a dynamic sense at the intersection of the mutual projective identifications between patient and analyst. Bion (1962) extended the understanding of projective identification to include a communicative function, which carried the idea of therapeutic growth via intercourse of internal objects and parts of the self between the patient and analyst to a new level of understanding.

124   *Kimberly Boyd and Christopher Lovett*

In the case to be discussed, the function of the container-contained and the analyst's use of *reverie* was largely carried out in the realm of play through a young boy's passionate interest in staging musicals. The invention of characters, the fashioning of staging and scenes, and the singing, at times on the part of both the patient and analyst, filled the playroom with a vibrant, emotionally expressive and continuous dialogue, or duet. The work carried out by this analytic duet included transformations in play and the disruption of play when the analytic pair encountered the patient's scenes of infantile trauma that had not yet been sufficiently metabolized. These disruptions seemed to be a function of difficulty the analytic couple experienced together in the effort to extend their jointly created dream capacity to contain the disruptive and fragmenting experiences brought into the treatment. The analyst in this case is the first author of this chapter, although it is important to point out that the work was discussed on a nearly weekly basis with the second author and a consultant very familiar with the issue of the place of the erotic in the analysis of children, Anne Alvarez.

'Mason'

In discussing this case, (a treatment that continues through the present), we would like to consider with the reader questions that pertain to the fate of erotic life for a child who did not have the benefit of stable caretaking in his early life. Green (1986) has discussed the importance of the mothering figure in fostering the birth of instinctual life and its psychical binding, even going so far as to suggest that the principle aim of maternal love is to make raw experience, particularly the experience of instinctual pressure, tolerable for the infant. When a stable and available maternal object, or container for the child's projections of intense longing and, very often, frustration, is not available, as in this case, Green suggests that, 'everything happens as though it *were impossible for the order of the world to appear*', and that, instead, in the infant's experience it is, 'as though all were chaos, chaos to which the chaos of destruction responds' (p. 247). In the analytic work with Mason a repeated experience of chaos was an important feature, as seen through the collapse of the narratives involved in his productions in play. This seemed to refer to a time in the patient's early life when containment and reverie were too little in supply and led to a collapse in Mason's nascent feeling of being a loved and cared-for object.

Mason, now a 13-year-old boy, was raised for his first nine months in an Eastern European orphanage, then adopted by an American couple and brought to the United States. Alvarez (2012) reminds us that, 'The normal baby is attracted to his objects, and if they give him time to ponder and linger over his experience, this, in itself, is highly integrating' (p. 117). But what of the baby receiving fragmented and mechanical care from multiple caregivers? What of the child who had no such early object who allowed him to linger, in other words, the baby who, as a result, is poorly integrated? Or, in terms employed by Bion and Freud, what of the child who is insufficiently

The tears of a clown   125

'contained' and without the kind of 'binding' of his various impulses and affects that allows for relative freedom from infantile anxieties concerning intrusion or loss of vital object ties at a very early point in life? How might the child's erotic life be shaped by such experience? In the work with Mason, his analyst continually wondered whether a child so fragmented could bring the various pieces of his scattered self into a transference in which a healthy experience of loving and eliciting love in another could be created.

Mason was born in a place not simply foreign, but a faraway land that most in the west might consider as exotic. Like all children he fell into a world, marked and defined by a language, and into a culture with different sights, sounds, smells and tastes from the one into which he was adopted. His coloring and bearing are distinct from his adoptive parents, who are both darker-complected and more broadly framed than he is. Though problems with infertility led them to him, during the waiting period prior to his adoption, his adoptive parents conceived twins, born only months after he arrived. If Mason was deprived of an early experience of significant others and thus the presence of others around him for whom he was an object of desire, his arrival in the midst of his new family was anticlimactic.

Mason entered treatment with one of the authors (KB) at age seven, smiling and gentle, wearing a tee shirt on the day of his first meeting that was drenched and tattered from his chewing on it. Immediately, he seemed an especially sunny fellow who was also anxious, disorganized, poorly regulated and, in a certain essential way, soft. His principal interests were in fashion and storybooks, and his favorites were what seemed a rather uninspired series about little girls drawn into difficult fixes from which they were rescued by characters described as magical fairies. They were sparkly creatures, distinctive by way of their varying hair and skin tones, and Mason described their outfits in some considerable and enthusiastic detail. Most importantly, they were special, because they were always there when you needed them.

As chaotic as Mason was, his use of the treatment space, in its form, at least, was quite predictable and consistent from the beginning of our work together, or, one might even say reliable and disorganized at the same time. In marked contrast to his early environment, this consistency provided part of the containing function of the setting and the treatment in general. Almost invariably, Mason would sit next to me at my table, and from there he would create stories, which over time evolved into a complex musical theater, complete with staging, lighting, special effects and costume design. He communicated his productions to me verbally, and they were complex and rich in both the level of imagination and dramatic action they featured. While much has changed from the early days in treatment, over time Mason has gradually emerged as enormously creative and talented.

Discussions between the two authors came to include reminders of the eventual career of the first child analytic patient, Little Hans (Freud, 1909), who grew up to become an opera director and producer of some considerable renown. This shared set of associations seemed to suggest a converging sense of

126   *Kimberly Boyd and Christopher Lovett*

hopefulness and admiration in response to Mason's talent and 'gifts' that may have been, in part, a reaction to the very deep impression that he had not been 'given' very much in the way of holding or attention as an infant. Alvarez (2012) has written about the child or adolescent's desire to 'make someone's eyes light up' and the child's 'need for a responsive interested object capable of being delighted' (p. 126) as crucial to the baby's feeling of being potent enough to awaken interest and delight in others. It seemed clear that this boy's capacity to stimulate excitement in his analyst and her colleague was a form of erotic responsiveness. As such, Mason began to assume the role of an 'object of analytic desire' in the form of a young person whose emerging 'potential' had awakened his analyst's imagination and interest in the futural dimension of their work together, the yet-to-be-realized that seemed to hold so much promise at that time (Wilson, 2018). In an important sense, this development seemed an expression of the field, one in which a creation story was being recast and reconfigured to include the possibility of a 'new beginning' (Balint, 1968) with a renewed set of hopes attached to the 'new arrival' in the analytic space.

It is important to note, however, that initially Mason had been difficult to join in play. I found that I could enter in through the music he created, at first by keeping the beat as he sang, then sometimes singing, too. At first, this was only an occasional practice, but later it assumed the nature of the real give and take of an improvising duo. This singing, like all music can, involved progressions from regularity and predictability, to novelty and surprise, and back again.

It was as if we were participating in the primordial rhythms that take place in the bodily interaction between a mother and child, like breathing and an awareness of a heartbeat. Rhythm, of course, and the sharing of it, is a regular, repeating embodied experience that serves to lay down the very earliest feelings of unison. Rhythm involves movement, and synchrony, which like dreaming seems to propel the subject's experience into a universal moment of playing – dreaming that in its rehearsal of separation and reunion, disintegration and integration, reinvigorates the erotic and the role of Eros in the earliest stages of development (Civitarese, 2016). In addition, the singing and operating together in a rhythmic and tonal exchange also invoked the early conversations between mothers and infants that take place before words. It was a communicative movement between us that was not only musical (Malloch and Trevarthen, 2009), but created in the field an atmosphere of safety and vitality. Along these same lines regarding rhythm and the development across many realms, Molinari (2014) has observed:

> The innate forms – that is, the abstract, aesthetic, geometric, musical forms of rhythm – organize the early relational experiences and become the essential element from which thinking and feeling develop – a bridge between the body and the mind – and the capacity to wait develops. From that comes the trust in the other-outside-oneself and the hope to be supported.
>
> (p. 240)

The tears of a clown 127

While the form of sessions with Mason had been predictable, the content had, at the same time, proved to be highly stimulating to overstimulating. There had been on offer a plethora of descriptions of visual sensory experience, particularly related to costume design. Sheen, color and material would all be specified by Mason, creating complex images, which were exciting, yet seemed empty of meaning, except as a spectacle. There was also an element of periodic auditory overstimulation in which Mason's masterly musical lines would be replaced by an irritating cacophony or a dialogue delivered through a form of squealing reminiscent of the high-pitched, 'Valley girl' type speech. The musical theater created in the hours during this period often started out as they always had, featuring a pleasant overture and the introduction of characters. In short order, however, the show would become fractured and fragmented, often consisting merely of elements from multiple fairy tales or musicals seemingly thrown together into a jumbled tangle, signaling the reentry of chaos into the work and then abruptly labeled 'a show'.

Continuously, my experience with Mason was one of feeling drawn to him, hopeful, yet intermittently overwhelmed and lost. I entered every hour eager to find him, often working particularly hard to pull together what felt like the shards of material strewn about in his wake through the hour. I became aware that I was working overtime to make some coherent meaning of it all and, by this means, hopefully to re-find some meaningful connection with him. Again, I also found myself feeling some quality of awe at the sheer enormity of his 'creative machine', which often produced smart, witty and sophisticated pieces of dialogue, plotline or lyric. Yet I also felt desperate and scattered, at times feeling as though I struggled to recall the trajectory of a single session. Meltzer's (1967) description of 'gathering the transference' came to mind, in which the various pieces of the patient's internal object world are constructed in a concentrated fashion in the transference. Given the degree of fragmentation that had pervaded the field, however, I felt in more immediate need of some means or method to gather my own thoughts as a way of providing some greater capacity for holding in the analytic hours. In an uncharacteristic move, as compared to my usual approach, I decided to take notes during the sessions, thus making a kind of script of the production unfolding in real time. Interestingly, both of us came to refer to these notes, and this joint activity, as the provision of a 'third' in the form of the recording of a history of the present. The shared scripts seemed to enable us to begin a slow shift in the work toward some stable and coherent narrative base that we could reclaim and occupy together.

Greenberg (2018) suggested in a commentary on Klein's ideas regarding psychoanalytic technique that, 'Only the analyst who has been disturbed has been receptive to the patient's projections; this receptivity must precede containment and reverie … The analyst's mind – altered by her receptivity to the patient's projections – is a vital source of information about what is most central to the patient's psychopathology' (p. 983). Initially, I understood the fragmented nature of Mason's 'shows' during this period to reflect his chaotic and poorly integrated internal experience. Simply put, I believed that he was not capable of putting together anything more meaningful. With time, however, I came to feel that something was occurring that was more meaningful, and, either consciously or unconsciously, something more pointed had come into our play that signaled a shift in the work. A demand for work was being placed on the analytic field and its dreaming function, though it seemed now to assume the form of something more intensely sensory, while at the same time seeming without any sense (i.e., neither sensual nor meaningful). In retrospect, it seems in keeping with a perverse erotic field, one characterized by fracturing and fragmentation.

Etchegoyen (1999) has described the workings of the perverse erotic, which involves elements of both deconstruction and overstimulation. In this period of work with Mason, the process of putting together, or 'creating' a story, devolved to the conjoining of fragments and then declaring it a 'story'. In its overstimulating aspects during this time elements that, as before, were often shiny or sparkling, came to seem the product of a fragmentation and its manic repair. Rather than a simple reflection of some 'deficit', I began to understand that this period of seeming mayhem and bottomless confusion represented a projective identification of the way in which Mason felt he had been constructed as an infant. The erotic 'madness' described by Green and present in the form of a descent into chaos in the clinical hours had emerged in the field between us. It was not simply perverse in its effect of blocking access to any coherent meaning or connection, it also represented a meaningful, communicative projection of Mason's very early experience in which he was repeatedly abandoned and left to his own devices.

In light of this experience in Mason's and my work together, the answer to the question, 'What is the fate of the erotic in an unintegrated child?' includes the possibility that the internal chaos, so well described by Green, may become fetishized and highly erotized in a perverse scenario. After the initial period of dislocation and loss of any secure analytic stance, it now seems that the perverse, destructive excitement pulled the analyst in, prompting me to redouble my efforts to try to make meaningful contact in some recognizable format – that of the scriptwriter and copy editor.

Over time, I again began to feel that something more deliberate and purposeful emerged in our analytic work and play, as his shows changed in character and casting. Increasingly, they featured a real plotline, now of his own making again, though they were often dark, even cynical, and the characters flat or wooden. Even so, at various points, his hours, and the stories that represented them, devolved into a regressive chaos, silliness or a return to manic overstimulation in relation to his analyst and the entire space. Mason would become quite charged up and excited during these moments, while I was able to articulate to him that he had left me, or one of his characters in that day's show, feeling the confusion and sense of being blocked or stymied that felt so threatening to him.

The tears of a clown 129

One such show began with a mysterious death in the year 2046. Central Park had burned down, and a 1000 story tower had been erected from the ruins. The tower was sleek, brightly lit, made of glass. It seemed to me that Mason was narrating his own recovery from the previous period of destructive activity through imagining a grand incarnation that might undo all the losses that the ruins seemed to represent. Blue Neon lights illuminated a sign that noted the passage of time in announcing, 'Three Weeks Earlier'. Avery, an adolescent boy, was now alone on the stage, having been 'dumped' by a girl at the end of a date. Avery continued, 'My name is Avery. I've never been dumped before. I'm genetically perfect. Instead of being conceived naturally, my parents sought other means. I'm smart and social, but for some reason something is out of my reach. Happiness. I live on the top floor. They live far away and visit sometimes, not often. But people want to be my friend. Who wouldn't want to be friends with a robot?'

I felt moved by the character of Avery – the perfect, perfectly unhappy robot who seemingly has so much, but, in actuality, has so little. I saw Mason as functioning robotically, without feeling, or rather obscuring what might lead to any feeling, so as to not be overwhelmed. Poignantly, he asks if I think it's a good show. I respond in a way that connects him to his production, though not in a saturated, directly interpretive mode. I said that there are important questions in his story, not only about death but also about what makes a person, what makes someone worth knowing and loving, and, finally, what makes for happiness.

Then, brutally, Mason set to dismantling the narrative that had assumed some form involving the expression of feelings of profound loss and loneliness, the survivor of an internal catastrophe that had flattened his world. As the director, Mason now brought onstage Celia, Avery's girlfriend, an expression of the previous event of being dumped – or feeling uncontained by his analyst in her interpretation. Celia proclaimed in a crescendo of frenzied silliness, 'My name is Celia. I went to rehab. I murdered my cat with a paperclip … You know, at rehab there was this girl who brought a rhino home, and it killed her Mom and Dad. Now she thinks the rhino is her mom and dad'.

In this hour, as in many similar moments, I felt drawn into the promise of some feeling of resonance or mutual realization, but this hope then suffered a fracture. Mason had constructed a story, and then deconstructed it when the emotion in the analytic space became too much to bear. I found myself moving toward becoming quite active, providing affect for the characters and expressing a sense of alarm, even protest at the abandonments and fracturing of the world only just created, as Mason himself had been abandoned and suffered a fracturing of his nascent self soon after his birth. Mason, however, still excited and buoyed by a sense of sadistic glee, persisted, saying that he 'liked it'.

Following this decisive hour, I began to understand the transference-countertransference and the communication of something vital within the analytic field of Mason's early experience. In an omnipotent fashion, he was now in control of all comings and goings, not stuck in a crib in a cold,

130 *Kimberly Boyd and Christopher Lovett*

institutional setting. At the same time, like many of the characters in his plays, I was reaching, grasping, hoping, looking, but feeling myself as unable to capture the desired other. The repetition grew increasingly meaningful, as it now seemed clear that the repetition itself provided a form of containment and shelter for that part of Mason that felt overstimulated, desperately seeking and repeatedly abandoned and disappointed in the shattering experience of his early caretaking environment. Yet, despite such realizations on my part, it remained the case that a perverse enactment was taking place, as for Mason chaos and the experience of disintegration itself had taken on an erotic, and at times sadistic charge. Although I did not consider him to be intensely sadistic in his overt behavior, he was at the same time clearly finding pleasure in something I found uncomfortable and at times noxiously overstimulating. My own persistence to remain engaged, perhaps was a response to anxiety about losing Mason, the once shiny and promising boy, to a darker turn in his developing adaptation. I knew that outside the treatment setting he was suffering greatly from the withdrawal of others whom he had hoped to engage. Again, I was struck by the evolution of the erotic elements in the development of this child who had suffered from states of unintegration, as the early disintegrative experiences had become fetishized and highly erotized as part of an emerging character defense.

Through the processes of metabolization of my own intensely difficult experiences with the 'original madness' that had entered the field like a whirlwind, what had only been enacted began gradually to become available in the field in symbolic form. Themes of abandonment and disappointment became increasingly central in the analytic hours. They assumed a focal place in Mason's storylines and, importantly, in the transference as well. I continued to concentrate on providing a receptive, though not passive or submissive container, so that I might be able to hold the feelings that Mason could not as yet.

One day, Mason made his way by public transportation all the way to my office, only realizing upon his arrival that he had 'forgotten' that I had planned to be out of town on that day. Later, he denied any disappointment, though in a now familiar sequence I felt enormous sadness at the thought of him alone at my locked door. His show that followed was about a 'crazed', neglected wife whose husband was engrossed in watching television and realized only when it came on the news that she had tumbled off the balcony of their apartment building. On another occasion when, again, I had to cancel an appointment, he constructed a show about a nanny who left her employ. When I again related the story to my absence, his association by way of a next show was about multiple superhero fairy tale princesses who were able to fend for themselves – like a Rapunzel who could escape her tower on her own.

I commented that I thought he was saying to me, 'I don't need you, Prince. Thank you very much!' At this point in our work together, despite his denials, Mason now at least appeared unconsciously aware that he felt some greater sense of loss in response to my absence. It had become obvious, at least to me,

The tears of a clown   131

that the deepening connection between us now included an increased ability on his part to tolerate the feelings of vulnerability that came along with that development in the erotic field.

In a fascinating turn, one that involved his using his own persona as the medium, we were able to make increasing contact with the sadness that lay beneath Mason's 'sunny' exterior. Around this time, he had begun to experiment with makeup, largely in the context of his involvement in the theater, but now he began to wear eye makeup outside of the home, both to school and to our sessions. The emotional impact of the eye makeup was compelling, as if it signified an appeal, or even a return, to an earlier, lost object. I found myself seeming more and more to look into his eyes, and, reciprocally, he more into mine, entering a greater level of some interconnection. This meeting through mutual gaze was, in retrospect, both a vehicle for an experience of emotional unison, as well as a necessary precursor and facilitator of his emerging integration and expression of feelings of sadness. The makeup was, typically, quite subtle, nearly skin toned, though one day he augmented it with shiny white strips at the inner corners of his eyes. I commented to him that the white markings looked like tears, and he told me that a classmate had said the same, but he added that we were both wrong. I believe that his classmate and I were, first, seen as together and so placing him in the position of the excluded third, but, in addition, we were wrong in our way of 'seeing', as from a different vertex, one outside of his omnipotent control. The makeup in this way functioned both to express and disguise his sadness, like the tears of a clown.

It was in a session shortly afterward that for the first time Mason spontaneously acknowledged feelings of sadness. That day almost immediately after his show began, he announced a shift from the usual process, now able to anticipate a developing story and create a genuine narrative, 'Once upon a time people were happy. Not anymore'.

It turned out to be a show about a scientist, one whose creations were creatures assembled from various body parts. These assembled characters were sent to an island where everyone was said to be happy. This arrangement, in fantasy an island inhabited by characters constructed from the debris, or fragments of other lives, or selves, was idealized as perfect, until a child arrived, the first and only child, one who, 'was different from all the other creations'. The others on the island were frightened of this child and tried to lock it away, because there had been a mistake in the child, the first mistake ever made. This child had no name, no personality, nor any gender. As Mason described this figure, it simply existed, and yet it was not merely and exclusively happy. It also had a 'range of emotion'. Locked away and deprived, it was fed multiple times each week by a boy who would let it out in order to feed it.

I commented that I found myself feeling a different way, hoping that this child could be freed, yet also afraid to hope too much. In this way, through a form of 'analyst–centered interpretation' (Steiner, 1994), one that avoided attributing my reaction to some aspect of his emotional life too soon, I attempted to convey in an 'unsaturated' way how an 'other' might feel in response to the dramatic scene he had constructed.

It seemed that, together, Mason and I were also beginning to invite out and to nurture the 'feeling' child within him, albeit still quite dissociated and defended against. There had emerged in the analytic hours an increased coherence in the affective realm. A development that included an increasing connection with me. Mason and I were now seeing 'eye to eye', and in concert with the greater sense of holding this seemed to allow, his shows became increasingly less splintered and were now merely incomplete. Still emblematic of his own evolving story, as yet unfinished, this seemed a reflection of a sense of his own continued feeling of inhabiting 'a potential beginning … prevented from developing' (Laplanche and Pontalis, 2018 [1967], p. 224). Feelings of disappointment, previously manifested in a form of pan-cynicism, had begun to coalesce into the disappointment of a promise of a love unfulfilled. This brings to mind Kohon's (2005) observation regarding the importance of the erotic transference to the development of the capacity for love, 'Can we conceive of an analysis without transference, without the love generated by transference?' (p. 78).

I was more clearly now the container of hope, but also of the feelings of disappointment, as again and again in his dramas the promise of something good took a downward turn, a loss or even a feeling of disaster, that I was asked to endure and articulate. These were expressions in the transference of both love and disappointments in love for this adopted child, previously not sufficiently lingered over, but rather given up and encroached upon prematurely by a multitude of infant siblings and roughly held together fragments of experience.

At this juncture in the treatment, the nature of the erotic in the field had shifted away from an atmosphere of perverse enactment toward an object related and now embodied love.

I have long pondered over the character of the embodied erotic for Mason and children like him, those who have enjoyed relatively little bodily contact and care early on when the proximate of the physical is a primary venue of relating. I have assumed that in Mason's case his highly developed visual and auditory registers might have somehow developed as part of a compensatory movement in response to a dearth of early touching. As this stage of the work continued to deepen, in addition to eye contact, I began to notice this highly visual boy now taking in my form as we walked down the hall toward the playroom, as the visual mode of contact and identificatory processes evolved to include some greater range of appreciation of the unique qualities of his objects. At the same time his play has shifted to a focus on a world where people don't grow old, where a 13-year-old cold fall in love with a 50-year-old in a 13-year-old's body and then be heartbroken. It was apparent to me that I was becoming an embodied figure for him and, at the same time, an object of transference love. For my part, I began to notice him growing tall, or that he does have

The tears of a clown 133

lovely eyes. All of these emerging elements were indications of a leading edge of some shift in the erotic field created between Mason and his analyst.

This development was followed by a change in the structure and quality of Mason's narrative capacities in the play, as he began to produce stories that were complete and coherent, some of them quite explicitly exploring different kinds of love. One, a Cinderella tale, opens with a song about beautiful moonlight, thus already featuring a romantic image, but now sensual in its quality, rather than merely sensory.

In this story, Ella, the protagonist, is described as a *'normal'* girl who dances when her stepfamily is out, clearly enjoying her bodily sensuality and capacity to move in rhythm with an imagined other. Ella wants to go to the Ball, and, perhaps, to have a chance at love. After finding an invitation on the ground, she says quietly to herself, 'Don't wish. You never get what you wish for'. This sense of apprehensiveness and fear of disappointment lasts only a moment before it gives way to a feeling of hope and longing, 'But I just have to wish'.

In this brief sequence it is apparent that Mason is now able to contain the ambivalence about hopefulness within the character herself, and thus within the field, as well as the sense of risk. In the story that follows, a Fairy Godmother then appears, giving off a sparkling light. Less cynical now, Mason is able to be rather ironic instead, a distinction that we think reflected a still developing belief in the goodness of his objects, as well as expressing a tentative possibility of hope. Yet he introduces an uncharacteristic Fairy Godmother, one perhaps even scandalously critical, who exclaims, 'Ball! You can't go to a Ball. You have nothing to wear. How dumb can you be!'

An inflection point seemed to be at hand, both in the context of the story and, it seemed, in Mason's own development and the process of his treatment. Unclear on the show's trajectory, Mason outlines three alternative plotlines, each one offering a different kind of love story. First, the Fairy Godmother and Ella could fall in love, representing both a homosexual adaptation and an identification with the loving analyst; or, second, Ella would override the Fairy Godmother's ruling and set out to meet the prince (a heterosexual oedipal victory); or, last, Ella could just carry out everything herself (perhaps masturbatory and self-sufficient). Mason quite deliberately decides to pursue the first plotline, and a circuitous unfolding of this story of possibilities in identity and object choice ensues. As it turns out, the Fairy Godmother becomes a fortuneteller who beckons Ella for a hug, but Ella insists that she is supposed to be her Fairy Godmother. At this, the fortuneteller begins to spin around, patches falling off her cloak reveal a shimmering gown of white and brown beneath. Taking in this vision, Ella insists this is the dress worn by her Fairy Godmother, but the glittering woman responds in a grand gesture of transformation and reunion with an idealized, combined parental object, that this is impossible, because she is, in fact, Ella's mother, and a racially integrated mother of white and brown.

In this moment Mason seemed to discover the impact and meaning of his story, and so he backtracks, saying that maybe the two won't fall in love after all. I feel at this moment that it might be important to express a disagreement, though it is primarily directed to Mason's apparent anxiety in relation to an emergent feeling of erotic longing and developing sense of object choice.

Summary

From the point of view of the two authors, the analytic work involved in the treatment of Mason demonstrates a process in which 'playing' involves the discovery of the possible contexts in the analytic field created between a child and a child analyst. It is a process that includes the creation of new forms of living, new forms of integration or re-integration in a generative experience.

In addition, we feel that this brief depiction of analytic work carried out with Mason also demonstrates that a living analytic process, when it is working well, ideally assumes the nature of complex forms of play that allow for transformations of previously fragmented or unrepresented emotions into meaningful patterns and narratives. It can be likened to dreams of a fairy who comes to feel more like an actual mother as the desiring subject feels there is sufficient receptivity present in the analytic field to allow for processes of both mourning for lost objects and longing for new opportunities to emerge. The last story constructed by Mason also represents the completion of a cycle, Freud's (1905) finding and re-finding of the object. The analytic process in this case, like so many others in the treatment of children and adolescents, also involves the process of re-finding hope and desire. It is a process that allows for and facilitates a communicative atmosphere of vitality and an experience of unison between the patient and his or her analyst. In this case, the analyst and her young patient established a shared 'musical culture', one that featured a shared, rhythmic atmosphere that allowed for the dreaming of experience in both the imagination and in the body (Civitarese, 2016). Others have written about the evocation of a 'body reverie' that is libidinally charged and allows for an affective resonance between the subject and the other in an intersubjective relation (Hartung and Steinbrecher, 2018). This shared experience can become a shared dreaming and an expression of Eros, binding and, finally, of love in a transferential relation that is both new and a reconstitution – a 'creative repetition' (Reis, 2019).

The expressions of love within the transference thus far in the case example discussed are not yet fully embodied, and thus integrated into the sexual sphere. Movement into a more broadly erotic domain is likely to be multiple in its manifest forms of expression. The continued evolution within the treatment and for Mason will most likely include issues involving both object choice and gender identity, as indicated by a significant degree of fluidity in his current subjective experience and depicted in his playing and its shifting themes and positions of the various characters in relation to one another.

In general, the treatment approach with this patient focused on a style of interpretation that was designed to encourage the development of his narrative capacities, the processes of subjectivation and symbolization, and the growth of a capacity to metabolize emotional experience. While the treatment is certainly not concluded, Mason's level of integration and his erotic life have shifted considerably and in concert with one another. A mutually reinforcing benign spiral has been at work which serves to increase connection and to enable increasing coherence in his inner life and in relation with his principal object. In the beginning of treatment, Mason had sought omnipotent control over losses that he had never psychically experienced, yet were suffered by him with a sense of internal chaos and overwhelming emotions. A shiny edifice had come to overlay what felt unconstructed, empty, or despairing within him. The sheen had become a means of enlivening himself, his internal objects and keeping the magic fairies available to him in fantasy, perhaps as omnipotent and loving objects, always there when he needed them in his private theater of dreams and dramas. This narcissistic retreat also served as a protective shield against re-experiencing the sort of overstimulation that had characterized his early life, which at times was incorporated into a perverse erotic transference and nascent character feature that worked to foreclose connection with others and a sustaining involvement in his analysis. In the quote from Horatio Etchegoyen presented at the outset of this paper, he makes clear the healthy and *necessary* role that feelings of love and erotic transference play in positive developments in analysis. For Mason, the gradual evolution of an erotic transference allowed him to increasingly harness his capacity for creative elaboration in fantasy toward useful purposes, such as psychic elaboration and the binding of destructive or primitive mechanisms, and the expansion of his inner world. A perverse erotic that posed a distinct and problematic issue in the analysis for a period of time shifted into an erotic attachment that is closer to what Bolognini (1994) had in mind in speaking about transference as loving, affectionate and even sexual, which has facilitated Mason's continuing work of psychic integration and the expansion of the story of his life and of his erotic life.

References

Abel-Hirsch, N. (2001). *Eros (Ideas in Psychoanalysis)*. Cambridge: Icon Books.

Alvarez, A. (2012). Types of sexual transference and countertransference in work with children and adolescents. *The Thinking Heart: Three Levels of Psychoanalytic Therapy with Disturbed Children*. New York: Routledge.

Balint, M. (1968). *The Basic Fault*. London: Tavistock.

Baranger, W., & Baranger, M. (1961–62). The analytic situation as a dynamic field. *International Journal of Psychoanalysis, 89*, 795–826.

Bion, W.R. (1962). *Learning from Experience*. London: Karnac.

Bion, W.R. (1970). *Attention and Interpretation*. London: Karnac.

Bolognini, S. (1994). Transference: Erotised, erotic, loving, affectionate. *International Journal of Psychoanalysis, 75*, 73–86.

Bonasia, E. (2001). The countertransference: Erotic, erotised and perverse. *International Journal of Psychoanalysis, 82*, 249–262.

Civitarese, G. (2016). Masochism and its rhythm. *Journal of the American Psychoanalytic Association, 64*, 885–916.

136 *Kimberly Boyd and Christopher Lovett*

Etchegoyen, R.H. (1999). *Fundamentals of Psychoanalytic Technique, Revised Edition*. London: Karnac.

Ferro, A., & Civitarese, G. (2015). *The Analytic Field and Its Transformations*. London: Karnac.

Freud, S. (1905). Three essays on the theory of sexuality. In Strachey, J. (Ed. & Trans.) *The Standard Edition of the Complete Psychological Works of Sigmund Freud*, Vol. 7, pp. 123–243. London: Hogarth Press.

Freud, S. (1909). Analysis of a phobia in a five-year-old boy. In Strachey, J. (Ed. & Trans.) *The Standard Edition of the Complete Psychological Works of Sigmund Freud*, Vol. 10, pp. 1–150. London: Hogarth Press.

Freud, S. (1915). Observations on transference-love. In Strachey, J. (Ed. & Trans.) *The Standard Edition of the Complete Psychological Works of Sigmund Freud*, Vol. 12, pp. 159–171. London: Hogarth Press.

Freud, S. (1920). *Beyond the pleasure principle*. In Strachey, J. (Ed. & Trans.), *The Standard Edition of the Complete Psychological Works of Sigmund Freud*, Vol. 18, pp. 1–64. London: Hogarth Press.

Freud, (1940). *Outline of psycho-analysis*. In Strachey, J. (Ed. & Trans.), *The Standard Edition of the Complete Psychological Works of Sigmund Freud*, Vol. 23, pp. 139–208. London: Hogarth Press.

Green, A. (1986[1980]). Passions and their vicissitudes: On the relation between madness and psychosis. *On Private Madness*, pp. 214–253. Madison, CT: International Universities Press.

Greenberg, J. (2018). Klein's technique. *International Journal of Psychoanalysis*, 99, 979–989.

Harris, A. (2009). *Gender as soft assembly*. New York: Routledge.

Hartung, T., & Steinbrecher, M. (2018). From somatic pain to psychic pain: The body in the psychoanalytic field. *International Journal of Psychoanalysis*, 99, 159–180.

Kohon, Gregorio (2005). Love in a time of madness. *Love and Its Vicissitudes*. New York: Routledge.

Laplanche, J. (1989[1987]). In Macey, D. (Trans.) *New Foundations for Psychoanalysis*. Oxford: Blackwell.

Laplanche, J., & Pontalis, J.-B. (1967). *The Language of Psycho-Analysis*. New York: Routledge.

Malloch, S., & Trevarthen, C. (2009). Musicality: Communicating the vitality and interests in life. In Malloch, S., & Trevarthen, C. (Eds.), *Communicative Musicality: Exploring the Basis of Human Companionship*. Oxford: Oxford University Press.

Meltzer, D. (1967). *The Psychoanalytical Process, Revised Edition*. London: The Harris Meltzer Trust.

Molinari, E. (2014). Action across emptiness. *Journal of Child Psychotherapy*, 40, 239–253.

Molinari, E. (2018). Variations on a theme: Child and adolescent analysis. In Ferro, A. (Ed.) *Contemporary Bionian Theory and Technique in Psychoanalysis*. New York: Routledge, pp. 176–216.

Reis, B. (2019). *Creative Repetition and Intersubjectivity: Contemporary Freudian Explorations of Trauma, Memory, and Clinical Process*. New York: Routledge.

Steiner, J. (1994). Patient-centered and analyst-centered interpretations: Some implications of Containment and countertransference. *Psychoanalytic Inquiry*, 14, 406–422.

Wilson, M. (2018). The analyst as listening-accompanist: Desire in Bion and Lacan. *Psychoanalytic Quarterly*, 82, 237–264.

Editor's Introduction to:
A boy's terror and fascination with the male body

In this chapter, we meet 'David', an early adolescent boy who entered treatment two years after a near fatal diabetic ketoacidosis. His analyst asks here, 'How do emerging erotic interests and desires change when a child or adolescent suffers a medical trauma that becomes a chronic condition?' Tyminski describes David's preoccupation with horror films as a way to grapple with the catastrophe that had come from within his own body – his body had seemed to turn on itself.

As David recovered from his medical catastrophe and acclimated to his ongoing diabetic condition, his analyst tells us 'I noticed him at times looking at my arms, my legs, my sideburns, and my beard. The look was often one of concealed excitement, as in "What's that?!"' David's own parents seemed well meaning, but too remote. In one session Tyminski notes David staring at his forearm and then 'accidentally' rolling his arm over his analyst's arm. This occurs while watching a brief clip of a horror film David has asked to show his analyst in which the anti-hero 'transforms'. Tyminski grapples with mentioning the physical contact, knowing David could feel sensitive or rejected by any comment. Tyminski finds a way into noting the potential pleasure of an accidental touch (meanwhile keeping the medical accident in mind) and remarks that David could be curious about his (Tyminski's) body. In this poignant clinical material, a boy's longing both to *see* and hope to eventually *be* a healthy man is evident. Here David must grapple with his health restrictions, but he is able to experience pleasure in male bodies and male closeness.

In this chapter, the erotic field is different that the intensity of the erotic experiences depicted by me in Chapter 2 and Jackson in Chapter 10. I was reminded here of Moss's (2012) contention that to identify with a man is to love a man – and that endless complications result. Moss (2012) asserts object love and identification are inter-penetrative. Tyminski braved his pre-pubertal boy's interest in his body and thus directly and indirectly communicated how normal it is to be interested in and enjoy a body a boy hopes he may also be able to grow into.

Reading this chapter I am reminded that at times the concrete gender of the analyst is salient, all caveats to the need to imagine ourselves into the other

DOI: 10.4324/9781003266303-15

gender or into gender fluidity aside. Here it seems that the physicality of his analyst stimulated an emerging desire in David and Tyminski was brave enough to engage his patient's interest in his body.

Reference

Moss, D. (2012). *Thirteen Ways of Looking at a Man: Psychoanalysis and Masculinity*. New York, NY: Routledge.

8 A boy's terror and fascination with the male body

Robert Tyminski

How do emerging erotic interests and desires change when a child or adolescent suffers a medical trauma that becomes a chronic condition? This chapter explores developments in the analytic field between David, a 13-year-old boy, and myself regarding our male bodies. My patient became curious about my body and he also feared unexpected discoveries about his masculine development. David came into treatment after being hospitalized and diagnosed with juvenile onset diabetes (type 1 diabetes or T1D). When we first met, he was in a state of shock, as he took in a foreign and upsetting daily routine of insulin injections and glucose monitoring. It took some time for his blood sugar to normalize. As he gradually came out of this state, David became fascinated by horror films, which offered him an outlet to express his own personal horror over what had happened to his body. On the cusp of puberty, bodily transformations took on terrorizing meanings for him. Like many children and adolescents dealing with chronic illnesses, David's awareness of *eros* as a life force became confused with other feelings of anguish and foreboding.

During the 1980s, I completed a rotation on a psychiatric consultation service at San Francisco General Hospital, and I was embedded in a diabetes clinic where I frequently saw adolescents and young adults who were in various states of profound emotional upset about their diabetes and struggling with ongoing management of it. Many were in outright rebellion at it. Throughout my years in practice since then, I have often had patients with diabetes and other chronic illnesses such as Crohn's disease, HIV/AIDS, sickle cell anemia, epilepsy, and severe asthma. Especially for children and adolescents, these conditions are terrifying and confusing, sometimes propelling them into omnipotent fantasizing, a loss of reality testing about their needs, and psychotic denial of limitations. Working with children and adolescents who have chronic illnesses usually involves complicated conversations about their bodies, their developmental horizons, and their hatred and rage about what has happened to them. Projective identification, as defined by Klein (Segal, 1974: 9, 27), is common when an analyst faces such anguished psychic states. Containing these projections within the analytic space can be

DOI: 10.4324/9781003266303-16

140   *Robert Tyminski*

challenging, for example, because of the analyst's countertransference feelings such as anger, panic, and disorientation when being forcefully rejected.

A theoretical frame that I use in working with adolescents relies on two of Bion's important ideas. One is that we all have psychotic, or regressed and quite disturbed, parts of our personalities that can become ascendant over the healthier nonpsychotic parts (Bion, 1984). Without going into too much detail here, Bion makes many valuable points about this struggle. First, the psychotic or regressed part can actually attack the ego and diminish a capacity for reality testing. Second, the psychotic part is prone to projective identification, leading to fragmentation. And finally, third, reality itself is hated, and representations of it are felt to be persecuting a person's psyche. Each of these three factors contributes strongly to how an adolescent deals with a chronic medical condition. For example, many adolescents with type 1 diabetes (T1D), which is insulin dependent, can engage in risky eating patterns that threaten to make them *hyperglycemic* (too much glucose in the bloodstream), and others might overdose their insulin threatening *hypoglycemia* (too little blood glucose). The hormone insulin regulates the body's blood sugar or glucose level. Both hypo- and hyperglycemia produce changes in psychic functioning. Hyperglycemia can cause headaches and fatigue and escalate to confusion and loss of consciousness. Hypoglycemia can result in irritability and anxiety, resembling panic attacks, and lead to abnormal behavior like shaking and seizures. Hyperglycemia has the potential to become diabetic ketoacidosis, which can lead to coma or even death.

The second idea pertains to Bion's notion of container-contained, which is useful in considering the tasks of therapeutic engagement when someone is more regressed and revealing their disturbed parts (Bion, 1983). In such states, rawer emotions can be discharged into the analytic space. 'Container and contained are susceptible of conjunction and permeation by emotion' and this conjunction can lead to growth (Bion, 1983: 90). When an analyst and a patient are not conjoined in this way, the patient may feel a lack of containment and a refusal by the analyst or therapist to accept the more disturbing parts, resulting in serious problems.[1] When the body as a container feels diseased, adolescents can resort to massive projective identification in order to empty themselves of dangerous internal parts. In such a situation the analyst represents a container for the adolescent, who may begin to hate the analyst. This hatred can break down therapeutic discourse and turn into a refusal for help. To better orient ourselves to the case, it will be helpful to provide a brief overview of the particular medical and mental health concerns pertaining to type 1 diabetes.

Diabetes and mental health

T1D is a pancreatic autoimmune disease that depletes cells manufacturing insulin (Kawasaki, 2014). There are 1.6 million persons in the United States with T1D, including nearly 200,000 children and adolescents; and in 2017, diabetes was the seventh-leading cause of death (see www.diabetes.org). Since the 1970s, diabetes has been recognized as a medical condition with unique challenges. The term *brittle diabetes* (or *labile diabetes*) refers to a minority of patients whose lives are constantly disrupted by oscillations between hypo- and hyperglycemia (Tattersall, 1981). These families are usually thrown into dynamics of constant anxiety, which they may try to manage with tyrannical attempts at control, against which most children and adolescents rebel. Commenting on the psychological dimensions of diabetes, Tattersall notes that 'Diet is the *sine qua non* of the treatment of diabetes and some patients may come to think of food as poison' (1981: 487). Children and adolescents rely on their families, their medical teams, and school nurses to help them learn how to stabilize their diabetes, not disrupt it with poor dietary habits. Psychological problems are typically more pronounced early in the course of T1D. Failure to treat T1D may lead to nerve damage, kidney disease, vision loss, vascular damage, stroke and heart attack, and amputation.

Many of those with T1D commonly present with needle phobias. Insulin infusion pumps now help to bypass that issue and allow for flexible dosing of insulin throughout the day, thus offering more stability for a person's glucose level. Studies have noted that one-third to one-half of adolescents with T1D have some kind of psychiatric disorder (Szydlo, van Wattum, and Woolston, 2003; Carroll and Vittrup, 2020), with the prevalence of depression being two to three times higher than that of adolescents without T1D. Intentional insulin misuse, a kind of substance abuse in adolescents with T1D, can be related to self-harm, weight manipulation, gorging on junk food, and feeling 'high' when hypoglycemic (Carroll and Vittrup, 2020: 140). The mortality risk is six times higher for adolescents with T1D compared to the nondiabetic population (p. 140).

T1D frequently affects a person's self-image in complex ways (Greydanus and Hofmann, 1979), especially the perceptions coming from a child's or teen's peer group. Often, the diagnosis of T1D can lead to a feeling of great difference that, in turn, creates isolating behaviors when children or teens separate themselves from others. Over a period of time, such isolating mechanisms can become entrenched into a developing personality. In that case, alienation coupled with more troubling psychological problems can emerge. Many early intervention programs now offer support groups, summer camps, psychoeducation, and intensive retreats to connect children and adolescents with others just like them who are living with T1D (Greco, Shroff-Pendley, McDonell, and Reeves, 2001).

Some research suggests that there can be minor and subtle cognitive changes associated with T1D (Szydlo et al., 2003). For instance, some patients show slower information processing speeds, as insulin receptors in the hypothalamus play a role in memory (Riederer et al., 2017). Hyperglycemia can cause permanent cognitive impairment. Mild to moderate hypoglycemic episodes likely affect the developing nervous system. The onset of T1D can be traumatic, as in the case example that follows. When ketoacidosis follows a

142 *Robert Tyminski*

hyperglycemic crisis, the body is literally poisoning itself. The loss of a healthy body is traumatic and can fuel fears 'that something terrible might happen in the future', much like Winnicott's fear of breakdown, in which an awful event has already fragmented the psyche and a person fears it will happen again (D'Alberton, Nardi, and Zucchini, 2012, p. 306).

Descriptions of individual psychotherapeutic treatments with children and adolescents with T1D are rare in the existing literature. Murphy Jones and Landreth (2002) report somewhat ambiguous results of a study of children with T1D with a mean age of just older than nine, who received twelve 30-minute play therapy sessions during a summer camp. Although the children's anxieties did not appear to improve, their understanding of diabetes did. Watson (1990) describes a psychodynamic psychotherapy with an 11-year-old boy who had T1D. However, she concludes that his psychotic process stemmed more from attachment difficulties than from his diabetes, which she believes was secondary.

Case example

David is a 13-year-old boy who I began seeing two years ago after an acute hospitalization for diabetic ketoacidosis. The younger of two children of a gay couple, David was diagnosed with T1D, which had apparently gone un-diagnosed for a while. He was admitted to the hospital and he nearly died. This medical crisis shattered David's world, and he was in shock for a good three months of his initial psychotherapy with me. I was reminded of Bion's idea of catastrophic change, when life events break the mind's usual capacity to metabolize what has happened and a psychotic reaction occurs (Bion, 1965). David presented as lethargic, collapsed, and severely depressed. He looked quite thin for his height, and his skin tone was markedly pale. His most common verbalization was 'I don't know', which his parents affirmed they heard constantly at home. To me, this response seemed like a mindless ex-pression of derealization that showed a psychotic aspect of David's struggle with his T1D.

During this first phase of our work, I made space for David's traumatized and psychotic parts. I did not push him to answer anything and I waited a lot. Eventually, he became more responsive. One day, he spotted the game of Jenga on my shelf. Jenga is a building game in which wood blocks are criss-crossed to build a tower. Players then remove a single block from the tower and restack it on top. The whole thing usually becomes wobbly until it falls. During many weeks of playing Jenga, David became more animated, and he often intentionally tumbled the tower toward me so the blocks fell on my lap. He laughed with delight whenever I said, 'Everything's falling on me and I don't know what to do!' I attempted to voice helplessness in the face of an impossible situation, much as I imagined he had felt when his life tumbled precipitously into dangerous circumstances. In an initial sandtray, David placed knights, soldiers, and pirates around the tray as they engaged in fights. In the center of the tray, he put a mummy sarcophagus. The center of a sandtray is often thought to convey the most pressing psychic problem; in David's case, that appeared to be death and mortality, around which furious battles were being fought.

David made steady though slow progress during the first year of his treatment. He struggled in school, partly because he attended a large school that did not have extra resources for children in unique circumstances. He passed sixth grade after some advocacy from his parents helped the school better understand the psychological aspects of T1D. Mixed in with his Jenga play, David began describing in detail various horror films he had watched. He repeatedly assured me, 'These never scare me', which I understood as a counterphobic defense against his actual terror of death. I interpreted little and instead encouraged him to express what he saw in the movies as well as his reactions to them. The horror genre is more popular among boys and men and is often associated with difficulties in empathy (Martin, 2019). It also can be viewed as a way to master paranoid anxieties that threaten a person's safety with invasion and domination (Ballon and Leszcz, 2007). For David, the primary existential threat came from inside him, and his fascination with horror, gore, and violent films seemed to express his helplessness and rage about what had happened to him.

The following excerpt occurred about 14 months into his psychotherapy with me. Some background on his family will be helpful: David has two fathers, one who travels a lot and is not often at home, and another who is very introverted and intellectual. Neither man has felt very physically available to David. At times, I have wondered how David makes sense of his body because neither father appears to offer him anything that is physically robust or exciting. David also has an older sister who is already away at university. As David became more engaged with me, I noticed him at times looking at my arms, my legs, my sideburns, and my beard. The look was often one of concealed excitement, as in 'What's that?!'

In this excerpt, David wants to show me video clips on his mobile phone from the movie *Joker*. This film is about a psychotic character who turns to violence to show his rage over the humiliations and shame he has suffered. It was immensely popular among boys and young men, and I had heard a lot about it, particularly from David, but also from other adolescent boys in my practice. It depicts alienation in a way that speaks to them, a complicated topic I discuss in a recent book (Tyminski, 2018). David had gained access to a website that shows pirated films, and he had been secretive about it with me.

RT: How are you?
David: I don't know.
RT: All right, I think I know that reply. (There is a pause.)
David: (Smiles) Okay, I guess. Not much is happening. I've been taking videos of my dog to make a movie. A horror film.

RT:	Horror?
David:	Yeah, me and Josh [best friend] have been working on it. We get my dog to play dead, and then someone screams, and we run out of the house acting crazy. On the way out, we jump over a knife we put on the floor with ketchup on it so it looks like blood. Wanna see?
RT:	Sure.
David:	(He gets up from the couch, comes over next to my chair, and crouches beside me. This is a relatively new thing for him to do.) Here it is. (He holds his phone, and I watch a short video, maybe two minutes, of jagged camera angles, yelling, the dog, and their running as he had described.) We're going to add more, like scenes of empty streets and trash bins.
RT:	Ah, to make it look creepy. I imagine there'll be more action too.
David:	(Smiles and leans toward me. I can see him glancing at my beard and trying to avoid me seeing him do so.) Yeah. We haven't figured that out yet. Josh wants to do something with people walking like they're zombies, but I don't think that's right. There's already so much zombie material.
RT:	You'd like something more dramatic and newer.
David:	I guess so. I like the empty street shots and hanging branches, and we can put tense music to it.
RT:	That sounds eerie, like a person would have no idea what to expect next.
David:	Right! That's exactly what I told Josh when he brought up zombies. Everyone knows what zombies do. (He stands up and looks at something on his phone. He smiles slyly at me.) Can we watch a clip from *Joker*?
RT:	Oh, the top secret website for catching pirated videos. I think it's all right to watch for maybe five minutes and then we can talk about it. How's that sound?
David:	(He rolled his eyes when I said 'talk about it' but in a pretend way like he felt he had to do it to show some displeasure.) Okay. (He crouches again and holds the phone on the arm of the chair. His arm and mine are about four inches apart.) Look at this scene. It's the subway, when Arthur [Joker] loses it. Watch. (Arthur, in clown makeup, is beaten by three men. He shoots two of them, then chases the third onto the subway platform and kills him too. While watching, David's arm slips closer to mine. They are nearly touching but not. I look at our arms and then at him. He is looking down at my arm and not watching the clip at all. He seems fascinated.)
RT:	Well, how about we stop it there? (He refocuses on his phone and stops the video. He is still leaning toward me and slips 'accidentally' so his arm rolls over mine. He quickly pulls it away and giggles. David moves back to sit on the couch.)

David:	I like that scene.
RT:	I could tell. How come?
David:	Because Arthur becomes Joker then. It's when he changes and isn't going to let others just laugh at him.
RT:	Hmm, he's angry. (I am wondering here whether to go into the movie, as I feel he wants, or how I could say something about the physical contact that just occurred. I know how defensive David is when I make remarks about him and me, and I wonder if I can't finesse it somehow so he does not shut down and withdraw.) I'm wondering, David, would it be all right if I said something about what I noticed as we watched together? It's not about the movie.
David:	(Looks skeptical) Maybe.
RT:	Well, how about I say it slowly and in parts, and you can signal if you want me to stop?
David:	Okay.
RT:	It is fun to watch something together with another person because it gives us a chance to feel close when we're doing that, just like with us when we were watching *Joker* right now.
David:	(He squints but nods, so I accept this as permission to continue.)
RT:	It was also funny how your arm slipped, and for a moment, it was on top of mine, and when something like that happens, with a person you feel close to, it's all right to like …
David:	(Interrupts) It was an accident. Totally an accident.
RT:	Yes, but aren't accidents occasionally enjoyable? Not every accident is a disaster. (Of course, I am thinking about his accident here with diabetes and his hospitalization, and I realize I could be seriously misstating this idea for him.)
David:	(Grins) Yeah, like when me and Josh tripped over Snowy [the dog]. It was sort of fun.
RT:	So, if I can say just a little more. (He looks right at me, which is a good sign from him.) I imagine sometimes you look at me and wonder what kind of guy I am. And one way we might start figuring out something like that is by looking at how a person looks, not just how they dress, but maybe also we sneak looks at parts of their bodies because we like them and we're curious about them. (He keeps looking at me.) I think sometimes, you want a closer look at me, maybe to see how I look as a man, maybe to imagine how you'll grow, and maybe sometimes just for the fun of it.
David:	(There's a pause.) Josh's dad plays tackle with him. He asked me if I wanted to play too, but … (He looks at his arm with the glucose monitor attached.)
RT:	Ugh, that sucks. You would've liked to play tackle with them and you weren't sure you could because of the monitor and pump. (He nods and has the slightest trace of tears in his eyes.)

Discussion

This complex excerpt shows how David brings different parts of himself into the analytic space. He begins by noting that he is trying to create something, a shift from his depressed, collapsed, and traumatized self into someone who can play and enjoy it. The content still refers to horror, showing the continued emotional processing for David of his terror, although making a movie puts him in an active role of mastering the content. Accompanying this is another change, namely, David's approaching me and getting physically closer. The first time this happened, I hesitated because I wondered about muddying our frame. Children often get more physically into an analyst's space as part of playing and exploring. I thought about David's trauma that disrupted childhood for him, and it therefore seemed worth seeing how our proximity would affect him. I also understood his approach as a further sign of his making use of the containment he gets in psychotherapy — that he wanted to test my tolerance for this and also satisfy his own curiosity about me.

At this time, David had not shown noticeable physical indications of puberty. He still looked and acted like a boy younger than 13. I was also aware that he did not have much physical contact with either of his fathers. A model of robust physicality seemed missing in their household, and David often expressed admiration for the male action heroes he saw in violent films. Their physical prowess and muscularity appealed to him and unconsciously tugged at what seemed lacking in his family. When I noticed him looking at my beard, I wondered about saying something to him then, but realized it would likely fall flat. In a way, had I done so, I would have been stepping outside a kind of play he desperately wanted.

My remark about not knowing what to expect next resonated for him, and when I said it, I had in mind his medical trauma, being the passive recipient of invasive procedures and medications that he has to submit to. His disagreeing with Josh about the script of their video sounds promising as an assertion of what David wants and a willingness to be in conflict about it with a friend. I suspect that the deeper relevance of my remark about unpredictability led to his bringing up *Joker*. Feeling held by me, David shows a more disturbed and psychotic part of himself, for that is what I believe Joker represents. Thinking about his nascent ability to tolerate conflict, I set a limit on how long we can watch the video and add that we will talk after watching it. His protest is bark, not bite, and performative to let me know he can object to how we proceed with the talking.

The scene we watched is horrible. Arthur's humiliation and then rage are raw, and a viewer feels hurtled about in the claustrophobic interior of the subway car and then to the violent revenge on the platform stairs. David is bringing close to me his feelings of rage, powerlessness, and wish for vengeance — his Joker part — and wanting me to see them and tolerate them. During this, he looks attentively at my arm. I am wearing a short-sleeved shirt and guess that he is examining the hair and muscles of my forearms. When his

A boy's terror and fascination   147

arm slips closer to my arm, I feel anxious and nearly move away. However, I choose then to stay put, in part because I want to hold the space for David, and in part because I believe he would take it poorly if I withdrew right then. This is not an easy choice, although keeping in mind that I am witnessing David's Joker-self helps to give me confidence in remaining present for him.

When I mention that the five minutes has passed, the 'accident' happens when his arm rolls over mine. I am reminded of the times in working with children when touch occurs because they are physically oriented and expressive in ways that adolescents usually are not. David seems much younger, which his giggling reflects. He is rarely a boy who giggles with me. So, in addition to his Joker-self, at this moment in the session, I am seeing his pre-diabetes self; he wants me to play with him. I consider his fathers – how one is mostly not at home, and the other is not a playful or physically active man. I wonder what developmental steps David might have missed when he would have enjoyed playful contact, 'accidents' that can lead to giggles rather than horrors.

While David explains why this clip is one of his favorites, I find myself in an analytic mode of part-reverie and part-dream when I imagine possibilities about what to say, including saying nothing at all. I decide to attempt to say more because of the scene with Arthur about which David remarks, 'It's when he changes'. This could be an invitation to change something between David and me. Previous attempts to talk about our relationship have often floundered. I sometimes felt that he took my comments in this direction as being painful, like injections for which he was unprepared. Now, I hope for a different exchange, although it seems fraught.

Thinking about his evolving active self, I frame it as my talking, but putting him in charge of how much I will say. He accepts this, and I decide to start with the closeness, but wording it so as to give him room to dispute it. His nod allows me to continue and I mention the actual contact. I want to note the enjoyment such moments offer because I feel David's longing for them. Defensively, he interrupts me to claim it was 'an accident', which at the time I think brings us back into the psychic territory of his traumatized self. I want to exercise caution in how I reply, so I take the tack of framing accidents as not always meaning disasters. I do not know if David will accept this differentiation; it is possible he will reject it and assert that all accidents are terrible, which for him was, of course, somewhat beyond dispute. I am aware of hoping to connect enjoyment as an experience of contact, and with that idea in mind, I offer that accidents could, in some instances, be like surprises we might like. This is an interesting moment in the session because I have no intuition how it will go. The traumatized David might withdraw; the Joker David might argue; the young boy David might feel ashamed. Instead, David links affirmatively and creatively to an incident that happened when he and Josh tripped over the dog while filming their video. Because of his response, I feel an opening to risk saying more about our accidental contact.

148 *Robert Tyminski*

I probably ventured too much, but I wanted to offer a possibility for David's erotic self to be acknowledged. I reflect how looking is a natural way for us to recognize one another and that looking, even when sneaked, can be pleasurable. I try to remark just briefly on the vitality of bodies, to speak to his desire to feel close to me, and to provide a prospective understanding for his curiosity about growing up. And finally, I want to emphasize that our erotic parts belong to us, just as our Joker parts might too, and that we hopefully can enjoy them. During the pause after I have said these things, I feel David's presence with me and he seems fuller in that moment. His response about Josh's dad appears to be an unconscious derivative that I have captured an essential aspect of David's erotic self and his conflict with his body. His poignant recollection about wanting to play tackle and his worry about his medical equipment seem to directly express anxiety about his future growth. His emotional response of sadness also shows David grappling realistically with what his body might and might not be able to do. A few weeks following this exchange, David comes into my office and announces he had a medical checkup. His physician told him he is starting puberty.

A short technical comment is perhaps helpful to explain my way of interacting with David. For a long while, he tended to recoil from more relatedness with me. I thought this was partly because his insides did not feel safe to him. How could he trust further possible intrusion from outside? Alvarez (2012) makes a valuable point about patients, often depressed, withdrawn, and apathetic, in need of a 'vitalizing level' of relating before they can learn about how to relate and make greater meanings: 'Certain patients need to be helped to be able to feel and to find meaning, sometimes via an experience that something matters imperatively to someone else; then, feelings can begin to be identified and explored …' (2012: 11). I believe, even in this shorter excerpt of David's work with me, that this mattering 'imperatively' was evident, for example, in David's taking a risk to let me speak about the 'accident'. Children and adolescents with chronic illnesses may benefit in their treatments by attending to their needs for psychic vitalization.

Conclusion

Working analytically with children and adolescents with T1D presents certain questions about containment because of their experiences with catastrophic bodily change. In the aftermath of such crises, it is not unusual for more disturbed and psychotic parts of the personality to surface and appear predominant, especially as the ego suffers from the medical trauma. Bion's ideas about the psychotic part of the personality and about container-contained present a valuable therapeutic framework for understanding how an analyst or psychotherapist can help children with chronic illnesses. It is important to make analytic space for all parts of the child's or adolescent's psyche and for analysts to let patients know they see them. Further, container-contained incorporates all of a patient's emotional responses, no matter how raw and agonizing these might seem for the analyst. Medical trauma can cause extreme emotional disturbance around incidents of humiliation, passivity, incomprehension, and the rapid speed with which they often occur.

With this case example, I have shown how my patient David had a paternal transference of a particular cast with me. He longed to see a male body that was present and robust. He wanted fatherly attention and affection that did not feel distant and remote to him. In many ways, David needed more an erotic father experience than a limit-setting one, and the excerpt demonstrates a point at which this happened between us. The 'accident' could easily, in David's mind, have been incorporated unthinkingly as another catastrophe. Because he felt his Joker-self could have room in my mind and not be repelled, he appeared to open himself for more awareness of his desire for erotic playfulness.

David's body felt to him like it had been invaded and poisoned. His preoccupation with horror films and violent action movies expressed this terror at being invaded and taken over by something foreign and highly dangerous. During the first period of treatment when he was in shock, David was minimally aware of his body. During a later phase, it seemed that he regarded his body as a war zone. In the excerpt, however, a new attitude is emerging when David expresses sadness around his body's real limitations. He is no longer submersed in a horror fantasy. He is simply a boy who would love to play tackle and is not sure that he can.

Note

1 Maier (2016) has written a fascinating article about how Bion might have come upon container-contained when he attended one of Jung's Tavistock lectures in 1935.

References

Alvarez, A. (2012). *The Thinking Heart: Three Levels of Psychoanalytic Therapy with Disturbed Children*. London, England, and New York, NY: Routledge.

Ballon, B., & Leszcz, M. (2007). Horror films: Tales to master trauma or shapers of trauma, *American Journal of Psychotherapy*, 61(2), 211–230.

Bion, W.R. (1965). *Transformations: Change from Learning to Growth*. London, England: Heinemann.

Bion, W.R. (1983). *Learning from Experience*. Lanham, MD: Jason Aronson.

Bion, W.R. (1984). Differentiation of the psychotic from the non-psychotic parts of the personality. In *Second Thoughts*, pp. 43–64. London, England: Karnac.

Carroll, N.C., & Vittrup, B. (2020). Type 1 diabetes in adolescence: Considerations for mental health professionals. *Journal of Child and Adolescent Counseling*, 6(2), 137–148.

D'Alberton, F., Nardi, L., & Zucchini, S. (2012). The onset of a chronic disease as a traumatic psychic experience: A psychodynamic survey on type 1 diabetes in young patients. *Psychoanalytic Psychotherapy*, 26(4), 294–307.

Greco, P., Shroff-Pendley, J., McDonell, K., & Reeves, G. (2001). A peer group intervention for adolescents with type 1 diabetes and their best friends. *Journal of Pediatric Psychology*, 26(8), 484–490.

150 *Robert Tyminski*

Greydanus, D.E., & Hofmann, A.D. (1979). Psychological factors in diabetes mellitus. *American Journal of Diseases of Children, 133*(10), 1061–1066.

Kawasaki, E. (2014). Type 1 diabetes and autoimmunity. *Clinical Pediatric Endocrinology, 23*(4), 99–105.

Maier, C. (2016). Bion and C.G. Jung. How did the container-contained model find its thinker? The fate of a cryptomnesia. *Journal of Analytical Psychology, 61*(2), 134–154.

Martin, G.N. (2019). (Why) do you like scary movies? A review of the empirical research on psychological responses to horror films. *Frontiers in Psychology,* 10. 10.3389/fpsyg.2019.02298

Murphy Jones, E., & Landreth, G. (2002). The efficacy of intensive individual play therapy for chronically ill children. *International Journal of Play Therapy,* 11(1), 117–140.

Riederer, P., Korczyn, A.D., Ali, S.S., Bajenaru, O., Choi, M.S., Chopp, M., … Cukierman-Yaffe, T. (2017). The diabetic brain and cognition. *Journal of Neural Transmission,* 124(11), 1431–1454. DOI: 10.1007/s00702-017-1763-2

Segal, H. (1974). *Introduction to the Work of Melanie Klein.* New York, NY: Basic Books.

Szydlo, D., van Wattum, P.J., & Woolston, J. (2003). Psychological aspects of diabetes mellitus. *Child and Adolescent Psychiatric Clinics of North America,* 12(3), 439–458. DOI: 10.1016/S1056-4993(03)00006-3

Tattersall, R.B. (1981). Psychiatric aspects of diabetes – A physician's view. *British Journal of Psychiatry, 139*(6), 484–493. 10.1192/bjp.139.6.485

Tyminski, R. (2018). *Male Alienation at the Crossroads of Identity, Culture and Cyberspace.* London, England, and New York, NY: Routledge.

Watson, A. (1990). The blossom tree and the number 4: Some ideas about thought disorder in an adopted, diabetic boy. *Journal of Child Psychotherapy, 16*(2), 99–110.

Editor's Introduction to:
The play of Eros: the story of an adolescent boy, his body, and his analyst's body

Bruce Reis's chapter brought Neville Symington's enlivening (1983) paper, 'The analyst's act of freedom' to mind. Symington relates a moment with a patient when he realizes he has been functioning under an internal fear or stricture and is able to shake free. Symington says, '… the soul of analytic technique is to free analyst and patient from the normal social constraints and so favour development of the inner world. The problem is when "classical technique" becomes the agent of a new social constraint' (1983: 260). There is a sort of shaking free I imagine for Reis in this chapter. Though highly versed in theory (see for instance Reis, 2020) his aim in this chapter is to break free of it. Bion's warning to clinicians that any theory can turn to an impenetrable crust also comes to mind. Perhaps we could say that the analyst must stand naked, without resort to his or her favoured theories in order to see what that feels like. Reis accomplishes that here.

Adolescents help us with such shaking free. They are alert to convention and stuffiness. You can see why Reis chose an adolescent case to disencumber himself of his theories.

Reis is a good writer. I think again (I have often throughout this volume), of the broader meanings of Eros − of pleasure in ideas, of pleasure in relationships. How could anyone fail to enjoy Reis's affectionate description of 'Manny': 'Manny's body was shaped like a giant bean. He was the kid you might have seen at Disney Land with a white XXL t-shirt coming down to mid-thigh'. I was immediately rooting for Manny, and for Manny and Reis.

The erotic field braved in this paper is different than the intense emotions between myself and my patient in Chapter 2 or that you will come upon in the next chapter by Jackson. As Reis says, 'I never did feel an eroticized attraction to Manny, and I don't believe he felt one to me. Our playing with Eros instead took the form of playmates who could feel Eros with each other'.

I would see the 'braving' here as that Reis was able to inhabit his own adolescence in being Manny's alter ego. He was able to allow Manny to be unique and to allow Manny's treatment to be unique. One is left with the sense of the radical uniqueness of each pair: Reis and Manny, Manny and Reis. A better world for it.

DOI: 10.4324/9781003266303-17

References

Reis, B. (2020). *Creative Repetition and Intersubjectivity: Contemporary Freudian Explorations of Trauma, Memory and Clinical Process*. London & New York: Routledge.

Symington, N. (1983). The analyst's act of freedom as agent of therapeutic change. *The International Journal of Psychoanalysis*, 10, 283–291.

9 The play of Eros: The story of an adolescent boy, his body, and his analyst's body

Bruce Reis

As I continue to practice psychoanalysis, I become increasingly suspect of the metapsychological structures we ascribe to and wonder if patient's improvements really have much if anything to do with the hypothesized mechanisms (e.g., fields, projections, figurations, recognitions, mentalizations, etc.) we imagine to be operative and whether our internecine arguments about such mechanisms amount to our arguing about Angels dancing on the head of a pin. Patients probably get better for reasons other than those we have dreamt in our philosophies. My intent here is to tell the story of my treatment with Manny as a story: as a story that'd be faithful to what clinical life is actually like, hence there'll be no arc to the story and no neat resolution. Rather than a case report grounded in the literature or one that necessarily covers the expected bases (because even to the extent that those bases were covered, I want to stress my feeling that they were not the most important parts of this treatment). **My aim** is to tell this story as honestly as possible without appeal to abstract theory.

'Manny' was a chubby, introverted pre-adolescent when he came to see me with his mother in my downtown Manhattan office. He was shy and frequently looked away, speaking in a low voice that made discernment of his words often difficult. She did most of the talking, telling me of her husband's departure from the family and how it impacted her son and his younger sister. Manny had been a good student, but his grades had begun to slip; he began to stay mostly to himself and play video games. His mother found it hard to reach him and was worried about her son. We agreed that Manny and I would meet, at first in a twice a week psychotherapy, later with increased frequency.

As we worked together over many years, and as my patient grew into adolescence and eventually left for college, I developed strong feelings of fondness for this lost boy. At times I was obviously a transferential paternal figure with all its superegoic and 'paternal' functions; more often I was a transferential peer, connecting with parts of my own adolescent self to be-with Manny in the ways he needed a companion to be with him during some troubling revelations about himself, his father, and his family. Over time we explored issues of male aggression and sexuality, male passivity, a boy's relation to heterosexual sex and to homosexuality, his fondness for psychic retreats, what may make a man leave (i.e., retreat from) his family,

DOI: 10.4324/9781003266303-18

154 *Bruce Reis*

issues of loneliness, isolation, the power of violent phantasies, ethics, his body and the ways it functioned, and shame. You won't hear about all of those topics in this chapter though.

As a countertransferential experience treating adolescents for me is like going back to visit a part of a city one used to live in when younger. Maybe there were good times spent there, perhaps some lonely times, things done that one still feels ashamed of or wished had been different. You know your way around, the streets, the buildings, it's all familiar, because even though you don't live there anymore, a part of you still does. In some ways it is 'brave' (Chapter 2, this volume) to go back to visit. It's easier to take refuge in the narrative of a linear development that puts that time in the past. Indeed, there is something of an intolerance of childhood that often permeates our efforts to treat adolescents, with super-egos all over the place urging quicker, more appropriate change in the direction towards adulthood. This attitude runs the very real risk of not allowing the space of childhood to remain open and unpredictable in a treatment. Which is to say that the analyst's defense against himself being child-like is an instantiation and communication to his patient about what will and will not be tolerated in the space of the treatment.

Playing was the most important part of this treatment. What was crucial was an intimate, frequent contact between two human beings meeting for the purposes of helping one of them deal with loss and cope with change. Thus, this was a play that involved us both, but asymmetrically and was not without the technical parameters pertaining to a psychoanalysis and the analyst's reflection on its process. I am hoping with this writing to yield a different report of a treatment, and I discuss different factors in the therapeutic relationship and consider different goals.

I continue to think of Manny, not frequently, but sometimes. And when I do, I wonder how he's getting along; and I let myself imagine how things may be for him now that he is what we euphemistically call a 'young adult'. It must be nearly a decade since termination of a treatment that began in pre-adolescence and lasted until his departure for college. In remembering him here in this chapter on Eros and adolescence, I want to remember Manny not as a case, or a treatment, but as something closer to a playmate, who I watched and helped to grow up. And if the erotic has also to do with love then it's appropriate to speak of Eros here.

I'd like to remember the story of my time with Manny, because this treatment, now that it's so many years past, appears like a chapter in my life too.

Manny, his body, and me

Manny's body was shaped like a giant bean. He was the kid you might have seen at Disney Land with a white XXL t-shirt coming down to mid-thigh. Maybe he was the kid you'd walk right past on the streets of New York, not looking twice at as he shlepped his overpacked book bag home from school,

The play of Eros 155

head down, in a half-dream state. His appearance was remarkable and un-remarkable at the same time. When his mother brought him to my Manhattan office for consultation, she did almost all of the talking, and Manny, as giant as this little fellow was, nearly disappeared.

Manny's slipping grades were easier for his mother to focus on than her husband's departure for another woman. That Manny was terribly hurt and drew further into himself following his father's leaving the family caused his mother real concern and pain. This was a mother who cared deeply for her son and feared losing him too. She knew she couldn't reach him much anymore, but she hoped someone else might be able to. And she had the foresight to think of consulting a male analyst. I still have the memory of Manny's sitting in a chair in my consulting room, having been brought there like you might bring a sack of potatoes and plunked down. He said about as much as those potatoes might have and he looked away the whole time, offering only a confirmatory 'yeahhh' in response to his mother's calls for his participation.

I don't know what it was, but I liked this kid from go. Call it 'the field', call it a countertransference, call it an identification, call it what you will. There was something about this bean-like boy that felt endearing and sweet and wounded. At the same time, I could feel a formidable depth to Manny, like when you're standing in front of the ocean and can somehow feel the volume of what's before you. It's tempting on the face of it to think that it may have had to do with his physical presentation, but I don't know that it was that at all.

I'll call it an analysis; we certainly met frequently enough for it to have that label attached. But calling it that could give the mistaken impression that for the first couple of years we did NOT predominately talk about the online multiplayer video game that Manny had become obsessed with and spent a large portion of his time playing, '… you know, going on quests, and doing magic and shit'. The obsession entered the analysis, I learned everything about this game, and I mean, everything – how players could assume different forms (appealing to Manny right away) how playing the game was not like what I associated what playing a game was, in that it took hours and hours and ex-tended over days and days; and how a particularly adolescent style of relating was honed in interaction with other online 'friends' who played. Avatars entered the stage of the analysis, like characters, each holding a different part of Manny, and expressing the many voices of his pain, wishes, and defeats. Through these conversations I was aware of an internal pressure inside of me to shift to 'serious' matters like his father's leaving or his declining grades. I simply noted that pressure and its superegoic demand to pull Manny out of the space he had found that felt safe to him, and let that go, so we could talk about what felt important to him.

Yes, it was a psychic retreat. Yes, it was also an opportunity to 'escape' his large body and inhabit an adult male body that in more or less of a fashion looked like my own. Yes, he was creating a virtual world of fantasy and phantasy in which he could live out themes of power and autonomy that would eventually become a part of our discussions. And yes, what young teenage boys speak about amongst themselves, when they're sure adults are not listening, can be shocking and revelatory and a window into a world you and I do not live in. Instead of trying to reach Manny I joined him where he lived, and I interpreted none of it.

The boys on the game trash-talked each other constantly. It's a form of male aggression that can be very biting, but also very tender. For instance, Manny described how it was common for them to call each other 'gay'. But, he emphasized, they spelled it 'ghey', which was their way of reclaiming the word. I came to understand this as a complex polymorphous verbiage, at once purposely dissociated from its most frequent usage, and simultaneously re-purposed as a term of same-sex affection. Functioning at once as both a denial and a put down and an expression of love and caring, 'You're so ghey', or 'that's totally ghey' was the lingua franca of disembodied boys scattered around the island of Manhattan, each trying to work out their own attractions, drive states and their antipathies.

Manny could be a warrior, with a sword. He could save the day. He could band together with other players to defeat other bands of players, conquering them in victorious glory. He had agency, he had strategy, he was strong and capable. Manny's avatar was well muscled, and his skin was a different colour than Manny's. Playing was a playing with possibilities for this young man who was forming himself online and in life. Here in the fantasy of the game though, Manny could be whoever and whatever he wanted to be. He was making and unmaking himself, creating himself defensively to be sure, and at the same time substantially in the realm of imagination, as someone who could be the winner of a battle, who could be strong, who might have a different body. Our talking about avatars and battles and guilds felt like being in the game with him, not an oneiric space so much as a transitional space, in which it was all important to not interpret or point out the reality of situations, but just to play, or witness his play, and be right there with him. Identity formation is so rapid in ado-lescence and these young people have a particular sensitivity to whether someone else has a good sense of who they are, or if they don't. If you are not comfortable in your own skin, they will feel it and then anxiously attack it or simply withdraw from the relationship. So being there with the adolescent is not as simple as one might think.

The experience of conscious conflict never really mattered much, not when there was so much power to be wielded, so much blood to be spilled, so much revenge to be taken. Yet still, even when he switched the game into 'God mode' so that he could have control over everything, he was left with a feeling of dissatisfaction and boredom because nothing could surprise him. He learned that one can't live in God mode, and that omnipotence is a powerful defence, and not an end unto itself.

I believe my own willingness to stay in the play allowed Manny to keep that part of his childhood that lived (i.e., was safeguarded) in games and phantasy without demanding he engage in adult conversations about 'real' issues of his

The play of Eros 157

father leaving or his declining grades. The game was the treatment, as it so often is in work with children and adolescents – not simply something that would lay the ground-work for the more serious conversations to follow, or interpretations about the game, but the thing in itself.

Manny was increasingly animated in telling me about the game over time. I learned of his triumphs and his defeats and in the telling we established our own unconscious rules of engagement – I wouldn't be a psychoanalyst, at least not the kind who would talk to him about the concerns of everyone around him or interpret experience in him that had not yet taken a conscious form. I was just the guy he talked to about video games four times a week for several years.

Manny's body and Eros

Okay, that was an overstatement. We did talk about other things too. There were parties, and sometimes there were girls at the parties. Games were played there too – kissing and frotteurism in a cloud of consent fueled by adolescent wishes to be popular, accepted, and successful vis a vis the other boys/girls. Manny was at least as interested in hooking up with girls as he was to not feel separated from the group of boys by way of an unsuccessful standing out. What Manny did in the darkly lit rooms of parentless apartments around the upper East and West sides of Manhattan felt different to what his father had done, and I never linked these experiences in discussion with him. Manny's father's actions were transgressions, but Manny was exploring the contours of desire, his own and those of his adolescent partners in the polymorphous space shrouded in darkness that would allow not so much a use of objects but a relating to them, and of their relations to him as a similar object (for development). If anything stood out about his explorations, it was how tentative and shy he could sometimes be about them. I recall that sometimes he would adopt a tone of voice that was tentative and questioning. It was halting and unsure, reaching out for support and guidance from me, and assurance that it was alright, he could explore.

Yet at other times when we talked about girls, he'd adopt an adorable bravado. Jennifer may be cute, but she also failed to live up to his standards; or in Manny's words: 'I'd do her, but I wouldn't date her'. Imagine if you will a boy under five feet tall, bean-like with long hair spilling into his face, uttering these words. Manny could talk some shit, but his prowess with girls was nearly as virtual as his exploits in the video game. Both were ways of imagining himself into more mature and ideal roles from the interstitial space of adolescence. Sure, we talked as if he were an OG, a real player. And I often called him 'man' as in, 'alright man', treating him at these times like the man he wished to be and become, the ideal object, a phantasied sexual avatar. The different things Manny needed contained by his analyst determined the shape of the container: when his developing and nascent sense of masculinity and sexuality were in play, I 'alrighted' him; and in those moments that Manny did

158   *Bruce Reis*

talk about what his family life was like in the wake of his father's leaving I'd tell him that not having a father there was painful and that boys need fathers there to help them grow up, that not having one there was sad; and sometimes silent tears would run down his puffy cheeks.

The fact was, Manny had a fair amount of success hooking up, and you might think that when he was rejected or unsuccessful he would have felt ashamed, about the experience or about himself. But that didn't seem to be central to his experience. Like the video games, these parties and the hijinks that went on there were as much about the boys' and girls' imagination as about the bodies that were touching each other; and more about having *had* an experience than about *who* one had that experience with, or even the particulars of the experience. Manny and I talked about how he wanted to be successful sexually and how his father's actions inhibited his feeling comfortable being sexually assertive. His father's affair left Manny feeling that to 'go for it' could be harmful and damaging, so Manny, despite the shit-talk, was the most cautious and tentative of paramours. It was hard to not think in navigating Eros that Manny wasn't also working something out for himself about his father (identifications and disidentifications) as well as the Oedipal situation that left him 'the man of the house'.

I recall feeling there was something vital about Manny's moving in this world of bodies and Eros. It was the unbound and polymorphous energy of sensorial and affective forces within him that one could barely make out in everyday mumbling speech, but which flashed brightly in his eyes as they opened wider in recounting what went on in darkened living rooms: 'Okay, so listen Man, we all went up to Charlotte's place cuz her parents were at their country house for the weekend. We played this game where you have to take off one piece of clothing every time you lose, and, OH MY GOD, the lights were almost off so I couldn't see everything, but, OH MY GOD, DUDE'.

I never did feel an eroticized attraction to Manny, and I don't believe he felt one to me. Our playing with Eros instead took the form of playmates who could feel Eros with each other. It was an unusual transference-countertransference experience, different from how I would think of such a configuration were it to happen with an adult patient. If that were the case, I would wonder what the patient was doing in the transference to induce erotic feelings in his/her analyst. I'd wonder what function(s), or effects sexual story telling had in the field or the analytic space. With Manny I felt the function was in the service of development. He was telling his adult male analyst stories as much as he was asking him questions – about interacting with other boys, with girls, about how his body functions, about what it feels like and is supposed to feel like. Our discussions, about which I don't go into detail here, were quite frank and very open. Neither Manny nor I felt shamed or censorious; and as importantly our discussion of these matters did not quickly slip into braggadocio or defensive silliness. The Eros that was in play did not feel to be Eros between us, it was the Eros of two men talking about their bodies and their attractions and how confusing and exciting and frustrating it all can be,

The play of Eros   159

trying to make sense of all of those things together, holding it all, more or less, in a package one could call 'masculinity'.

Isn't it interesting that in this chapter having so much to do with Eros that love hasn't yet been mentioned? Well, it's past time to say it: Manny loved his Mother. I hadn't thought about it at the time, but Manny's worry for his mother was a part of that same package. She'd brought him to see me because of her worry, but he was worried for her as well. He saw her as broken from the experience of his father's leaving the family. He could see her depression from under her patina of resilience and he felt he wanted to protect her, but there was just so much a 14-year-old boy could do, or could understand. His arguing with his sister didn't help his mother, nor did his own adolescent need to separate from her in clumsy or at times defiant ways. Mother had her own analyst to help her navigate her own and her children's reactions to changes in the family. She supported her son's treatment, phoning me to leave messages about things she was concerned over so that I'd be aware of them, and largely allowing Manny to have the experiences he needed to have in treatment. Over time Manny would return to her and become significantly more emotionally accessible to her, but the Manny who returned was not the same one who had entered treatment. This young man had developed a gravitas and self-assurance over the years, partly as a result of making a number of poor choices.

When Manny got caught plagiarizing on a high school paper, he realized his attempted shortcut led to more grief for his mother and himself − nearly getting him expelled from school and nearly losing the scholarship that allowed him to attend a school his mother, now the single wage earner for the family, otherwise wouldn't have been able to send her children to. I remember being struck by how Manny immediately understood what he'd done. There was no pretense of rationalization or defensive justification. Manny knew he'd royally screwed up and he felt terribly that he did. Manny felt deeply ashamed and he spoke openly and contritely about his actions, with no need for me to play the role of 'do you know what you've done' authority figure. I imagine the school administrators saw Manny's reaction for what it was, and that their seeing that might have been what saved him from expulsion. I said earlier that there was something about this boy that felt deep and powerful, and this was an expression of that − of his character.

Manny also made mistakes with girls, like hanging out with one who was more sexually expressive but who he had no real feeling for. We talked about how that wasn't as satisfying as he'd imagined it'd be, and Manny wanted to know from me what the most respectful way of exiting that situation could be, so we played out several scenarios and he chose the one he felt would be best for him. If I was a paternal figure for Manny during times like these, I was one who was present and involved rather than absent or disinterested, as Manny felt his father was after leaving the home. But what was most valuable in these discussions was my learning over time that prior to his leaving Manny's father hadn't been especially involved with his son's interior or external lives, despite a measure of idealization that whitewashed the narrative of family life before the split. Rather than turn away from male authority, which may have been an entirely reasonable adaptation, Manny was left hungry for it. Thus, it was important for me to access my own adolescent experiencing to be-with Manny in the ways he needed me to play with him while also always remaining the adult he needed me to be.

It's not like this with all adolescents, but Manny's maturation seemed to simply be waiting there for him to claim. It's like he had it already, and he just needed to access it or find his way to it. One way he found it was through mistakes at school and with girls. Those mistakes also helped him square things about his past and come to realizations such as the one just mentioned regarding his father's closeness. By moving forward, he was learning about and addressing his past; and in addressing that past he was gradually becoming someone he could feel proud about being. Over time Manny talked less about playing online multiplayer video games and began dating one girl from school he seemed to really care about. Their relationship reminded me in some ways of my relationship with Manny, in that it was a friendship through which the two discovered things about themselves and played. Manny grew into that relationship, developing noticeably different ways of talking about her, and about his feelings. When it came time to apply to colleges he kept in mind where she was applying too, with the hope that they'd wind up geographically close to each other. That didn't happen. Instead, Manny was admitted to his dream school and decided to leave New York behind for another, distant part of the U.S. He and I celebrated in session, talking for months before his departure about what it'd be like in college, his ideas about what he wanted to major in, how he'd get by being so far away from his mother and his sister – his hopes, his anxieties, and his excitement for this new chapter in his life.

I continue to think of Manny, not frequently, but sometimes. And when I do, I wonder how he's getting along; and I let myself imagine how things may be for him now, and I can't help but smile, thinking that he's alright, and that if he's not, he knows where to find me.

Acknowledgements

I'd like to acknowledge my appreciation for the helpful comments and suggestions of Drew Tillotson and Terry Owens on an earlier draft of this chapter.

Editor's Introduction to:
Too close for comfort: the challenges of engaging with sexuality in work with adolescents

This chapter presents erotic transference/countertransference situations somewhat like the one I discussed in Chapter 2, only here with a male therapist and two different female adolescent patients. Jackson helpfully differentiates between erotic feelings that emerge almost immediately as the treatment begins and those which emerge after a significant period of work, (such as in the later period with Sarah – the second patient he describes here). The early work, with Hannah could be described as a teen who enters treatment over-stimulated by aspects of her home life. She sees her only value as her sexuality – if she attracts someone, (including her analyst) it only proves his vacancy. While Field Theory is not the language Jackson uses here, he makes clear even at this early point in a treatment how difficult it is to say, 'whose feeling is it?' The subtleties of what can be felt as a seduction or a rejection on the therapist's part are very well described here.

Jackson also rightly grapples with his own discomfort at stepping into the erotic feelings in the consulting room, he says, 'sometimes we seek false comfort in reassuring ourselves that it is our patients – rather than ourselves – that we are protecting'. Clearly, he bravely grapples with the feelings in the field between himself and Sarah after she begins to use the couch. He describes that his patient tells him, 'she had kissed a close friend of her boyfriend. The intensity of the impact this had on me was startling. I experienced it like a personal assault – a body blow, affecting my whole physiology and evoking something not far off a sense of outrage, as if she had actually been unfaithful to me'. The work of the pair at this point is moving and Jackson is straightforward (not avoidant) in dealing with the explosive feelings in the room.

Along with the similarities between the feelings in Jackson's work with his female patients and my work with my male adolescent described in Chapter 2, I am also struck by the background societal/gender differences in the cross-gender pairs in these two chapters. An older male therapist with a female patient is different culturally than the reverse. Nabokov's *Lolita* comes to mind as a disturbing cultural trope that male therapists must consciously and unconsciously contend with. Culture is in us and we are in

DOI: 10.4324/9781003266303-19

162   *Too close for comfort*

culture. Hannah, the first patient Jackson relates, seems initially trapped in a stereotype of seductive femaleness that seems cut off from much real pleasure or sense of authenticity. The older woman/adolescent boy pair in Chapter 2 has a different quality to it – much less common culturally – and so in certain ways more taboo. There I found myself pulled to disguising warm and affectionate feelings behind the maternal, which certainly risks the inauthentic.

10 Too close for comfort: the challenges of engaging with sexuality in work with adolescents

Emil Jackson

Introduction

This chapter explores some of the powerful, provocative and disturbing ways in which sexuality can intrude into the consulting room in psychoanalytic work with adolescents. In particular, I shall examine some of the challenges that confront us when sexuality emerges within the transference and countertransference, threatening to disrupt our thinking and shatter our psychic equilibrium. Given the profoundly unsettling nature of this area of work, coupled with our fear that we might further disturb our patients by addressing it, we should not underestimate our propensity to avoid, negate and defend ourselves against these dynamics, even when we are conscious of them. The central focus of this chapter is therefore on the clinical encounter and the way this can be experienced, evaded and responded to by both patient and therapist. This includes exploration of those experiences which are sexualised in nature: experiences emerging within the transference and countertransference which patients want us to receive, need us to process and which, if we can bear them, may eventually be effectively and therapeutically interpreted. As well as conveying my belief about our potential to facilitate significant transformational and maturational developments through careful engagement in this area of work, I also hope to highlight the potential consequences to our patients, as well as to the depth of our work when we fail to do so. This chapter also addresses some specific challenges relating to technique, in particular the challenge of how to find safe ways to engage directly with sexuality and the question of whether and when interpretation of the transference is necessary and helpful. Most importantly, this chapter aims to stimulate thinking and discussion about an area of work and technique which is not only too infrequently discussed in the literature, but also rarely receives attention in our clinical discussions, supervisions and even analyses.

Types of sexual and erotic transference

Although the intention of this chapter is to focus on the clinical encounter rather than to offer a theoretical exposition which delineates between different

DOI: 10.4324/9781003266303-20

164   *Emil Jackson*

forms of transference, it may nevertheless be helpful to summarise briefly some central ideas about these differences to help contextualise the clinical material and reflect on technique.

In his paper on transference-love, Freud warns us that the management of the transference is the most serious of difficulties needing to be addressed. He writes: 'The psycho-analyst knows that he is working with highly explosive forces and that he needs to proceed with as much caution and conscientiousness as a chemist' (Freud, 1915: 170). The explosive potential of these forces is greater still when they are at risk of being ignited by adolescents, whose burgeoning sexuality so often leaves them feeling out of control in their minds and bodies, especially when their psychological development lags behind their physical development rendering their experience all the more overwhelming and incomprehensible. But it is not just adolescents who can feel overwhelmed by the nature of their experience – so too can all those most closely connected to them: parents, siblings, teachers[1] and therapists too. Nevertheless, as Freud continues: 'But when have chemists ever been forbidden, because of the danger, from handling explosive substances, which are indispensible, on account of their effects?' (ibid.: 170–171).[2]

More recent literature refers to several different types of transferences – erotic transference, erotised transference and sexualised transference to name but a few. The defining lines between these different concepts is not always clear however, resulting in their being used somewhat interchangeably at times (e.g., erotic transference and transference love; sexualised transference, eroticised and erotised transference). In his 1994 paper 'On love and lust in erotic transference' Gabbard offers some helpful distinctions. He draws on Person's definition of erotic transference as 'some mixture of tender, erotic, and sexual feelings that a patient experiences in reference to his or her analyst and, as such, forms part of a positive transference' (Person, 1985: 161, quoted in Gabbard, 1994a: 398). Bollas similarly suggests that erotic transferences allow for a psychic bridge to be forged between the object of the instinct and the alive other who makes instinctual representations meaningful and possible. Although Bollas notes the potential for the erotic transference to result in 'resistance to free association', he equally notes its potential to 'facilitate embodiment and personalisation', including a capacity for the patient to erotically cathect the analyst's presence (Bollas, 1994: 581).

In Bollas' view, erotic refers to 'any subject's private imaginative use of the object of desire'. He writes: 'Much of the pleasure of erotic life is derived from the absence of sexual realisation, perhaps because the love object is simply not available. The subject, then, must live with this absence, but such unavailability actually increases the intense longing for the object, and leads to its enlargement in the subject's mind' (ibid.: 588). Bolognini also comments on the forbidden or inaccessible nature of the object in the erotic transference, perhaps because it risks a transgression of generational boundaries or those relating to social status. Although Bolognini writes that this situation presents

Too close for comfort   165

the 'greatest risk to the analytic attitude', he draws on authors who share a view that '… intense, long term erotic transferences persist only if the analyst unconsciously colludes' (Bolognini, 1994: 75–76).

Bollas distinguishes between the erotic transference and the sexualised transference, suggesting that the latter refers to 'the analysand's urgent demand to have intercourse with the analyst' while the erotic transference 'implicitly recognises the passion of a love relationship … Sexuality (in instinct theory) does not. The instincts do not love the object of desire; they seek to be discharged of their tensions through it' (Bollas, 1994: 589). Gabbard (1994a) also differentiates between the erotic transference and a situation in which there is an overt sexualisation of the transference but instead uses Blum's (1973) term for this of the 'erotized transference'. Implicit in their descriptions is the idea that the sexualised or eroticised transference is underpinned by a breakdown in the capacity to symbolise, partially rooted in a defence against separation and individuation, and that this form of transference is closest to psychosis (Bolognini, 1994).

If the literature base in the field of the erotic transference remains thin in relation to work with adults, it is especially thin in relation to psychoanalytic work with children and adolescents. A thorough review of the history of psychoanalytic ideas on childhood sexuality is, however, offered by Alvarez in her 2010 paper in which she explores the applicability of some of the adult literature to work with children, as well as the place of the positive countertransference. The research led by Moses and Egle Laufer into the broader process of adolescent development and breakdown has also been extremely influential. In particular, it emphasises the central significance of the impact of puberty on the relationship to the body and emerging sexuality during adolescence (Laufer and Laufer, 1995). Furthermore, although Feldman's paper on the manifestation of the Oedipus complex in the inner world does not refer directly to the erotic transference, his descriptions of the impossible dilemma faced by a father with his daughter on his knee certainly alert us to its emergence in the transference and countertransference. To take his daughter on his knee may, for example, inadvertently '… stimulate her belief in their excited sexual alliance against the mother. Not to take her on his knee may be to reject her perhaps giving evidence of his unease about the situation and thus confirming … the child's oedipal phantasies' (Feldman, 1989: 105).

As Brenman–Pick states:

> Like the young child, the patient is … consciously and unconsciously acutely sensitive to the way we interpret his difficulties in confronting the important issues, his labour in getting in touch with his infantile self – his propensities to become sadistic when he feels neglected or jealous or envious, when he feels mother/analyst is engaged with a new baby, and he feels himself to be the unwanted party.
>
> (Brenman–Pick, 1988: 40)

166 *Emil Jackson*

She further notes the likelihood of these issues stirring up reactions or excessive defensiveness on the part of the analyst as well as patient and reminds us that: 'It is our professional task to subject these reactions to scrutiny' (ibid.: 40). By their very nature, reactions and defensive reactions such as these can be extremely evasive, and it is these therefore that I wish to scrutinise through an exploration of psychotherapy with two adolescent patients. Given that the erotic transference often '... occurs early on in the treatment situation' (Symington, 1996: 75), I focus particularly on the starting phase of therapy with both patients which, for understandable reasons, is also the phase so often marking the greatest discrepancy between the intensity of the transference phantasies activated in the patient, and the therapist's awareness of and/or reticence to address these. In discussing the second patient I also examine some experiences later in the therapy when the transference was more established.

Clinical example 1: Hannah

Background and referral

Hannah[3] is an attractive 17-year-old girl who was referred after she dropped out of school in her final year. She had taken a potentially serious overdose when she was 15. At the time of referral, Hannah had withdrawn from re-lationships and activities outside of the family other than with her boyfriend. Instead, she spent most of her time at home watching television or cleaning in a way that seemed designed to empty her mind of any thought, anxiety or concern about her stuckness and the passing of time.

Hannah's presentation during the assessment had a strange and incongruous feel to it. She spoke, for instance, about how isolated, unhappy and over-looked she felt at home and school but there seemed to be only limited *felt* concern about this or ambition for things to change. Instead, she complained bitterly that her mother always prioritised father, paying him more attention than her own children when he was '... not even a blood relative! ... they are only married it's not as if they love each other or anything!' There was no irony or humour in the way she spoke. She was being quite serious.

Hannah did not, initially, have a coherent narrative for what was happening around the time of her overdose, although we later understood it to have been triggered by her experience of being psychologically ill-equipped to manage the demands of puberty, adolescence and, more specifically, her first experi-ence of sexual intercourse. More concerning, at the time, was her story of how, when her mother found out about her overdose, she took her straight back to school on discharge from hospital – perhaps signposting early on something about the considerable difficulty her mother, and internal objects, might have in receiving, containing and processing her communications and projections. Father was described as either a non-entity or a rival for mother's attention. Hannah reported, rather dispassionately, that she felt much closer to him growing up, more like a daddy's girl, but they had become distant in recent years.

Alongside the content of these discussions there were some striking features to the process of the assessment. Firstly, I was aware, from the outset, of an intense and gripping atmosphere in the room which was not easy to make sense of. Hannah always arrived early but presented as if she couldn't care less about coming. Meanwhile I noticed the difficulty I had in finishing on time and how hard she made me work to engage and interest her, as if all the desire for contact was located in me. In puzzling contrast to the intensity of contact made in sessions, I had the bizarre and disconcerting experience of finding it virtually impossible to remember anything about her in between sessions.

Second week of two times weekly psychotherapy

Hannah returned from the first weekend break to tell me that she hadn't been to college all week and had felt low after the previous session. She relayed an argument with her boyfriend after he had flirted with another girl right in front of her, becoming tearful as she described how rejected she felt by him and also by previous boyfriends who had left her feeling used (sexually).

In the session, I was initially aware of having a range of thoughts about the impact on Hannah of starting twice weekly therapy and of how she might have felt more keenly 'dropped' by me over this first weekend break. However, as Hannah continued to speak almost non-stop in an *apparently engaged* way, my connection to my thoughts and to what might have been going on for Hannah, became increasingly compromised: I found myself feeling silenced and agitated, struggling to contain or process my experience and increasingly propelled by an impulse to evacuate it by making my presence felt. At the time I could not make adequate sense of what was happening. Retrospectively however I wonder how much I might have been defending myself against experiences which were much closer to Hannah's than I was aware – for instance against the experience of feeling forced to witness her metaphorically flirting with her thoughts in front of me in a way that was simultaneously directed at (and into) me and experienced by me as absolutely annihilating. If this was the case, these defences would have left me all the more blind to the way Hannah may have interpreted my agreement to take her on for psychotherapy and her experience of this first weekend break in the same way as she interpreted her experience with her boyfriend – as my *intentional* and even sadistic wish to provoke her with jealousy and possessiveness.

There was further indication of this when I let Hannah know it was time to end the session. I was conscious at the time of feeling somewhat guilty for cutting her off before she was ready, all the more because of the hurt and dejected way she left the room. Only much later was I able to consider the momentary glimpse of triumph I would have unconsciously felt at being able to reassert my presence and authority in enforcing the time boundary. The likelihood that Hannah detected this immediately however – probably through what would have been my somewhat apologetic and *apparently* compassionate tone and manner – can be seen below in the striking way she presented in the following session and the unnerving impact it had on me.

I could already smell Hannah's perfume from half way down the corridor to the waiting room. It was like walking into some sort of intoxicating mist that immediately started messing with my mind. Hannah gave me a bland greeting. In the consulting room she dropped her jacket rather disdainfully on the couch and sat down, moving the angle of the chair slightly towards me. She wore black fishnet tights and a tiny mini-skirt. She had dressed similarly before but this time it felt different, made worse by the way she now sat facing me with her legs slightly parted, exposing her underwear, simultaneously inviting and repelling my attention. Having greeted her, I looked away, feeling uncomfortable and not knowing where to look or what to do or say. In the initial silence, I felt tense, self-conscious and blank – perhaps because I was concentrating so hard on not appearing uncomfortable or inadvertently glancing at her, all other thoughts escaped me.

In the next few minutes, a range of thoughts and feelings started to surface … Why did she come dressed like this? How did she hope I would respond to her? How did she expect me to think about her? Was she doing it on purpose? Did she want me to look and notice? Surely, she knows what she is doing? Or is this just me and what's going on in my head? It gave me a headache.

Hannah looked miserable and reluctant to speak. She shuffled on her chair and put her hands between her legs as if to cover herself. Momentarily I felt bad as if she had done this to protect herself from me – but then I wondered whether she was sitting like this, not only to protect herself from my gaze but to invite it. As she sat looking disconcertingly calm, I felt agitated and angry – both intrusive and also intruded upon ….

After a few long minutes I felt compelled to say something and commented on her reluctance to say much. Hannah spoke about feeling angry with everything at the moment. She complained about her boyfriend, friends, her parents and the way everyone treated her. I acknowledged this and wondered whether, on top of everything else, she might have felt fed up when I ended the previous session, adding that I had the impression it might have left her feeling dismissed and even used by me, especially after opening up a bit more. In saying this, I was aware of my apprehension and discomfort at saying the word 'used'. Hannah looked at me searchingly. It felt important to hold her gaze – almost as if I needed to stand by my belief in what I had said despite the apprehension in my tone. Hannah then agreed. The atmosphere eased.

After a pause, she began to speak more vehemently about how people can't be trusted and how she thinks all relationships are really just 'lies'. She spoke about how even her relationship with her 'boy best friend' is a lie because there is so much he doesn't know about her. I commented that she seemed to feel that unless a relationship is absolutely exclusive, almost like living alone on a desert island, then it is a lie and not to be trusted. Hannah responded in an assertive way. 'Yes. That is how it is!' She gave me a slightly embarrassed smile.

Too close for comfort 169

In the silence that followed, a range of thoughts came to mind, most significantly in relation to the demand for an exclusive transference relationship and her refusal to accept the validity of anything less. I decided against addressing these thoughts directly however, for fear of exciting rather than containing the situation. Instead, I made a safer link with what she had told me about her relationship with her parents, wondering whether she might therefore also feel that if her mother has any relationship with her father then it means her own relationship with her mother is a complete lie. Hannah responded in a passionately angry way, telling me how she and father are in competition for mother's attention. She conveyed a conviction that her father felt exactly as she did. She continued to tell me how there was a time when her parents were always arguing with each other but then something changed and they fell in love again. She paused, fell silent and seemed suddenly hesitant. I said that she seemed to have come up against a difficult thought. Hannah burst into a tirade: 'It's disgusting! … They do "it"

I commented, with some feeling in my voice, on how awful it was for her when she felt her parents got together in a couple like this and were so busy with each other, having sex all over the place. I said that I thought it left her feeling completely filled up and tormented by the sight and sound of them and completely abandoned by them at the same time. I acknowledged that it could even feel as if they were doing this to her on purpose – like they must know what they were doing. Hannah sighed and slumped back in her seat. She said that she supposed she didn't object to her parents having a relationship with each other but 'they should always love their children more and put them first'.

She then seemed to come up against another uncomfortable thought. Cautiously she added 'It's not that I want to be in there with them while they are doing it. It's just that …'. She got stuck and looked at me awkwardly. I eventually said '… but you don't want to be left out of it either?'

'Exactly! …' she replied. More gently, she said that sometimes she even had to shout at her parents to shut up when they were making too much noise. Her brother just put his fingers in his ears and tried to ignore it. She did once confront her mother about it but her mother just said, 'What are we supposed to do? You stay in all the time and never go out so when are we meant to do it?'

Despite remaining upset, Hannah seemed relieved that it had been possible to begin to put her experience into words, including her reluctance to leave her parents alone. Although there was still an intensity in the room, I was aware of how the atmosphere had changed and how her appearance now seemed less sexual, distracting or threatening.

In many ways, some important and convincing psychic movement took place in this session. This included a shift in Hannah's awareness about her fierce resistance to the idea of her parents as a couple in their own right – something which will almost certainly have been contributing significantly to her difficulty in managing separation and the transition towards adulthood more generally.[4] There was also a considerable shift in my own state of mind – from one in which I felt overwhelmed and defended in the face of the disturbing experience I was having at the start of the session, to one in which I could not help but feel relieved to have a sense of my sanity restored when the nature of my experience made so much more sense. Rather than feel almost angry with Hannah for what she was doing to me, I could then begin to consider, with greater compassion and concern, how invaded, overwhelmed and driven mad she must at times feel – all the more so if her actual parents were behaving in such a sexually uncontained, provocative and worrying manner.[5]

However, while I believe this progress was meaningful and valid, I am nevertheless left with questions about what I did and did not address with Hannah and how to draw the defining lines between what is safe and containing as opposed to something that might be *rationalised* as safe and containing but which is essentially evasive and defensive on the part of the therapist. For example, while the changed atmosphere *felt* much better, might this have come at the expense of her internal parents who bore the brunt of her feelings, partly on account of my having decided against more direct interpretation in the transference? In a similar vein, retrospectively, I also wonder how blind I was as to how Hannah might have interpreted the way I had 'shut the door' in the previous session (the hint of triumph) together with my apprehensive tone in this session (when re-employing her word 'used' now in relation to myself). Might she, for example, have interpreted this as evidence that, like everyone else including her parents, I was a liar and a user out to satisfy my own narcissistic needs at her expense?

Towards more direct interpretation

Soon after commencing twice-weekly therapy, Hannah was able to return to college and re-engage with her studies. While she was positive about this, it forced her to recognise how problematic her relationships with her peers had become. In one session, for example, she asserted that 'Girls, were jealous bitches not to be trusted. Boys were only interested in her looks'. She looked directly at me as she said this. I said that she must then also believe that either I would be jealous of her looks like the girls or just another boy who is only interested in her because of her looks. This seemed to resonate with Hannah as it led to her conveying her underlying dread that she had nothing good inside her, nothing she believed would *really* interest anyone, including me. It was then possible to get alongside her in acknowledging how caught between a rock and a hard place she must feel – on the one hand relying on her looks for attention and dreading the prospect of anyone really getting to know her, while equally dreading the prospect of never feeling known, which would leave her relentlessly mistrustful of any attention she does get.

A couple of months into the therapy, Hannah seemed to confirm this when she told me that she and her 'boy best friend' had got together. However, rather than feeling hopeful that he was interested in her personality first and foremost, she felt insulted, as if her looks obviously didn't attract him. I commented on her belief that her trump card was her looks and seductive capacity and that anything else came a poor second. She agreed emphatically saying that she may as well not bother. She slumped in her seat and told me how any other time this has happened the person has gone off her within weeks. In subsequent sessions Hannah conveyed her hatred of any sense of neediness or vulnerability in herself and the way she managed it by using her seductive prowess to project interest and desire into others:

When I found a way to comment on this dynamic, Hannah told me how she had done it to her boyfriend that very morning when she was waiting to meet him at the bus stop. He was late. Another boy was chatting her up and even though she wasn't remotely interested she let the conversation continue until her boyfriend arrived and felt provoked. I took up how her seductiveness not only distracted her from having to wait, but ensured that it was others, the boy and her boyfriend, who were clamouring after her attention. Apprehensively, I added that perhaps she felt her 'seductiveness' was the only way she had to secure my attention.

'I don't think I try and seduce you!' Hannah retorted scathingly. 'No, of course not, it's different here', I said, taking immediate flight from my own comment. However, I did then manage to stop and catch myself. 'Well let's just hold on and think about that for a moment actually', I said. 'Of course, it is different here, but I still think that it does happen in all sorts of subtle ways.' I went on to comment on how hard she needed me to work to prove I was interested before she was prepared to tell me anything; how often she started saying something but then fell silent mid-sentence, wanting to stir my curiosity. Hannah looked seriously at me. Then, sounding exasperated with herself, she said: 'It's true, I do that with everyone, even my parents and sister. I hate it that I do that!'

In this session I did find a way, albeit clumsily, to take up more directly how Hannah could use her seductiveness (and implicitly her body and sexuality) to control me. Rather than exciting her, heating up the atmosphere or generating shame in either of us, Hannah seemed receptive and able then to recognise some valuable, though challenging, hitherto 'unthought knowns' about herself (Bollas, 1987). This shift was also evident in the following session when she returned presenting in a way that seemed *outwardly unchanged* (in relation to her appearance and what she was saying) but which *felt* quite different in the countertransference.

Hannah arrived at the following session in a rush telling me she had something exciting to tell me: 'It will sound silly and it probably won't be exciting to anyone else, but it was to me.' She went on to tell me how she had been out with her boyfriend and had a really nice time. She only meant to go for a short while but enjoyed it and stayed out late. Usually, she would get up early to get ready but this morning she overslept. At first she gave up, thinking she couldn't possibly get to her session, but then she thought, 'Stuff it, I can do it, I can just get dressed and leave and that's what I did and I got here in time! … Sorry about my bed hair and my morning look', she said with a smile. Then, more thoughtfully, conveying a sense of bewildering liberation from her usual grooming regime she added, 'It's strange … I'm wearing more or less the same clothes but the whole process was completely different.'

There are, of course, many lenses through which one might examine this material, for example in terms of the possible implications of Hannah's excitement and comments about her bed hair and morning look. However, what

172 *Emil Jackson*

felt more significant than the meaning of any specific content was my different experience of her presentation – engaging, attractive and even flirty, but without the intoxicating or seductive edge. I was also struck by how more direct interpretation in the transference in the previous session helped to facilitate a shift from behaviour that seemed primarily projective and evacuative, designed to relieve Hannah's instinctual frustration, towards something that felt more symbolic and rooted in development. After all, as Alvarez notes:

> … flirting need not be seen as a purely seductive act. If it is occurring on the symbolic level, it can involve a type of playing, of acknowledging attraction but under safe conditions where the internal Oedipal triangle of which Britton (2003: 55) has spoken is kept intact, respected and acknowledged.
>
> (Alvarez, 2010: 216)

My own impression was similar – that Hannah was here conveying to me a rather new and fresh experience, that of feeling herself to be much more like an ordinary 17-year old who was pleased to come to her therapy, feeling she could, at least momentarily, trust that she might be accepted for who she was without having to intrude into my mind or stimulate me instinctually with her stories, her appearance, smells and sexuality (see also Klauber, 1986: 50).

Clinical example 2: Sarah

I now wish to describe work with a second adolescent patient. I have selected material from two time points to illustrate and examine some of the difficulties we encounter in recognising the intensity and complexity of what is being communicated and how it impacts on both patient and therapist. The first of these time points focuses on the impact of starting therapy (as in Hannah's case). I then turn to material from a later point in the therapy which marked the deepening of the transference.

Referral

Sarah was referred for assessment at the age of 18. At the time of referral she had recently returned early from her 'gap year' having broken up with her boyfriend with whom she was travelling. Sarah reported feeling depressed and suicidal. She described self-harming behaviour, daily use of cannabis and eating difficulties. Following the assessment with a senior colleague, Sarah was referred for therapy three times a week.

Starting therapy: the initial impact on patient and therapist

Sarah presented as a young woman who was potentially attractive but who (unlike Hannah) dressed down in a bland way that detracted from her femininity and sexuality. Despite her androgynous appearance, the initial contact she made was intense and engaging. On her way out at the end of the first session, for example, she asked whether she should come 'straight to my room' next time. I answered pragmatically, letting her know she needed to check in with reception first, but was aware that her question did not feel straightforward.

Although Sarah said she rarely remembered her dreams, she returned to the second session surprised to have had a vivid dream:

> *She was in Africa with her ex-boyfriend Simon. There was another couple there too. There was an office in the house with a light on. She thought Simon was inside the office. She felt torn between wanting and not wanting to know what was going on behind the closed door. She thought about whether she should give him a warning before going straight in.*

On hearing her dream, I was aware of feeling both excited by and cautious about the start Sarah was making in her therapy. I had to remind myself to manage the pace – especially as a male therapist working with a female adolescent.[6]

When I asked for her thoughts about the dream, Sarah told me how she and her ex-boyfriend broke up after she discovered he was into internet porn and was having an affair. She had thought something was going on for months but 'couldn't use the information in her head to do anything about it'. I commented on the impact of starting therapy and her mixed feelings about knowing more about what goes on inside her mind. When she agreed, I also took up her uncertainty about what sort of a person I was, what went on in my mind and whether I could be trusted. Sarah responded by telling me about how she had once read her father's diary and discovered intimate secrets about his private life. Towards the end of the session I said that I had the impression that she wanted a space to bring her thoughts but that she also needed me to understand her concerns about the speed at which things might happen here. Sarah agreed and then suddenly remembered a fragment from a second dream the previous night in which she had been on a journey somewhere and had passed a 'Quick Fit' garage.

Within this brief material from the first two sessions, there is already a huge amount which deserves further consideration and scrutiny, including several signposts to the excitement and anxiety that was immediately being activated by the therapeutic encounter. Some of these I was partially aware of and able to address. Retrospectively however, I think I was responding to and defending against much more powerful and unsettling communications than I was conscious of at the time. For example, while I was aware that Sarah's question about coming 'straight' to the therapy room left me somewhat suspicious about its underlying meaning, I prematurely reassured myself that I had managed the *boundaries of the setting* in not allowing her to bypass the clinic reception with all its oedipal symbolism. Meanwhile, Sarah returned to the

174 *Emil Jackson*

second session not only reporting a dream the content of which was engaging, but doing so in a way that perhaps contributed to my excitement and narcissistic interest by telling me rather seductively that it was 'unusual for her to remember her dreams', almost as if it was a special gift. While, in her dream, Sarah questioned whether she should warn her boyfriend before going 'straight in', I was rather blind to the fact that she had *already* bypassed the *boundaries to my mind* and come straight in!

Building on this further: in exploring the dream with Sarah, I did take up her mixed feelings about knowing more about what went on, not only in her mind but also in mine, including whether I could be trusted. At the time, I understood her response to me – telling me about the discovery of intimate secrets about her father's life – to indicate some confirmation of my interpretation. But perhaps what I failed to consider was how my interpretation itself might have been understood by Sarah as inadvertent exposure of my own intimate secrets and private life – and that this is what led to her response about her father. If so, then I would also have missed the way she might already be experiencing me, in the transference, as an object who simultaneously invites (sexual) intrusion and leaves her feeling (sexually) intruded upon in what Rosenfeld might call an 'intrusive identification with the object' (Rosenfeld, 1971). Perhaps then, the content of the dream together with Sarah's associations to it, not only communicated her hope that therapy might enable her to make better use of 'the information in her head' but also her fear that I would 'fit' too quickly with her in finding it equally impossible to maintain a functioning mind that could pace itself when captivated by the lure of illicit sex, porn and infidelity.

Controlling versus containing the pace: the dilemmas of whether and when to interpret

When faced with difficulties such as those described above, we frequently, and understandably, gravitate to somewhat compensatory attempts to slow down the pace when the temperature rises, rather than stay with our discomfort and find safe ways to contain and address the speed and heat generated in the transference and countertransference. Some of these dynamics could be seen when Sarah returned from the first weekend break feeling depressed, angry and frustrated.

Sarah returned, complaining that she had no real friends and didn't 'fit in', becoming tearful as she conveyed her fear that therapy would make her more depressed, especially if it unearthed hostile feelings towards her parents. She referred, in particular, to her parents' violent separation when she was five after her mother walked in on her father in bed with another woman (whom he subsequently married).

In the final session that week, Sarah was dominated by a conviction that she was boring and unattractive, telling me about a man from university whom she fancied but who was not interested in her. This escalated into a rant about how she would have to settle for 'second best' in relationships as she was always drawn to people 'out of her league'. Sarah then told me about an older man, a musician, who did gigs at the pub. She had always quietly flirted with him but last night he had asked her out. After feeling momentarily triumphant, she felt devastated as if some sort of important boundary transgression had taken place. She started crying as she noticed how quickly she tends to reject the very thing she longs for as soon as she has it.

At this early and delicate stage of therapy with a vulnerable adolescent, I was unsure about what could be helpfully or safely explored in the transference. For example, I chose not to take up how violently displaced Sarah might feel at the weekend when she imagines me in 'another couple'. Nor did I feel confident enough to interpret what an impossible situation she found herself in with me – hating the idea that I was out of her league as much as she dreaded the possibility that she might succeed in seducing me – like the musician in the transference.

Sarah returned from the second weekend break to tell me she had slept with the man from university – the man she was sure was 'out of her league'. She spoke excitedly of how 'connected' they were after spending the weekend alone together. I, meanwhile, was kept at arm's length – allowed to listen and filled with thoughts but silenced sharply as soon as I said anything.

There are, of course, many good reasons for pacing things carefully at this early point in a therapy, all the more so in work with adolescents for whom intimacy and sexuality can be so easily confused. But sometimes we seek false comfort in reassuring ourselves that it is our patients – rather than ourselves – that we are protecting. After all, as Symington notes, it can be 'thoroughly alarming' for us to realise how our 'innocent actions ... can have an effect that penetrates a person's emotional sexual life' (Symington, 1996: 77–78). For example, is it true to say that my decision to play safe and to avoid making any more anxiety-provoking transference interpretations really protected my patient? Or rather, was it precisely my inability to process and interpret the transference and countertransference more directly that may have inadvertently contributed to a precipitous sexual acting out – an encounter which ended just as quickly as it began, leaving Sarah feeling all the more rejected and desperate about herself?

The deepening of the transference relationship and the use of the couch

I shall now focus on a period, two years into the therapy, when the intensity and impact of the transference and countertransference were felt more acutely in relation to Sarah's growing interest in and eventual move to using the couch.

As psychotherapists, our experience of using the couch will be varied. I have neither the wish to idealise the importance of the couch nor to underestimate what can be achieved without it. However, I think there are some issues, with some patients, that are simply very difficult to address sitting face to face.

176 *Emil Jackson*

This is especially the case with the erotic transference where there is a greater risk that the thoughts and feelings generated will be experienced concretely, resulting in a premature flight from treatment, and not only by the patient!

Although Sarah acknowledged a growing interest in the couch, she was conscious of her fear that using it might result in an unsafe unravelling of her mind. This fear was further fuelled by unconscious anxieties that use of the couch would leave her at the mercy of an insatiable appetite, unbearable curiosity and intense phantasies of a sexual and oedipal nature. Aspects of these anxieties can be seen in the following dream:

> *I was in a large warehouse. My bed was in the corner up against two walls. There was an expanse of space next to my bed. There were automatic doors coming into the warehouse. They had an ominous feel to them which unsettled me. There was a man and woman conducting some sort of dance. There were lots of other people there too. The woman was very happy but wanted to be on some sort of an island.*

Through her exploration of the dream, Sarah was able to acknowledge how the prospect of using the couch disturbed her, both because it might allow more automatic access to her mind and because of the space it would be likely to open up. In part, she seemed to feel it threatened to confront her with important 'facts of life' usually barred from thought (Brenman, 2006). These included fantasies about my private life: wife, children and other patients, fantasies which had, so far, been most noticeable by their absence.

However, it was not just Sarah who was feeling threatened. Although at times it felt deeply unsettling, it was also essential that I engage with those anxieties that I too most wished to avoid (Strachey, 1934; Brenman-Pick, 1988). Primarily these related to the possibility that the couch might feel more like a bed, resulting in the intensification of some sort of 'desert island' erotic transference which threatened to tip into something more akin to a sexualised transference and countertransference. A number of core anxieties, therefore, needed to be addressed within my own mind as well as directly with Sarah. These included the anxieties that she unconsciously signposted at the start of treatment: her wish to seduce me, my own fears about being seduced, her fear that I would succumb to her seduction and her dread that I would be impervious to it – all of which were felt to be potentially devastating.

Equally unsettling was the periodic presence of something more akin to a positive or loving transference – something that both Gabbard (1994a) and Alvarez (2010) note can be harder to stay with than the negative, all the more so when there is any 'felt' sexual component. At times, for example, I noticed how I could experience Sarah as being something like the clinical 'apple of my eye', leaving me with the impression that there were important aspects of Sarah's internal history that needed to be recovered – or re-written – with me, as Bolognini describes it, as a therapist/father 'able to see in her a potential princess, capable and deserving of arousing charm' (Bolognini, 1994: 82).

The move to the couch felt like quite an adjustment. For the first few weeks Sarah seemed tense, lying on the couch with her knees up as if she felt like a terrified virgin on her wedding night. This was poignantly represented when she told me how her new travel card gave her freedom to go wherever she wanted but left her worrying about whether she could manage the increased cost. She was able to recognise how the 'cost' in the transference connected in part to the increased access she had to her fantasies about my 'private life' and her hatred of feeling so excluded from it.

However retrospectively, I was unaware of the extent to which I was also struggling with Sarah's move to the couch and the increased freedom it offered me to travel to new places with my patient. This was evident when Sarah returned from the first major break since moving to the couch to tell me that she had 'done a terrible thing': she had kissed a close friend of her boyfriend. The intensity of the impact this had on me was startling. I experienced it like a personal assault – a body blow, affecting my whole physiology and evoking something not far off a sense of outrage, as if she had actually been unfaithful to me.

Making sense of what had happened in terms of the impact and significance of this news, took some time. It also forced me to reflect on the difficulty I had had in adequately being able to address the earlier impact of Sarah's move to the couch either in myself or with her. Just as at the start of treatment, I think this difficulty probably contributed to another compulsive repetition of sexual acting out that had its roots much further back in her life history. Only when this second enactment had been given due attention did things begin to shift.

As we approached the next weekend break, I more robustly interpreted the impact of both the weekend and Easter breaks and how they could feel like a violation of the therapy and therapeutic relationship. Sarah fell silent. The atmosphere then seemed to heat up rather suddenly until she said that she thought she kissed the boy to hurt me more than her boyfriend. She linked this to the Easter break. I acknowledged the importance of what she was saying about how angry, jealous and cheated on she felt by me over Easter, adding that perhaps now I needed to know what that was like – including what it was like to feel sexually jealous. 'Yes', she responded seriously. The temperature then seemed to cool down just as quickly as it heated up.

Discussion

Maintaining a therapeutic equilibrium on the tightrope of the erotic transference

Klauber notes the way we can overlook the strain that the analytic method imposes on both patient and analyst. He writes: 'The development of transference is always traumatic for the patient, as is the longing for relationship with the analyst as a result of their intimacy' (Klauber, 1986: 45). In this

178   *Emil Jackson*

respect, it is not just our patient's seductiveness that we need to attend to, but also their experience of our own: for instance, the way they might feel we are seductive with our interest and attention, running the risk of teasing them by constantly arousing emotions that we will never satisfy, requiring them instead to be content with interpretations alone (ibid.: 47). Klauber further notes that: 'The development of psychoanalytic objectivity and distance, which have to be combined with ready empathy, are similarly an arduous task for the analyst' (ibid.: 45). This is especially relevant in work with adolescents where the potential dangers to one's work and person are all the greater due to the adolescent's own developmental needs and conflicts (Laufer, 1975).

In her paper on 'Working through in the countertransference', Brenman-Pick (1988) builds on Strachey's (1934) paper on 'The nature of the therapeutic action of psychoanalysis'. She highlights the apparent ambiguity between what Strachey viewed as a 'true transference interpretation' – that being one which the analyst 'most feared and most wished to avoid' – and his belief that it is necessary to convey an interpretation in a calm way to the patient. The whole idea that, as therapists, we 'should' remain calm deserves further interrogation. What happens, for example, when a patient has little sense of the availability or penetrability of their object? What if, as in Sarah's case, my apparent calmness exacerbated her sense of impotence, making her feel that even her best attempts to seduce or provoke me were futile? What if she *really* needed me to be emotionally aroused and to bear not feeling calm?

There have certainly been times in my work with both Hannah and Sarah when my internal sense of calm was shattered in all sorts of disturbing ways. I remember one particular occasion, when the already heated atmosphere was made immeasurably worse by the way that Sarah lay on the couch in silence, sliding her fingers back and forth inside the hem of her skirt and playing with the top buttons of her blouse, exposing nothing but inviting everything. On that occasion I felt compelled to turn away and shield my eyes to protect myself against what felt like an overwhelming intrusion into my mind – an intrusion of the wish to intrude itself. How do we then, as Brenman–Pick so clearly puts it, walk the 'tightrope between experiencing disturbance and responding with interpretation that does not convey disturbing anxiety' (Brenman–Pick, 1988: 34)? Is it not, as she suggests, precisely 'The process of meeting and working through our own experience of both wanting to know and fearing knowing … [that] facilitates … a deeper and more empathic contact with these parts of the patient and his internal objects? … If we keep emotions out, are we in danger of keeping out the love which mitigates the hatred …?' (ibid.: 39).

Protective factors

To my mind, there are a number of factors that help to stabilise us on the tightrope of the erotic transference. These include: the experience and

Too close for comfort   179

protection offered through our own analyses; the state of our personal life, relationships and sense of internal security; the extent to which we feel supported and contained within our teams and workplaces; and rigorous, emotionally safe, on-going supervision both individually and in groups. Such supervision regrounds us, when necessary, in our knowledge that the patient's 'falling in love is induced by the analytic situation and is not to be attributed to the charms of his own person' (Freud, 1915: 160–161). It also helps us not to treat the positive transference 'defensively, as something wholly bogus or incongruous' and supports us to remain 'depressively conscious' of the need to tolerate the 'possible unpleasure of renunciation' (Bolognini, 1994: 84).

Bolognini draws on a range of sources to enumerate what he describes as 'guarantee factors' which he believes are important in providing the analyst with the correct attitude so that he can cope with the 'highly explosive forces' of erotic transferences.[7] In addition to some of those already described, he includes the constitution of a good psychoanalytic superego and the clinician's group of patients amongst whom the available countertransference resources can be shared (ibid.: 83–84). This latter point would be all the more pertinent for clinicians working predominantly with patient groups who invariably evoke intense countertransference responses such as those who have been sexually abused and/or who abuse.

While the knowledge that we should never feel alone in our struggles with our patients is something we might easily take for granted, Gabbard offers a sobering reminder that 'most of us do not avail ourselves of consultation as often as we probably should' (Gabbard, 1994b: 1102). At a personal level, I distinctly remember sharing the disturbing experience of needing to turn away from Sarah with my clinical supervision group. Being helped to examine this robustly, and to make greater sense of it within this more exposing group context was supportive, validating and had a transformative impact. Instead of feeling judged or shamed, it left me feeling noticeably safer inside myself and resulted in a greater sense of freedom to receive, explore and interpret my patients' communications, trusting that I was accompanied by solid enough internal and external chaperones.

At a technical level, our therapeutic equilibrium is also likely to be better secured when we keep in mind some well-known considerations that are, all too often, neglected. Are we clear enough, for example, about why we are pursuing a particular line of thinking or inquiry? Can we, as Moses Laufer (1975) believes is sometimes necessary, explain, even to ourselves, why we have asked a question and what we might do with the answer? The inverse of this is also true. Are we, for instance, clear about why we are not pursuing a line of thinking or interpretation? For even when we do not dare to address the nature of our patients' phantasies, might it at least be important to acknowledge the presence of thoughts, feelings and impulses that, for now, it does not seem possible to address in a way that feels safe enough. At least we would not then be at risk of joining the patient or their objects in turning a blind eye (Steiner, 1985).

180 *Emil Jackson*

It is also important to follow the process of the session closely, along with the impact that any given interpretation has on the patient. What is their experience of and response to it – and us? Does it, for instance, excite and further intensify the anxiety and shame? Or does it result in a reduction of anxiety and the emergence of new thoughts, associations or dreams? The same questions are equally essential to ask of ourselves. In other words, when we make an interpretation in a potentially toxic area like the erotic transference, we need to follow not only our patient's responses, but also *our own experience* of our interpretation and of our patient's response to it. Do we get more excited with the direction of travel or, rather, does it help to restore our sense of internal containment and psychic equilibrium?

The developmental potential of addressing sexuality and the erotic transference

I have always felt reassured and encouraged to discover that my attempts to address some of the most uncomfortable areas of the transference and countertransference in a matter of fact way – paradoxically treating them as being as ordinary as they are – could significantly reduce anxiety and result in important shifts, not only in my patients' thinking, but in my own. This is facilitated when we are able to help patients establish a dual state of awareness in which there is simultaneously a recognition of active wishes that were previously repressed and a dispassionate reflection on the meaning and significance of those wishes (Gabbard, 1994a). One example of this 'dual state of awareness' can be seen in Sarah's response to a very direct interpretation I made about her difficulty in being anything other than my number one, exacerbated by her belief that she would be excluded from a place of any importance in my mind if I was not actually sleeping with her. My interpretation did not seem to excite either Sarah or myself. Instead, she reflected quietly for a few minutes before responding movingly by telling me that she noticed she was finding herself drawn to different kinds of relationships – relationships that were likely to be good for her. She said she was really pleased about this … but that it made her sad too. Suddenly she burst out crying. Sarah then continued to talk about her father's relationship with his wife, the person with whom he had had the original affair. No longer did she want to disown her father and murder her stepmother. Instead – hardly able to believe what she was saying – she spoke about how she now recognised that they had had a really good relationship for 15 years – and she hoped that one day she would also be lucky enough to have a relationship like theirs.

Summary

In adolescence, as we know, the life blood of the internal world is often experienced and channelled most vividly through the relationship to the developing body and sexuality.

This paper has focussed on my experience of working with two adolescents where an intense and sexual atmosphere was, at times, very much alive and all a bit too close for comfort for both patient and therapist. As well as exploring some of the challenges which face us in this kind of work, I have tried to illustrate how, from a clinical and technical perspective, it can prove possible and therapeutically effective to address some of these issues and anxieties in ways that are surprisingly direct. I have also tried to show how, even during the early stages of a therapy when we might most readily justify erring on the side of safety in relation to what we interpret and how we interpret it, our neglect of the transference and, in particular our neglect of the countertransference, is anything but protective of our patients.

Psychoanalytic work with adolescents, whose anxieties and phantasies about sexuality are part of healthy development and never far from consciousness, is inevitably going to be an anxiety-provoking experience, and one which can feel potentially threatening for both patient and therapist alike. Nevertheless, despite the discomfort it might cause, I hope I have been able to convey my belief that our patients need us to be able to receive, contain, process and eventually articulate the profoundly uncomfortable and disturbing experiences generated in the transference and countertransference as a critical, essential and developmental part of their treatment.

Note

Earlier versions of this paper were presented at the ACP Annual Conference, London 2011, the Birmingham Trust for Psychoanalytic Psychotherapy, 2011 and the Tavistock Clinic's Psychoanalytic Forum in 2015.

Acknowledgements

I would like to acknowledge my appreciation of Steve Dreyer and, separately, members of my clinical supervision group at the time I was working with the patients described in this paper, for their invaluable supervision and support through some of the most difficult periods of this work.

Notes

1 I have written elsewhere about the challenges that teachers have to manage in containing sexual anxieties in schools (Jackson, 2015).
2 There is a question here, worthy of further discussion, about whether a health and safety culture has diminished our willingness as therapists to engage with 'dangerous' sexual material, especially perhaps as a male therapist with female patients given this is the most common form of sexual power dynamics.
3 All names and identifying details have been changed to protect confidentiality.
4 One can see here how reductive it would be to describe Hannah's difficulties as 'separation anxiety'.

182   *Emil Jackson*

5 While not the focus of this paper, it is important to note that material such as this, did later result in additional and separate work with Hannah's parents being arranged.
6 The complex ways that the gender and sexuality of both patient and therapist manifest within the transference and countertransference is an important one, deserving of further exploration, though beyond the scope of this paper.
7 Personally I do not like the term 'guarantee factors' as I think the idea of a 'guarantee' may itself be a potential risk factor.

References

Alvarez, A. (2010). Types of sexual transference and countertransference in psychotherapeutic work with children and adolescents. *Journal of Child Psychotherapy*, 36 (3), 211–224.

Blum, H.P. (1973). The concept of erotized transference. *Journal of the American Psychoanalytic Association*, 21, 76.

Bollas, C. (1987) *The Shadow of the Object: Psychoanalysis of the Unthought Known*. London: Free Association Books.

Bollas, C. (1994). Aspects of the erotic transference. *Psychoanalytic Inquiry*, 14 (4), 572–590.

Bolognini, S. (1994). Transference: Erotised, erotic, loving, affectionate. *International Journal of Psycho-Analysis*, 75 (1), 73–86.

Brenman, E. (2006). The narcissism of the analyst: Its effect in clinical practice. *Recovery of the Lost Good Object*. London: Routledge.

Brenman-Pick, I. (1988). Working through in the countertransference. In Spillius, E. (Ed.), *Melanie Klein Today: Developments in Theory and Practice, Vol. 2: Mainly Practice*. London: Routledge.

Britton, R. (2003) *Sex, Death and the Superego*. London: Karnac.

Feldman, M. (1989). The Oedipus complex: Manifestations in the inner world and the therapeutic situation. In Steiner, J. (Ed.), *The Oedipus Complex Today: Clinical Implications*. London: Karnac.

Freud, S. (1915). Observations of transference-love. *SE*, 12, 159–171.

Gabbard, G. (1994a). On love and lust in erotic transference. *Journal of the American Psychoanalytic Association*, 42 (2), 385–403.

Gabbard, G. (1994b). Sexual excitement and countertransference love in the analyst. *Journal of the American Psychoanalytic Association*, 42 (4), 1083–1106.

Jackson, E. (2015). Work discussion groups as a container for sexual anxieties in schools. In Armstrong, D., & Rustin, M. (Eds.), *Social Defences against Anxiety: Explorations in a Paradigm*. London: Karnac.

Klauber, J. (1986). *Difficulties in the Analytic Encounter*. London: Karnac.

Laufer, M. (1975). Preventive intervention in adolescence. *Psychoanalytic Study of the Child*, 30, 511–528.

Laufer, M. & Laufer, M.E. (1995). *Adolescence and Developmental Breakdown*. London: Karnac.

Person, E.S. (1985). The erotic transference in woman and in men: Differences and consequences. *Journal of the American Academy of Psychoanalysis and Dynamic Psychiatry*, 13 (2), 159–180.

Rosenfeld, H. (1971). Contribution to the psychopathology of psychotic states: The importance of projective identification in the ego structure and objects relations of the psychotic patient. In Steiner, J. (Ed.) *Rosenfeld in Retrospect: Essays on His Clinical Influence*. London: Routledge.

Steiner, J. (1985). Turning a blind eye: The cover up for Oedipus. *International Review of Psycho-Analysis*, 12 (2), 161–172.

Strachey, J. (1934). The nature of the therapeutic action of psychoanalysis. *International Journal of Psycho-Analysis*, 15, 275–293.

Symington, N. (1996) *The Making of a Psychotherapist*. London: Karnac.

Editor's Introduction to:
Erotic, eroticized and perverse transference in child analysis

In this chapter Kohen de Abdala poses the challenge that the sexually 'traumatic situation must emerge into the transference in order to be analysed and, at the same time, it generates in us an emotional storm…'. Likewise, she helpfully posits the grave necessity of instituting boundaries for a sexually over-stimulated child, along with the concomitant danger that the child's negative feelings at being faced with limits may overwhelm the treatment.

Kohen de Abdala uses the framework of erotic/eroticized and perverse transferences here. This seems to help ground her in theory, such as when four-year-old Pablo asks her to turn her back while he masturbated and she felt paralyzed. Overwhelming experiences for clinicians rightly lead us to turn to theory to find our footing. The reader may consider whether this framework of erotic/eroticized/perverse assists the clinical work here. Kohen de Abdala's understanding that she was overwhelmed (in a state of projective identification), as her patient had been overwhelmed by a premature over-exposure to sexuality is central.

In this intense moment when Kohen de Abdala feels frozen as Pablo asks her to turn her back while he masturbates we might also ask — what is it that freezes us at such moments? I could certainly imagine it is the sexual explosiveness of the material. I also wonder if our psychoanalytic emphasis on interpretation could divert us from other modalities — here some gentle limit — (to suggest he wait until after the session, to take him to the bathroom to have privacy, etc.). I think such limits can have an interpretive or eventually interpretable function (for instance, implying that sexual over-stimulation precludes a child from developing their own sexual feelings more organically, gradually and in a manner that is not so catastrophically overwhelming).

Clarification can occur in a child's mind as he compares the difference between his analyst's and his parents' responses to over-stimulation. This may gradually allow him to notice problems in his objects instead of endlessly enacting over-stimulated states. Paradoxically, an action by the analyst (here a gentle limit on Pablo's masturbating with his analyst present) can sometimes allow a patient to begin to think. Sometimes an action on the analyst's part might be felt as more of a communication than an interpretation might. For example, if we interpret and a child continues to evoke overwhelming

DOI: 10.4324/9781003266303-21

stimulation, he could feel there is no such thing as protection. Some children have had little experience of action and thinking being linked – that we might do or not do something because of a consideration of our own or others' feelings.

With traumatically over-stimulated children protective limits may need to precede symbolically expressed thought in conveying meaning. Clearly Kohen de Abdala's work demonstrates this understanding – such as when she tells Pablo she will not let him throw himself and the naked Barbie out the window! Thinking through the psychological meanings of limits may assist us in finding our way at such intense moments as Kohen de Abdala courageously describes.

11 Erotic, eroticized and perverse transference in child analysis

N. Graciela Kohen de Abdala

This work is the fruit of my experience as a child psychoanalyst. I present here the analytic process of four-year-old Pablo, where transferential elements linked to erotic, eroticized or perverse states appeared along with the resulting countertransferential states.

Erotic, eroticized and perverse transference

It is important to differentiate erotic transference from eroticized and perverse transference in the child (as it is in the adult). According to Bolognini (1994), there are four types of erotic transference – erotic, eroticized, loving and affectionate – each with their respective origins, dynamics and repercussions in the analytic relationship.

The **erotic** is characterized by manifest demands for love; it is ego-syntonic and comes with the desire for sexual satisfaction from the analyst. It is a positive transference. However, the sexual fantasies that the patient has with the analyst confuse the patient who expects to convert these love situations into reality. Feelings of rivalry, jealousy, or intense love linked to oedipal desires also appear, that is to say, we are dealing with neurotic transference and, therefore, it can be interpreted.

Eroticized transference, on the other hand, is a perverse and repeated quest on the part of the patient who hopes to achieve bodily and sexual contact with the analyst. Children are continuously trying to touch the analyst, approach them physically, insisting on physical contact and engaging in attempts at seduction or actions which break down the distance necessary to even think. This can be seen in children with serious pathologies (narcissistic, borderline or psychotic) and in patients (as I show in the clinical vignette) who have been exposed to situations of overstimulation or sexual abuse) where the child's disorganization leads to the search for acting out that can put the analytic process at risk.

The analyst must be very attentive to conscious and/or subconscious demands for sexual satisfaction which at times can provoke vexatious countertransferential emotions or, even more seriously, which result in enactment or acting on the part of the analyst.

DOI: 10.4324/9781003266303-22

Erotic, eroticized, perverse transference   187

Etchegoyen (1978, 2009) defines **perverse transference** as the attempt, with the use of eroticization, by the patient (and I would here add 'or by the parents of the patient') to 'pervert the transferential link, putting the abilities of the analyst to the test'. This implies an undercurrent which impregnates the analytic situation. H. Etchegoyen highlights the technical problems that the ideology of the patient creates when they use perverse transference defensively. Lies and deceit are present and can be detected by the intuition of the analyst, or they could have emotions with a certain countertransferential confusion as they do not coincide with their ethics. Perverse transference is very different in adults and children: in adults it is surreptitious, appears to be more encrypted and we are obliged to look for it.

Loving and affectionate transference are clinical manifestations which belong to a healthier and more mature emotional development.

We must not overlook here the Field Theory that M. & W. Baranger describe in their seminal work 'The Analytic Situation as a Dynamic Field' (1961–1962: 3–54) which expands on the intrapsychic and the intersubjective. According to Bernardi (2009: 200), 'The conception of the dynamic field was essentially a theoretical-technical conception of clinical practice. It sought to conceptualise the central phenomena of analysis, understood to be the profound meeting of two intensely engaged subjectivities in the task of causing the psychic transformation of the analysand. The idea of the dynamic field offered up a new context which allowed for the linking of general concepts of psychoanalysis, such as transference, countertransference, resistance, interpretation, etc. with the phenomena of concrete psychoanalytic experience'. She goes on to explain that, 'in the encounter, new structures, unconscious and shared fantasies which are the product of the interplay of reciprocal identifications between patient and analyst emerge'. In that sense and accepting the concept, the dynamic field includes an erotic field. Guignard (2020) emphasized that the infantile in the analyst or the patient can also coexist in the dynamic field.

The consultation itself evokes emotional responses in the analyst in spite of their internal frame, their theories and their attentive openness. There are surely infantile and/or narcissistic aspects of the analyst that can appear. There is a need, as Etchegoyen (1986) would say, to connect with the frame and with the contract of an unusual asymmetric relationship.

I believe that, in the meeting with the parents, a situation unique to child analysis, we may think of different fields where the situation becomes more complicated, the characters become more numerous and the fantasies are transformed generating the dynamic of the field.

The different types of transference will appear in the process and will have a specific dynamic and mobility, taking into account that the characteristic of child sexuality is perverse-polymorphous, as defined by Freud, or perverse or polymorphous according to Meltzer.

188 *N. Graciela Kohen de Abdala*

Clinical case

In the psychoanalytic process with a child, the appearance of erotic transference, and especially transference eroticized by the level of acting of the patient, is a permanent threat to the evolution of the analysis and is a technical challenge for the analyst who must carry out an elaboration process which runs between the countertransferential impacts and the possibility to play, act and interpret.

Loving transference facilitates the relationship with the analyst but, when it appears or is transformed into a search for at times impulsive, reiterative physical contact, the play is stopped. In this case, the objective appears to be only the physical relationship with the analyst, and we are faced with a situation of eroticized transference.

'Pablo', age four, is the second child of a young, middle class family with a very active social life. He was brought for the consultation by his parents. They were worried because Pablo had had some episodes of vomiting and dizziness with no apparent medical basis. He then started sucking his thumb and entered a state of isolation from which it was difficult to get him out.

A few days before the consultation, the boy's older sister told their mother Pablo had told her that, when the parents went out for the night, the maid put Pablo to sleep with her 'meme' (breast). The parents reacted in very different ways to the comment: the father didn't believe it, saying 'It can't be true', while the mother spoke to the (foreign) maid who confirmed the incident saying, 'I treated him like a son'.

The central characteristic of the first interviews with the patient was the intense erotic transference which developed, and which remained for most of the analytic process. Then, and through the process, it intensified and is an example of an eroticized transference.

In the first hour of play, Pablo asked me if I could draw him a 'little giraffe' to which he added two balls, one on the mouth and the other on the head. Then, at a manic pace, he lay down on the couch and he placed a ball from the box of toys in his mouth. In the drawing it is possible to see this double inscription: on the mouth, the ball-breast, and at the mental level, where the ball represents the fantasized and ever-present breast. The intensity of the fantasy, which seemingly occupied all his mental space, was reaffirmed when Pablo also stuck the ball in his mouth in the session. After that, he went over to the small sink in the consulting room and drank water straight from the tap (Figure 11.1).

In my clinical experience, if at the end of the hour of play the child asks, 'When am I coming back?' and/or 'How many times am I going to come?' this as an indication of the start of a positive transferential relationship, with an awareness of the illness. It is the clear request for help to an analyst who offered space, time and a different way of listening.

The Bionian model of the pre-conception combined with a realization, results in a conception, which will always have to do with an emotional

Erotic, eroticized, perverse transference 189

Figure 11.1 'Little Giraffe'.

experience of satisfaction. This situation is such that, if there is analytic availability and disposition, and if the child accepts the necessity to connect with a new object, coming together will be achieved.

Extrapolating this concept to the clinical context and, specifically, regarding erotic transference, I was able to observe that the patient requests to be understood, but also to repeat with the therapist the sexual satisfaction he underwent. Money-Kyrle thought that the child is innately predisposed to knowing the truth and that, if distress exists in bringing this knowledge about, it is mainly emotional.

The question of 'when will I return?' condenses the need for help, the desire to clarify a truth, and perhaps the child's recognition that this analyst-patient bond will be possible. The meeting with the analyst will allow the child to unfurl their repetition, but with the possibility of a different resolution. Therefore, with an analytic attitude, an attempt can be made to mitigate the child's anguish and consequent posttraumatic symptomatology. The paradox is that the traumatic situation must emerge into the transference in order to be analysed and, at the same time, it generates in us an emotional storm which I describe in the clinical material.

The symptom, which at first was psychosomatic, transformed into a manifestation of the 'autistic enclave' (Houzel, 1993). It evoked Klein's conceptions of the experience of fusion, of unity with the mother and of security, which characterises prenatal life. It is represented here in the scene the parents related in which the patient lies down in the foetal position with his thumb in his mouth.

These manifestations represent an attempt to recreate a narcissistic union with the object–mother which in phantasy will protect the child and isolate him from the real situation of violent eroticization which amounted to abuse.

It is worth noting not only the abuse of the maid, but also a family environment which lacked necessary safeguards. On top of the trauma, we must add the boy's prior brusque weaning process as a result of the mother's third pregnancy. That is to say, the trauma magnified certain characteristics of Pablo's personality towards oral fixation. Furthermore, there were also careless situations concerning the parents' intimacy with respect to the children observing on a number of occasions the sex acts of their parents. Certain habits – such as the father wandering around the house in full view of the children while wearing only his pyjama top and exhibiting his genitals in a somewhat blasé way – created a very eroticized family environment with a lack of limits in the necessary child–adult asymmetry.

An important technical problem arises when an analyst meets a child who is so eroticized. The intense eroticization in the transference implies that the analyst must frustrate the attempt at satisfaction. There is a difficult balance aimed at not stimulating the development of a negative transference which in turn, when it appears, must be interpreted and differentiated. That is to say, the acting out of the repetition in the search for the eroticising object must not be allowed. At the same time, the analyst needs to be careful not to become a rejecting and persecutory object for the patient. From my point of view, this represents the greatest difficulty – and a permanent one – in the analysis of eroticized transference.

Erotic, eroticized, perverse transference 191

The person of the analyst

From a post-Kleinian perspective, the figure of the analyst will be linked at times both to the maternal figure as well as the paternal or fraternal one. It is not necessary to take into account the sex or gender of the analyst. Configurations and characters of the internal world are transferred in the transference–countertransference context. In psychoanalytic practice with children, the parents often evaluate who to consult. The gender of the analyst may be one of the factors considered. The choice will depend on different factors such as the gender or sexuality of the patient, their history, the conflictive element, the symptoms, the traumatic situation, age and empathy. I believe that the person of the analyst themselves could introduce a different tendency at the start of the analysis – speaking both in general and specifically – concerning the topic chosen for transmission.

In some cases, before I make a decision regarding analytic treatment, I make a diagnosis based on play hours and drawings. With the information gleaned, I give feedback to the parents and then to the child.

Case 'Pablo'

In the first play hour, Pablo takes two lions and brings them together saying that they are giving each other 'a little kiss'.

A: Who are they?
P: Mum and dad.
A: And what are you doing?
P: I'm biting my willy.

I believe that this expression refers to oral rage and to the identification between his penis and that of his father, self-mutilations which appear in the identification with the masochistic object. I associated it with the moment in which 'Rita' fears biting off her own *butzen* as punishment for castrating the father.

Fairbairn (1946/1996) notes that in the adult, libido can deviate from the genital to the mouth, in children libido can prematurely take the reverse path, from mouth to genital, if the breast-baby experience is compromised by situations of frustration. This particular deviation is associated with hysterical pathology and is common in childhood masturbation.

H. Rosenfeld (1987: 287) states: 'When the eroticisation with the breast is accompanied with strong erotic sensations, there could be a confusion between the nipple and the penis, a depreciation of the functional role of the breast and delirious fantasies (in psychotic cases) of a sexual relationship with the mother'.

During Pablo's psychodiagnostic evaluation the primal scene was personified in a number of sequences: when he hit two blackboard dusters 'which get the dust out' hard. Also, while trying to stick two markers together (one blue and the other red) and the lion with the lioness who were 'in love' and who were kissing each other. This was perhaps the expression of a response when faced with the pain and the anger of being, on the one hand, excluded while, on the other, being exposed without the necessary safeguards to excessive excitement. The defences were manic in the presence of the subjugation of his links in the primal scene. The violent necessity to open the door of the consulting room, shouting 'stop giving little kisses to each other', or the desire to 'pishar' (urinate) in the consulting room itself – evocative of the primal scene – were expressions of an overwhelming emotional state.

In the same diagnostic session, Pablo took a baby's bottle and gave it to a doll while laughing and touching the 'little hole'. He continued with the game until his body started to shake. I thought that the excitement originated in the confusion between the oral and the genital, which are so close in early states. When he said, 'I want to cut up glazed paper!' he seemed to be crying out for limits that would help him to calm down.

Again, in that same play hour, Pablo lay down on the couch and asked me if there was a 'little blanket'. He touched his penis and said to me: 'I'm dreaming of a little blanket', 'I'm very tired'. He seemed to be able to connect with the exhaustion that he was experiencing as a result of this unparalleled struggle; it was the desire for a little blanket that would protect him and cover him, and his own excitement.

Ferro (1999) describes the session as a realization of a dream; this scene, has the sensation of a nightmare. A short time later, Pablo left the consultation room and went towards the waiting room, indicating the persecutory anxiety turned the consulting room into a dangerous place. This seemed to be a repetition of his fear and excitement at having to stay alone with the analyst, just as he had with the maid. Acting blocked him off from a chain of displacements which would have helped him towards symbolization.

I believe that my gender perhaps allowed for the quick staging of this traumatic situation. The appearance of the traumatic situation challenges the analyst whose presence is composed of the real figure and their counter-transference, which becomes apparent in their interpretations and signaling.

Following the diagnostic meeting, Pablo started three weekly sessions. Even though a positive transference was present to some extent – he was talking and playing calmly – his play was invaded by eroticization. Pablo tried to lift up my skirt and climbed unexpectedly up on my lap, in an effort to touch my breasts.

Resistance to hearing an interpretation, via shouting to get me to 'shut up', was frequent. Negative transference was expressed openly. He destroyed his box or his toys, escaped from the consulting room. He tried to kick me or refused to come to the session.

In some sessions, Pablo escaped from the consulting room and threw himself onto the rug of the waiting room. Where, with his thumb in his mouth, he took up the foetal position. My interpretation of his necessity to be a baby united with his mother in order to feel safe when faced with the fear of being left alone with me (as with the maid) were, sometimes calming and he could return to the consulting room.

Erotic, eroticized, perverse transference   193

In a session when his father brought him in his arms, Pablo lunged towards the analyst whom he wanted to kiss and touch. He shouted, 'I want to be a baby, because only babies can be breastfed! I only want to be breastfed; I did it with María [the maid] when I was three!'

A: You also want to do it with me. You are afraid of growing up; being weaned is as if growing up meant being left alone. (The father was present.)
P: I hate growing up, because only babies can be breastfed.

In spite of limits being clearly expressed by the analyst, Pablo's insistent efforts showed his overwhelming anxiety when faced with separation. He attempted to recreate what had calmed him down previously. I believe that, in his acting, he was trying to recreate the ultimately traumatic scene as a communication to be interpreted.

Note should be made of the father as witness here. He had tried to deny the possibility of there having been abuse in the first place. It was as if Pablo was asking for action or limits from a father, who instead was a model of competition and hyperactivity, focused expressly on his professional career.

When this incident happened, I decided to add two piñata balloons to the box of toys. They were big and strong, and the patient filled them with water and put a knot in them in such a way that they clearly represented two breasts which he began to play with. Sometimes he sucked them or rubbed his face between them.

In a session before the separation caused by holidays, the analyst and the patient played hide and seek. He became very excited when each of us found the other. The situation intensified in that maximum eroticization presented itself. Pablo asked me to turn around and he masturbated. This was the first time this had happened to me. I was very troubled by the expression of an intense projection of exhibition at a traumatic level.

When Pablo finished masturbating, my first reaction was of 'distracting' him, trying to change the atmosphere of the session. So, I invited him to play at the table. Pablo chose to play dominos, possibly making a reference to how to 'dominate' his sexual impulses. Eroticized transference was repeated in the link producing in the analyst's countertransferential sensations of perplexity from which she rescued herself by thinking interpretatively.

When Pablo calmed down and I recovered my composure, I interpreted for him: 'You wanted to show me how alone you could feel because of my holidays, like when mum and dad go off on their own and you think how you can calm yourself'.

The material gives an understanding of the mechanism of projective identification. I was confused and felt paralyzed. I had to compose myself in order to be able to think about the interpretation and play as a means of getting out of the acting that had been triggered.

194   *N. Graciela Kohen de Abdala*

Meltzer (1968: 67), refers to this type of masturbation – the rubbing-penetrating type – as 'associated with the problems of possession and manic reparation, and related to sadism and projective identification'. Rosenfeld (1987: 288) concurs that, 'erotic transference is closely linked to projective identification'.

There was also a sadistic element in the acting that removed the analyst 'from their support role, possibly as a result of the frustration or envy of the patient' (Meltzer, 1997: 68). In children who have disturbed symbolization, great care must be taken in play, action and interpretation. Meltzer, (1997: 311), talks about the narcissistic core which is hidden behind this (eroticized) resistance, but also the importance of 'the person of the analyst' and of the countertransferential handling of these intense anxieties.

Eroticized transference can lead to patient or analyst acting out, which destroys the analysis. The guilt feelings which arise in children who are abused augment symptoms of self-aggression and isolation. Pablo threw the ball to the ceiling and let it hit him, even trying to hit himself off the ceiling (which is lower in one part of the consulting room). He threw himself onto the couch and asked, 'if you breathe when you have fainted'. I answered, 'Yes'.

He then asked what the analyst would do if he or the doll (Barbie, naked) threw themselves out the window. I answered that I wouldn't let him do such a thing and that what he was thinking – such as when he thought of or felt the desire for naked women – was neither as bad as he thought, nor should he kill himself for that, or punish himself by banging his head.

Pablo went to the sink in the consulting room and wet his head. I interpret that he wanted to 'cool down' his head when his thoughts became a little hot and angry. In the next session, Pablo drew a picture of me naked and told me that he dreamt of me like this, asking if he fainted whether I would.... 'Sprinkle some drops of water on me or give me a kiss?' He asked me to sprinkle his head with water and then he wet his head again.

We can also speculate that the two breasts represent eyes which graphically plot his attentive gaze but are also eyes which look and have paranoid aspects which appear in his fantasies. Child sexuality is seen in the polymorphous-perverse vignette (Figure 11.2).

Nearly two years into analysis, Pablo told me that he wasn't doing well at school and that he thought that he was a 'bad boy'. He said that 'the maid takes notice of me because I treat her as a tyrant' and also that he had felt 'a bad taste in the mouth'. He picked up a bottle of glue and squeezed hard, putting some onto a sheet of paper. I explained that he wanted to throw up the idea, like when he got sick, and punish himself because he believed that he had done something wrong, but that it is the adults who have to say 'no' to a baby tyrant.

Erotic, eroticized, perverse transference 195

Figure 11.2 'Dreaming of the Psychoanalyst'.

The symptomatology, added to the drawing, in this period was a learning disorder. In one of the last sessions before Pablo's parents decided to finish the analysis, Pablo suggested we play mother and father, explaining that 'we take great care of our children'. The oedipal elaboration was present with a weaker impression from the traumatic situation. A greater symbolic capacity was evident, as when Pablo said, 'When I grow up, I'm going to be a kisser'.

Summary

In presenting a clinical case, the author examines the erotic, eroticized and perverse transferences which appears in child psychoanalysis. This takes place both with the children in treatment as well as in the relationship with the parents of the patients.

In the case mentioned, we can observe how child sexuality, impacted by situations of abuse or marked by a sexuality that is not the child's own, appear during the diagnostic or psychoanalytic process in verbalization or in play.

Unlike adult sexuality – which Meltzer describes as modest, humble, private and lacking exhibitionist tendencies – child sexuality is perverse and polymorphous and reappears strongly during analysis.

The frame, analytic space, the analytic attitude and the availability of the analyst are reconsidered as factors which allow for the unfurling of the various transferences. The appearance of eroticized transference impacts the countertransference of the analyst. Considering this allows the analyst to create new contexts which will not satisfy the repetition that the patient is set on.

During the process, an important technical problem arose as the intense eroticization in the transference forced the analyst to be a frustrating object. This is a difficult balancing act, which ideally does not result in the development of negative transference, or where the analyst becomes an object that rejects or persecutes. This is the greatest difficulty, and a permanent one, that presents itself in eroticized transference. When faced with this, the analyst must resort to observation, play and, principally, interpretation in order to facilitate the elaboration of the conflict.

Bibliography

Baranger, W., & Baranger, M. (1961–1962). La situación analítica como campo dinámico. *Revista Uruguaya de Psicoanálisis*, *IV*, 13–54.

Bernardi, .B. . (1998). Un modo de pensar la clínica. Vigencia y perspectiva del enfoque de W. y M. Baranger. Revista de Psicoanálisis. Nuevos Desarrollos.

Bolognini, S. (1994). Transference: Erotized, erotic, loving, affectionate. *International Journal of Psycho-Analysis*, *75*, 73–86.

Etchegoyen, R.H. (1978). Some thoughts on transference perversion. *International Journal of Psycho-Analysis*, *59*, 45–53.

Etchegoyen, R.H. (2009). Perversión de transferencia. *En Los fundamentos de la técnica psicoanalítica*, pp. 220–235. Buenos Aires: Amorrortu.

Fairbain, W.R.D. (1946/1996). Relaciones objetales y estructura dinámica (1946), en Estudio psicoanalítico de la personalidad. Hormé: Buenos Aires.

Ferro, A. (1999). The Bi-Personal Field: Experiences in Child Analysis. London: Routledge.

Houzel, D. (1993). Los enclaves autistas en el psicoanálisis de niños. *Revista de Psicoanálisis con Niños y Adolescentes*, N° 5, p. 97–115. Buenos Aires.

Meltzer, D. (1997). Basamento narcisístico de la transferencia erótica. *Sinceridad y Otras Obras Escogidas*. Buenos Aires: Ed. Spatia.

Meltzer, D. (1968). *El Proceso Psicoanalítico*. Buenos Aires: Ed. Hormé.

Rosenfeld, H. (1987). *Impasse e Interpretación*. Madrid: Tecnipublicaciones S.A.

Editor's Introduction to:
A special boy: melancholic terrors of awakening the erotic man

Cameron introduces himself to his analyst, saying: 'I've come to see you because I'm still a virgin'. The erotic to be braved by patient and analyst in this chapter involves the meanings of stepping definitively into sexuality in the shadow of Cameron's mother's death. Well into treatment Cameron becomes obsessed with a fantasy of having done permanent damage to his face by 'popping a zit'. Following this period, poignant material emerges as Cameron encounters some baby mice abandoned by their mother. He is in fantasy either the abandoned, dying mice or the murderer and abandoner of his dying mother. The confusion regarding 'who is whom?' is palpable. Drew Tillotson understands his patient's sexual inhibition as fraught with the generational shift in 'killing the older generation', when in fact there is a real death too near.

A sub-theme of this chapter is the bravery that is required for an adolescent to come out as gay. I have written elsewhere about this issue (Brady, 2011) and the complications for adolescents who come out late and feel they have missed out on a period of experimentation that other teenagers have had. Alternately, it is not without complications to come out earlier and sometimes experience rejections based on other teens' discomfort and uncertainty about their own sexual orientation. Additionally, Tillotson tells us this adolescent's coming out was under the horrific shadow of the AIDS epidemic, lending an added pall on sexuality for this young person to grapple with.

Reference

Brady, M.T. (2011). "Sometimes we are prejudiced against ourselves": Internalized and external homophobia in the treatment of an adolescent boy. *Contemporary Psychoanalysis*, 47(4), 458–479

DOI: 10.4324/9781003266303-23

12 A special boy: melancholic terrors of awakening the erotic man

Drew Tillotson

Beginnings

'I've come to see you because I'm still a virgin'. Cameron looked at me searchingly in silence. 'I'm not exactly sure why I'm still a virgin, I have some sense of it, but really know I can't figure this one out on my own. He paused as I took this in. 'And I understand you have some expertise in sexuality'.

As we continued, I sensed a kind of precocity you see in young children, not a young man of 20 years. His manner had some demand in it, and it touched me because I gleaned that underneath there was fragility. Yet my first reverie was striking: I found myself looking intently at Cameron's face wondering what he would look like when he reached 40 years. Cameron was tall and lanky, handsome, with dark brown eyes that spoke an intensity. He looked boyish for his age: more high school student than college graduate. But I was to eventually learn there were layers of meaning in his boyishness. It became apparent that his sincere anxiety about being a virgin was deeply felt. He'd reached a crossroads where the pressures of adulthood were in conflict with what I was to discover was a wish to remain a boy; at least that was what I came to understand later.

Cameron was a self-described 'precocious' child. He began kindergarten early, and was gifted in academics and music. He skipped 2nd grade entirely. His mother and father were both highly successful professionals. His only sibling was a younger sister. For much of his early life, he was under the care of a nanny who cared for the children until they were both into adolescence. He grew very attached to her.

While talented academically, Cameron described a childhood and early adolescence filled with social isolation and loneliness. He preferred to play alone, and said he had 'no real relationship' with his younger sister. His mother was acclaimed in her field, and traveled frequently to give presentations. Cameron described his father, also a successful busy professional, as more reachable and available, the parent he and his sister sought out '*if we got scared in the middle of the night*'. Yet he also described his father as somewhat passive, kind and acquiescent. Cameron said his relationship to

DOI: 10.4324/9781003266303-24

his father felt 'similar to a sibling'. I wondered if this foreshadowed a competitive sibling transference with me.

He fondly recalled family vacations, but was aware his parents were intensely preoccupied with advancing professionally. Their daily family routine was to have dinner together, then his parents would go off to work in their respective home offices. His sister went to her room to play, and he would read or watch television by himself. He saw his mother as more preoccupied with her work than his father, with periodic 'spot-lit interest' in the family usually around holidays and vacations.

Cameron felt awkward around his peers. At 14 he became extremely depressed, to the point where he considered suicide. At 15 he attended an afterschool drama program for teenagers that helped with his shyness, and started to make friends and gain social skills he felt he lacked. His difficulties, in part, arose from a dawning awareness of his attraction to other boys. Depressive cycles also emerged due to being bored with high school, which I considered as a potential defense against his dawning sexuality. He'd do his homework while in class because he was bored by lectures, which eventually led to leaving campus for home at lunch then not returning for afternoon classes. In response, his parents found a private boarding school for academically advanced students a few hours away where he spent his senior year.

Cameron was accepted to a prominent university across the country. One month before he was to leave for school his mother was diagnosed with a serious form of cancer. She insisted Cameron continue with his plans to go to university. His mother's condition worsened during his four years away, and she died a few days after his graduation.

At the beginning of treatment, Cameron was preoccupied with his 'halcyon' days at university. He worried his former classmates were moving on with their lives, having relationships, developing careers and leaving him behind. He was terrified to initiate intimate contact with men and preoccupied with being a virgin. He felt sexually naive, and unappealing physically: he described bodily distortions, a feeling his chest was 'too concave' and feeling overweight, when he was slender and of average proportions.

Early in treatment I sensed that I was not an individual with a separate mind for Cameron. I came to feel some of what he might have felt in his early life with his parents: like a narcissistic extension of his mind. My office and mind were places to discharge his fears and fantasies, not to engage in them with me. He was unfulfilled in work and ashamed of being 'underemployed'. He'd held a series of day jobs, then secured a better position as a technical writer though he wished to be a creative writer. There was no movement in developing romantic relationships. He spoke about wanting to feel safe with a man before becoming romantically and sexually involved. Cameron increased from once to three times a week sessions over the course of three years. I eventually suggested a fourth session and using the couch. He agreed, saying he wanted to 'get more to the bottom of things'.

Analysis: the emergence of the erotic

Soon after starting on the couch, his transference became more complex and heated. Cameron started becoming more concerned about how I saw him, and what I was thinking about him. He made statements like 'I know what *you* feel about this' and 'I know what *you* think'. At one point I had to cancel some sessions with short notice to travel for a family emergency. Although I never disclosed the reason for these cancellations, Cameron sensed some distress in me, and expressed concern for my welfare by voicemail. This made me aware I was becoming more real to him and that he had developed more complex affection for me.

Cameron started to more openly express his upset in response to my interpretations. Soon after starting his couch work, I moved to a significantly larger and nicer office, and invested more in its décor. This aroused complicated feelings and fantasies for Cameron. During his first hour in the new office, he mentioned my 'moving up in the world, to the world of fancy analysts'. I explored the hypothesis that my move activated Oedipal issues of competition with my perceived success versus the pace of movement in his own life. 'I think you're very angry at me right now for moving, and this disruption', I ventured. Cameron paused for a bit: 'yes, it's possible … but it's probably because I don't want to have these doubts. I'm upset when it feels like we're having analysis to talk about how I *feel* about the analysis, like a self-contained unnecessary. This move is *very much* on my mind'. 'Yes, I can see that. It's placed our relationship front and center … it forces you to contend with changes I make that impact you'. He said quickly, 'yes, but this relationship is still in a box. There's no shared life experience, it would be *inappropriate* for overlap. I want relationships that aren't in a box. So isn't there something fucked up about investing in this? It's not my goal to get closer to my *analyst* than to anyone in the world!'

I thought about his envy: he couldn't allow himself to enjoy the new office with me. With my office move, dependence and competition were catalyzed. I also started to notice an erotic tinge in the air, a feeling of '*I hate it that I love and need you*', along with burgeoning curiosity about my private life.

A bit later in the hour, he grew more irritable: 'You have to pay for this new larger office with nice stuff in it. I find it increasingly hard to bear concessions you've made for me with a lower fee that lets me afford analysis. What I see around me here is a desire for something more deluxe. *I'm* not deluxe. But at the same time, I'm not deserving of concessions, there are people struggling more than me for whom you could make concessions. I'm out of place'. I said, 'so there really are multiple layers to this. I could feel your growing irritation and anxiety after the move, but I hadn't put it together until lately, and now it's on the table between us'. Cameron was silent, then said 'I think I'm more aware of the idea of your other patients. I know I'm not your only patient, but in your old office space, I felt like the *anchor* tenant. In some ways, I felt that place was all about me. Other people had come and gone in that office. *This* move feels like that place was no longer good enough for you, but it was still good enough for me. In a way, I feel you're always trying to get away from me. Like when I see all this, you're looking to the day when there are no discount patients, *only* wealthy full-fee ones. Part of me feels it's what you want, so let's just end it now'. I paused: 'you sound afraid I'll leave you behind, or that I want to'. 'Or that you'll resent me', he shot back, 'it seems you have a lot of ambition, that you always want more, and I think it's true that there are similarities between us. *I* want more – but it's my goal to stop feeling that way, to feel content with what I have, to not *need* more!' I felt he was saying to himself, '*don't change, don't grow up, stay pre-oedipal! Don't develop more to be able to pay more/play more*'.

Cameron gradually showed increased curiosity about my personal life, and eventually my romantic and sexual life. He inquired about where I lived, who I lived with, if I was married, divorced or single. He commented on and combed through artwork on my walls and objects on my desk and shelves for clues about my personal life. In one session he said he imagined I lost my virginity in high school, that I 'didn't hold back', and likely was 'very disinhibited sexually'. This was a new tightrope for me to traverse with Cameron, a tectonic shift in our relationship that left me feeling a lot more pressure. I tried to explore his curiosity about me without shaming him or reverting to silence while at times feeling on the spot or awkward about his frankness.

I also noticed I was growing fond of Cameron, and looked forward to our sessions. I'd been touched in the very first session with his precocity. He'd struck me as the boy in the front row of the class in grade school, the first one to put his hand up when the teacher asked questions. I thought he was like an adorable little boy who wants to engage vivaciously on all kinds of topics. Maybe I had wanted to be that boy myself when I was little? Clearly something about the transference-countertranference evoked a warmth in me, a desire to help this lost little guy whose mother died, who had a lot of promise, but no clear direction in his life. Even in heated moments when he might be critical of me or irritated, I didn't get annoyed. Rather, I thought he was using me in various ways in transference, and did not feel destroyed by his aggression (Winnicott, 1969). The eroticism felt more like 'a vitalization of the clinical situation – a libidinal force field … an expanded meaning of transference-countertransference, where both patient and analyst engage their erotic energies and where this engagement is not specific to (though it may include) erotic desire for the other' (Elise, 2019: 15).

During this time, he told me about a significant romantic and erotic rejection, a memory of being 16 and meeting an older teenager known as a 'bad boy' one summer when he and some friends went away for the weekend together. Cameron said they were on a beach and had made a bonfire: 'He put his hand on my leg', I thought '*oh gosh, I'm in love with this guy*'. He was flying off to college the next day, so I asked if he wanted to spend this last night in my cabin, and he said, '*that'd be great*'. My friend Molly who really knew him said, '*oh Cameron, for the love of God, Nate is such a jerk, don't fall for him*'. Later,

A special boy: melancholic terrors 203

Nate and I were eating in a coffee shop. He kept talking about hitting all these clubs after dinner. I said, '*we can go to clubs if you want, but I would like to spend time with you, alone*'. Then he said '*I said all that stuff to you because you were so infatuated with me and it felt good. But there's this guy with a really hot body that I'm hooking up with, so when I told you I would stay with you, I knew I would cancel. When you're older, you'll realize there's no such thing as love – there's only sex*'. As if he was saying '*I knew I would cancel – that was part of the fun for me*'. I was prepared to have my first sexual experience with this guy, and he took out a butcher knife and cut me up and down. All through college that stayed very vivid, the hurt, the betrayal, my inadequacy. So when I shied away from sex, I was thinking '*I can't leave myself open to devastation again*'. And I think that's why I haven't let myself remember it, because it still really upsets me. The first guy I felt something for was the *Devil*, not just a *jerk*.

Cameron was silent for a long time. Eventually, he quietly said, 'I think what we don't talk about are important things that don't *want* to be talked about, even with your help. When I lie here and regret all the dalliances I didn't have, and spend months blaming my upbringing – and have you feed it back to me – leaving out the time the guy ripped out my heart and ate it in front of me?' Again his voice grew louder: 'It happened at the *worst* possible time. Trying to open myself up this year to sexual experiences ... the more I have experiences where guys respond favorably to me'. He stopped himself, then continued, 'I'm not saying everything we talked about with my Mother – the dinnertime conversations about AIDS – wasn't important. But this window opened at 16, just like it is here and now in my life. A voice is saying '*I've gotta have it this time, let the chips fall as they may*'. I tried at 16, and it didn't work.

There was a silence, then Cameron said, 'I hope you agree on some level that *that incident* could not be whited out'. I thought for a moment: 'maybe you haven't felt safe enough, close enough to me to open it up'. Cameron replied, 'Maybe I haven't felt *able* to open it up. For a long time I felt that he was right, I'm not good enough, anyone would pass me up for somebody better. But now I don't feel that way. I'm starting to feel closer to my sexuality, maybe more capable today than ever before, but I think how unlucky that *that* guy crossed my path and I took the bait'. He paused. 'It's not something I've wanted to talk about. But I *still* have feelings about it. I desperately wanted to white him *and* my suicidal thoughts out at 16'.

Cameron was risking and letting himself be more known to me. Along with his curiosities about my erotic life, he was beginning to form an identification with me that might allow him to see himself as capable of adult sexuality. In seeing his father as more of a 'sibling', Cameron had avoided an identificatory process with his father's sexuality, that of course involved Cameron's mother, which was too threatening to consider. I was there to be used as an object both paternal and maternal. Cameron had always idealized his mother's success to defend against relying on her for more maternal aspects, which he transferred onto his father (the parent he sought out if he got scared in the

204 *Drew Tillotson*

middle of the night), but this made his father more of a rival (sibling) for mother's love. It also explained Cameron's irritation when I moved to a larger office: his fantasies about me advancing professionally made him envious and competitive while at the same time fearful I would leave him behind in my aspirations, like his mother who – while idealized – was preoccupied with her own career aspirations. His worries about her leaving him behind were flipped into an over-idealization of her and all she achieved.

Sexuality and love objects

Coming to terms with his sexuality complicated Cameron's move from adolescence to young adulthood. He'd become hopeful about potential romantic partners only to feel crushed when perspective partners abruptly stopped returning his calls. These painful events however led to Cameron telling me more about realizing his strong attraction to boys. He spoke openly about feeling unattractive as a young teenager, saying he felt 'so ugly'. During his senior year at boarding school he developed his first 'serious crush' and realized he was gay. He chose not to come out to his parents because he worried about his mother's reaction in particular, and her comments about AIDS. As a child, Cameron was aware vast numbers of gay men were dying of AIDS because his mother spoke openly at home how some of her colleagues were dying rapidly. He didn't want her to worry about him dying.

Another layer of conflict about being gay was a desire to be like his parents: 'I wanted to live up to the model of them in *every* way, to achieve something big, to raise a family and become a good dad'. He thought he couldn't fulfill that destiny as a gay man, and his future remained 'hazy': 'I had the fantasy I couldn't come out to them until I had it all figured out, and could prove it by having a boyfriend'. When he did eventually tell them during his first year of college, he said they'd expected as much, and he was relieved. Yet, in college, he described forming crushes on close heterosexual male friends, but couldn't allow himself to form romantic attachments to openly gay men he knew.

I came to understand Cameron was using me as a developmental object: both as an erotic love interest in the transference (serving as libidinal fuel for growth) *and* as a parent figure who could serve as a non–rejecting role model, someone who could be idealized, but who was there to help.

Oedipal crisis

In 'The waning of the Oedipus Complex', Loewald emphasized that the advancement of and responsibility for one's adult life is 'in psychic reality tantamount to the murder of the parents, to the crime of parricide' (1979: 757), which elicits much guilt:

A special boy: melancholic terrors 205

Not only parental authority is destroyed by wresting authority from the parents and taking it over, but the parents, if the process were thoroughly carried out, are being destroyed as libidinal objects as well.

(p. 757)

Cameron's difficulty mourning the loss of his mother, along with a truncated-now-activated Oedipal struggle were about to come to the fore.[1] A critical juncture occurred as Cameron's capacity to be more open with me deepened. His father, who'd remarried a markedly younger woman the year prior, told Cameron of their plans to have a baby. Cameron was outraged, protesting to his father he must not have a new child with this 'new mother'. Psychically, this threatened Cameron's attempts to 'keep the *real* family together'. Subsequent analysis revealed fantasies of the new baby replacing him in the family. In sessions, he accused his father of betraying his late mother by allowing a new mother into their family. A new baby, a new family configuration would destroy the memory of his mother, forcing Cameron to mourn her loss, a mourning heretofore he had been unwilling to experience.

This time in his analysis was ultimately fruitful, and rich with dreams and fantasies. Cameron continued to cling to an undead mother object as he strove to be accomplished, sexually powerful and viable (while watching his father remarry, have a new baby and be promoted to a prominent position). He seemed able to hear interpretations about his wish to keep mother, via his fantasies of their reuniting in fame, and the possibility of keeping her alive in his mind. We explored his fantasies of not being special, and not having unique gifts of his own to develop by moving forward in his adult life. I interpreted his grief at relinquishing the powerful melancholic object tie he'd maintained for years (Freud, 1917).

Also, during this phase, Cameron became markedly worried about his appearance in relationship to his father's 'unending ability to not age'. He said his father seemed '*supernaturally* youthful' at 62. This concretely took the form of obsessing about his own receding hairline. He feared he would start looking older than his father: 'he has a full head of hair, its remarkable how youthful he looks, easily 20 years younger – everyone comments on it'.

A dream illustrated Cameron's Oedipal struggles, narcissistic defenses and vulnerabilities: 'The U.S. President was the challenger of my father, and I was in the middle of it. I was staying with the President in a vacation house. In the dream I remember disliking his policies intensely, but thinking, *"well, he's a good host, it's a nice house."* Then when it was time to leave, my father picked me up and we drove somewhere with a lot of people. Hillary Clinton was there. She was joking around with my father, seeming more real, and funny. As we walked away, I said, "Well *that* was something." My father said he'd deliberately filmed it to make her image more palatable. I was crestfallen because that's more *my* kind of thing, to come up with something clever. So here my father was doing it on a much grander scale, and I felt completely minimized. After that, we ended up back at the President's house and we confessed what we'd done. Throughout the dream, I enjoyed being in the presence of power. I woke up relieved that my father hadn't shown me up again. I don't know why I would have that dream right now'. Cameron was silent, then said, 'in the dream, my father does this incredible combination of achievements. He goes straight to the center of power, writes a script, performs in it, then treats it like *"in my spare time I've influenced the outcome of the next election."* Oh, I remember a detail – when I was back at the President's house, someone said, *"you hang out with the President? Do you stand up when he comes in?"* I said, "I don't know, let's see." I was lying on a couch, much in the position I'm in now here with you. The President walked in, I turned to the person who asked, and said, "I guess I don't."'

I said, 'here in this dream, you're very important too, as important as these powerful men you describe, the U.S. President, your father'. Cameron said, 'I think I'm *not* important, but at least I don't kowtow to those who *are* important. (*This marked a significant change in the transference: although I am still way above him (analyst/President), he does not need to kowtow.*) That's what I grew up in: having prominent people around, being casually in their midst as an inside member of the supporting cast. I don't need to stand up when people in power come in. Part of me feels it's the closest I'll get to power, to be lounging *nearby* the important figure. Part of me feels I should be powerful too, a stubbornness in me: until I command respect I'm not going to give it'. I said, 'as in the dream, the way you were with the President'. Cameron replied, 'Yes. There's a contrast in the dream: I'm hanging out with the U.S. President, then I meet up with my father. He's a differing figure in the race. I'm sitting around, but my father helps define the next President. That's more powerful than lounging nearby. I thought *"Dammit, why can't **I** put a President in place?"*'

Cameron became quiet and we sat in silence. Eventually he said 'what's hard for me is there's more than one thing going on in my life. I hate my job. I don't know where I'm headed in life, and it frightens me'. I offered, 'your anxiety seems to be about doing something as important as your father and mother did. The dream is related to fears of *not* being valuable on your *own* merits'. He replied quickly, 'yes, I don't just want to be *near* the power – I want to have it. My father gets more invitations to speak than he can accept. Awards, dinners – it couldn't be further from my life. I've no one to blame for that but myself. I don't even have the power to get the neighbor boy to return my phone call. It's humiliating. It contributes to re-evaluating how I think of myself. Maybe I'm *not* disgusting. Maybe I don't have guys at my feet, but what if I'm just *pretty good?* Maybe I'm not a top writer. Sometimes I feel lazy, like in the dream, lounging on a couch when the President walks in. I've never had to be a hard worker. I graduated summa cum laude, and friends said 'How?? You were out partying every night!!' I'd study quickly so I could go have some fun. I was a relatively privileged kid from a good family, and a relatively stable upbringing. What problems have I had that constitutes more than whining? So I lost my mother at 20, I'm not one in a million to experience that. But everyone would think that was tragic. My mother knew what she wanted in life and went for it. Yet the last time I went to her grave, I was trying to imagine what she would say to me. She'd likely say, *'Enjoy your life, enjoy the people in your life, life is to be lived and enjoyed – not turned into a battlefield where there's something always to be proved'.*

When Cameron left, I suddenly remembered the odd reverie I had in the first hour, when I imagined what he might look like at age 40. My reverie was likely related to Cameron's unconscious wish to grow up into an adulthood of his own, a time when he would be mature and freed from the bonds of conflict regarding separation from his idealized mother. The hour also poignantly captured where we'd arrived in Cameron's analysis. Strands of core conflicts within him were coming together, forming neurotic knots layered with meaning. As his first attempts at romantic and sexual love somewhat collapsed around him, he was fearful of his own value without it being attached to successful and attractive parents. The material also shows Cameron in a deeply conflicted melancholic internal relationship with his late mother (Freud, 1917), unable to fully grieve her loss, to relinquish his special place as her special boy made all the more special by her professional achievements.

The task of entering young adulthood, with talents, intelligence and adult sexual desires proved daunting. This hour described above showed Cameron's growing wishes to be unburdened by the past, to live life more fully with greater pleasure. Cameron was at a loss as to why he could not become prominent or powerful; he'd been a gifted child, and his parents were so accomplished. It is as if he believed his adult accomplishments would magically come to pass, but he was masochistically self-denigrating. He struggled to see that his fears of moving away from mother kept him preoccupied, unavailable to the present, and fearful of an erotic life. In this session and hours like it, I observed Cameron oscillation between a growing awareness of the cost of clinging to a dead–yet–alive internal mother (Freud, 1917) and regressive anxieties about moving forward with his own life and ambitions: separating from mother was tantamount to killing her (Loewald, 1979).

By acknowledging the impact of his imagined pact with his mother, Cameron started pursuing sexual and romantic impulses. A particularly significant event occurred on a date in which he let himself have safe sex with a known HIV+ man. In facing his mother's death head-on, in allowing space to grieve and reflect, Cameron commented that it was different for him 'not being a person shrink wrapped in protective mylar for the sake of my mother's memory'. He started talking about a desire to enroll in a master level writing program.

Love dangers

With the awakening of his erotic self, Cameron sought romantic connections and exciting sexual encounters to explore his potency and desirability. To his delight, he met Paul by chance at a party. They started dating and Cameron fell in love. He said he'd found a kindred spirit, 'boyish, playful, sexy' and with many similar interests. Paul's love of music revived Cameron's lost interest in composing music, which he'd done as a child. Contact with Paul further fueled already entrenched fantasies of perpetual youth and specialness. It was a dream come true: to meet another boyish man caught in the struggles of maturing into manhood, a twin that mirrored Cameron's idealized qualities. However, things between them quickly became complicated. Paul's ambivalence to deepen things with Cameron led him to confessing he'd just gotten out of a relationship and was mourning its loss. Finally, one evening while in the midst of sex with Cameron, Paul stopped and explained he was too sad about his break-up and couldn't continue to date. Cameron fell into despair, and spoke of feeling humiliated that his love was 'not enough' to break through Paul's mourning.

Soon after, in a somewhat manic retreat, Cameron foreswore dating and plunged headlong into writing a memoir: he would revive his mother's name and career by making a mark of his own. I understood it as a reaction to feeling humiliated by Paul, and a defensive identification with his mother's success; that writing about her professional prominence, was also a way to be with mother again, retreating to the past to be the special child of a special mother with whom he could spend long hours in memory. In sessions Cameron described fears of how it might be a betrayal to write about her private struggles behind the scenes of becoming 'an inspiration to all who knew her', and thought the memoir would have the gravitas of exploring his history and his mother's success in detail. But could he tell a truthful story without exposing her flaws?

During this period, I found Cameron hard to tolerate; I grew impatient with sessions that seemed largely recitations about his writing, and I felt as though he was not allowing me to be more than a spectator, a fantasized audience. Cameron spent hours excavating old family letters and videotapes of his mother's appearances while claiming he wanted to write something that would define *him*. He was very protective of the project and threatened by my interpretations that seemed to separate him from his mother. He had fantasies about becoming famous in his own right, all while reminding the world to never forget how unique his mother had been. He also spoke of some anger at her for choosing to deny her frailty, for being so remote and protected about her illness. He spoke about her dying process, that now *he* should be given recognition for what he endured. Her expectation that 'we shouldn't talk about it', not openly acknowledging her impending death robbed him of meaningful conversations with her near the end. Cameron fantasized that the world had continued on and left him behind: his Father remarried with a new baby on the way, and his sister was moving forward with her career. He said he wanted to keep the four of them together as they had been, not acknowledging his mother's death as a true change for all his family.

A *special boy: melancholic terrors* 209

The more ensconced he became in writing the book the more he resisted analysis. He believed writing was his only therapy, conducted by him, without a need for me. He resisted my attempts to help him reflect on how he was using the book as a flight from grief and a retreat from his present life and future. He reacted irritably at my attempts to make contact with him. A dream from this period details his conflict and wish to be with his mother:

> I was in an open area away from the house and initially felt good. Then there were tigers stalking me from all sides. My mother's car was there. I had to jump on top of it to get inside through the sunroof. Then somehow I got into the house using the car. The tigers followed. They got trapped in the garage. I got inside the house and my mother was there in a nightgown. It was dark. I put my head on her lap, like a baby, even making little cooing sounds. I needed to know she was there and to hold onto her. There was no talking. I remember thinking '*the tigers are in the garage, I should let the garage door open so the tigers will leave*'.

(Then, his associations): I woke up, I wasn't frightened or disappointed. In the dream it was surprising she was there. I don't think I've ever had a single dream since she died that I didn't know that she was gone. Either she was coming back from the dead, or – like the dream – I was surprised and clung onto her, because in the dream I knew it had been forever. There was also a hazy sense in the dream, '*What about Jan?*' (his father's new wife) '*Does father go back to you now, now that you're back?*' Mom's usually compliant in dreams and I'm the one who is like, '*NO! You were here first, before Jan!*' In the dream I had that feeling but Mom didn't engage with my question, '*who goes with whom, now?*' There was a sense of '*this isn't so much about my father and Jan, I'm not back here for them. This is about us, me and Mom, not about her and my father or Jan.*' In the dream I got what I wanted … comfort, to be close to her, protected from the tigers. Then I thought, '*I think I'll even be able to get rid of the tigers, I have sequestered them.*' In a vague way, the dream seems easy to understand. But in a specific way, it's elusive. Even the threatening parts of the dream are filled with references to my Mom. It's her car. Tigers are fearsome but also majestic, to be respected and feared. Similar to lions. I think of Mom as a lion, powerful, dominant, proud, the feeling of protectiveness all being the same source. An 'only my mother can protect me from my mother' kind of thing.

Cameron's perception that I was trying to separate him from his mother (me as tiger) and thus his resistance to my interpretations paralleled the Oedipal father's intrusions into his child fantasy of being an exclusive unit with his mother.

In many hours, Cameron explored the effects of writing the book, of viewing archival images of his mother. He actively sought memories of childhood which evoked complex emotions and fantasies. Without her living

210   *Drew Tillotson*

presence, Cameron was constructing not only his childhood experiences but also what he imagined his mother was thinking and feeling. During this passage of treatment Cameron gradually allowed more grief. When deep sadness emerged, he shared it with me through words and tears. When grief became overwhelming, he digressed into ruminating about what to write in the book. In softer moments he allowed me closer, and we work together more peaceably.

Catastrophic change

After several months, Cameron realized he could not write the book. He read over all he'd written, and felt he'd failed to write the book he set out to write. He'd gotten lost in how to write about his mother in a way that would befit her legacy, and masochistically reproached himself (Freud, 1917). Also, he realized there was nothing to write in the book regarding his own accomplishments. It was all about her, he'd 'disappeared' in her story, and grown weary of the project. We were then more able to talk about how the writing had been a process of attempted mourning of his mother, and he grew more interested in a romantic relationship. He'd recently met Tom through friends, they'd started to date and their affections for each other were growing. Cameron said sex with Tom was the first time in his life he wasn't intimidated or self-conscious about performance; they had a 'sexy connection without a lot of drama'. Tom was attractive, funny, sensitive and a professional 'with his own aspirations that didn't involve having to put his career above everything else', a better love object.

Cameron simultaneously explored MFA creative writing programs. Writing the memoir, while ultimately disappointing, ignited a wish to write fictional works. With this rise in libidinal energy, Cameron was energized creatively and romantically, allowing his sexual life to become more disinhibited. Concurrently, he started to think more about his life outside the shadow of a reified but deceased mother.

While welcomed, this psychic movement catalyzed a catastrophic change (Bion, 2014 [1970]) which opened a regressive pull towards guilt for separating from his late mother. On a Monday, Cameron called me in a panic and left a message asking for an earlier hour than his usual afternoon appointment. I left a message that I was full through the morning but would see him as usual after lunch. He arrived distraught and explained that over the weekend he'd noticed the beginnings of a pimple, and had picked it. Now, he said, it had become a 'crater' on his face, and was convinced he'd created a massive scar on his face forever.

Cameron was insistent about this forever crater for the following two weeks of sessions. He was unable to do much else but stare into the mirror and ruminate about how he'd ruined his face forever. It held such a powerful grip on him that at points I almost got pulled into reassuring him I couldn't detect *anything* on his face. But I realized the gradual relinquishment of his gifted

A special boy: melancholic terrors   211

child identity for one that could engage in real relationships and be imperfect (the 'crater') had catalyzed an internal catastrophe (Bion, ibid.) manifesting as a psychotic process I had not seen in him before. I was shaken by the delusional nature of this fantasy. Cameron had never before spoken like this nor been this disturbed about something outside the boundaries of consensual reality.[2]

A visit to his general practitioner loosened the certainty he held about this facial damage. His physician said he could not see what Cameron was pointing out about his face, but prescribed a mild steroid cream if blemishes got infected in the future. I suddenly remembered that near the beginning of his work with me, he'd mentioned seeing a doctor about a rash in his groin area. His doctor explained he was physically maturing, that more pubic hair was emerging along his inner thigh near his groin, and the red bumps were actually emerging hair that had become ingrown. My sudden remembrance opened my mind to the symbolic possibilities of his current dilemma. Was leaving adolescence creating concrete preoccupations with bodily phenomenon as a form of displaced anxiety about separating from mother and becoming a man able to be independent, sexual, potent with ambitions of his own? Was this a form of guilt for leaving his mother, mourning her death and moving forward?

This final clinical example is a poignant session from that juncture of Cameron's analysis. It embodies much of the hard work we were in the midst of, revealing the last vestiges of his grip onto his maternal object. It highlights his toggling between murderous guilt (Loewald, 1979) and hope. He started the hour by telling me he had invited Tom and a few of his friends for a weekend at his family's 'country house' in a bucolic setting that Cameron's family visited regularly all during his childhood:

C: I went down into the basement to get some firewood, and heard something squealing … it was a tiny baby mouse, only a few days old. I thought 'what do I do?' So I called my father. He said, 'there's nothing you can do, it needs it's mother's milk, and it will likely die'. He told me to put it back where I found it, and maybe the mother would find it. So I did. Later, we heard more squealing downstairs. We went down to look and there were three more tiny mouse babies!! It was heart rending. My father said rodents are notoriously bad mothers. So I just left them there, but I didn't sleep well. In the morning, two of them had died, one died while I was standing there, and the last one was so weak, it looked very near the end. I didn't want to leave them there to decompose, so I put the dead ones outside on the patio. But the one who was barely alive, I just couldn't put him outside, I was afraid a bird would snatch him. It was awful. I remembered from my biology class how to put a mouse out of misery – you disconnect them at the neck – so I did it. And now I've become obsessed! I feel like a murderer … I know it touches on other things for me – but I feel terrible. The one that was lingering was grasping for a nipple … I feel now like I did an injury to myself I should have been able to foresee. To let nature take its course, he would have just died within hours … the whole sad story of the orphan mouse. The weird thing is that it didn't upset me immediately. It wasn't until a few hours later it became compelling. It felt like the right thing to do. But it's been tormenting me today in an obsessive loop of recriminations, then rationale, then counter-recriminations. I say, 'the mouse was comatose almost!' Then another voice says, '*but you did it*'. These blind creatures, grappling to find their mother, making noise so she would come. But there was no mother. I don't like to jump to metaphors, but today I feel like a murderer … and this idea of Mom, yanking their life away … these were field mice. I feel like a monster. But I couldn't be their mother! I feel sad and crazy, like 'maybe you did this to be monstrous, so you could be the Monster!' I've spent the day worrying about this hideous act intended as mercy.

A: I think when you let yourself move forward with your own dreams and desires to have a romantic relationship, to pursue a writing career, you feel like a murderer … you murder your mother, you become the Monster.

C: (pauses) The little paw reaching and reaching … the agony I feel seeing the gesture.

A: The gesture was reaching for a mother who wasn't there.

C: That baby mouse had only one motivation. 'Where's mother?'

A: You can understand that. You can imagine reaching for no mother there.

C: Then why did I have to do it? Why did I do it to myself? To give myself another unpardonable crime.

A: What were your crimes, Cameron?

C: Well, popping a zit on my nose and disfiguring myself for life. Crime or no crime, it's hard for me to go through life making daily decisions without doing something I subsequently will find wretched.

(Silence)

A: Just now I was thinking of the helplessness you felt around your mother's death. And you're reaching for a mother who can't be there now.

C: Why wouldn't I just let it be, let nature take its course?

A: Maybe you felt it was the one thing you could do to help.

C: This is my Achilles heel, to be able to do something…. I couldn't bear that I couldn't do something.

A: You wanted to end her suffering … you want now to end your suffering.

C: I didn't want the baby to be eaten alive outside by a bird. I couldn't bear moving him out of a place where he was protected from predators. To my mind the mother had the sense to deliver these babies in a protected place.

A: You wanted to protect the living baby. I think you're becoming the alive man who once was the mourning baby boy.

A special boy: melancholic terrors   213

C: (pauses) I don't have residual feelings about those two dead ones ... but the one I *killed*, I don't know how to get out from under it. I have no rational explanation for why I feel so bad. I don't think I did anything bad. But I feel *bad*. I feel held hostage by this loop of regret.

A: (Pause) You weren't able to be with your mother both while she was dying, and the day of her death.

C: Yeah ... yes. But even thinking about my mother makes the violence of my act so much worse. It implies I would have wanted to reach out and break Mom's neck. I don't associate the mouse to her because up until then I associate the mouse with me. 'Where's my mother? Why won't she come and get me?' By ending the life of this last mouse baby, I had the mistaken feeling I would end the reminder of that feeling. But maybe sometimes it's painful to let nature take its course. If I was going to be merciful with the mice, I would have done it right when I found them. But waiting? Why one and not the others?

A: You had some hope that mother would return to find its baby.

C: (noticeably relaxes a bit) It's strange. It's all more upsetting in retrospect than it was when it was happening. I was scared this morning but went ahead and worked on my personal essay for the grad school application. Then I got distracted, 'Am I just a fraud? Will I not stay true to this? Today I thought 'Get a hold of yourself! You'd go on feeling like a murderer forever more'. The notion that that's plausible reminds me of the frenzy I got into over the mark on my face. It reminds me of fragility, it scares me.

A: I think taking these steps to write your entrance essay – maybe there's a kind of murder in pursuing something for yourself that is not as big as what you feel your mother and father did, and it makes you very anxious.

C: I'm anxious about failing. Recently in talking with you, I've gotten a sense of impulses to move myself forward, to be motivated by that and feel it's genuine. I'm always nervous what I'm doing is fraudulent. These feelings of nurturance and patience that I've been trying to write about. *'You just broke the neck of that adorable mouse ... you are a monster ... you are not a good person'*. I would have nursed the mice, tried to save them, I wanted to. My father said, 'You can't do it'. He would have let nature take its course. I didn't have the fortitude. I thought I was brave to end the story. But I was cowardly. Nature has to take its course.

A: And that's your crime.

C: Well, I don't know exactly. Attacking the mouse. I wanted to love it, nurse it, be its mother, but I ended its life. A seemingly small thing can become a towering mistake at a time of great anxiety ... or a transition.

A: Yes.

C: I feel I struggle more with fear than I used to. I've had rough times but it's not uncommon for me to feel scared even though I'm making strides in my life. You don't think I'm going to be scared all the time permanently? (laughs)

214   *Drew Tillotson*

A: I think this is a particularly loaded juncture. It's not a goal you're pursuing because you are special, or a duty to be larger than life. You've found something you're pursuing that's meaningful to you, something of your own out of mother's long shadow. For the first time in your life, it's based on something you've been able to hold on to. You are the little mice.

C: They're all going to be saved … they're all going to be saved.

In this material, we see Cameron's fear that he failed his mother (let her die like the baby mice). We see in the mercy killing of the last mouse baby the guilt from the crime of not being able to stay with his mother: if he moves forward and creates a life of his own, has romance and a career he has murdered mother (Loewald, 1979). He calls his father (analyst) for advice on what to do about the dying baby mouse (mother object). His father (analyst) says, there's nothing to be done, nature must take its course, he can't save or feed the dying baby. Life will move forward. We see his grappling with my interpretations, warding me off even as he takes me in, in waves of guilt, remorse and some relief. If he succeeds, will that mean he is a fraud?

Conclusion

In this chapter I focused on two periods in the analysis of 'Cameron'. The first was right after he started using the couch, when his erotic curiosity and envy regarding the analyst's fantasized erotic life and professional success came to the fore. In the second period, bodily distortions emerged during the treatment as Cameron imagined capacities of the adult male's erotic body. Identificatory processes with me as his analyst, and concomitant relinquishment of boyhood evoked deep anxiety and catastrophic repercussions (Bion, 2014 [1970]). A melancholic hold onto a powerful mother object was threatened by emerging anger and grief over her death, leaving him without purpose or creative aliveness.

Using clinical material, I illustrated how for Cameron, the psychical reorganizations of puberty were delayed, and normal developmental erotic longings were thwarted by an object identification with a dead parent, a dread of potentially lethal sexual object choice during the AIDs era, and a delayed oedipal tussle with his attractive, successful father. This psychic knot left Cameron in a *prolonged adolescence* (Schlüssel 2005); or '*frozen adolescence*' (De Mendelssohn (2001: 495); or a prolonged *emerging adulthood* (Gilmore, 2019; Miller, 2017).

Acknowledgements

I am very grateful for Mary Brady's invitation to contribute to this project, and her help in conceptualizing this chapter. I am also grateful for comments and ideas from Michael J. Diamond, Caron Harrang, Bruce Reis and Nancy Winters.

Notes

1 It is beyond the scope of this chapter to discuss at length more contemporary ideas related to Freud's Oedipus Complex as they relate to gay male development. For further exploration, see Bollas (2000), Corbett (2009), Frommer (2000), Phillips (2001, 2003).

2 Loewald (1979) writes about 'certain gifted and articulate patients' who show psychotic-like traits: … they often give one the feeling that they are struggling with basic, primary dilemmas of human life in forms and contents that seem less diluted and tempered, less qualified and overshadowed, by the ordinary familiar vicissitudes of life than is generally true of neurotic patients … in the light of our growing understanding of the separation-individuation process, of the development of subject/object differentiation from primary narcissism during the early, preoedipal stages, it is reasonable to assume that the fundamental issues by which such patients are transfixed have to do with problems of this genetic depth and antiquity. Unquestionably there is something archaic about their mentality … Just as the Oedipus complex, the neurotic core, wanes but is never actually and definitively destroyed, and rises again at different periods in life and in different shapes, so, too, that more archaic, psychotic core tends to wane but remains with us. Indeed, the Oedipus complex and its sequelae, viewed prospectively rather than retrospectively from adult life, are later versions of archaic yet enduring, indestructible life issues. (p. 769–770).

References

Bion, W.R. (2014 [1970]). Attention and interpretation: A scientific approach to insight in psycho-analysis and groups. *The Complete Works of W.R. Bion. IV*, pp. 211–330. London: Karnac Books.

Bollas, C. (2000). *Hysteria*. London & New York, NY: Routledge.

Corbett, K. (2009). *Boyhoods: Rethinking Masculinities*. New Haven, CT: Yale University Press.

De Mendelssohn, F. (2001). Building a bridge to heaven: Notes on the construction, destruction and reconstruction of the Tower of Babel. *Free Associations, 8* (3), 486–506.

Elise, D. (2019). *Creativity and the Erotic Dimensions of the Analytic Field*. New York, NY: Routledge.

Freud, S. (1917). Mourning and melancholia. *The Standard Edition of the Complete Psychological Works of Sigmund Freud, Vol. XIV* (1914–1916): *On the History of the Psycho-Analytic Movement, Papers on Metapsychology and Other Works*, 237–258.

Frommer, M.S. (2000). Offending gender: Being and wanting in male same-sex desire. *Studies in Gender and Sexuality, 1* (2), 191–206.

Gilmore, K. (2019). Is emerging adulthood a new developmental phase?. *Journal of the American Psychoanalytic Association, 67* (4), 625–653.

Loewald, H.W. (1979). The waning of the Oedipus complex. *Journal of the American Psychoanalytic Association, 27*, 751–775.

Miller, J.M. (2017). Young or emerging adulthood: A psychoanalytic view. *The Psychoanalytic Study of the Child, 70*, 8–21.

Phillips, S.H. (2001). The overstimulation of everyday life: I. New aspects of male homosexuality. *Journal of the American Psychoanalytic Association, 49* (4), 1235–1267.

Phillips, S.H. (2003). Homosexuality: Coming out of the confusion. *The International Journal of Psychoanalysis, 84* (6), 1431–1450.

Schlüssel, A. (2005). Making a political statement or refusing to grow up—Reflections on the situation of the academic youth in postwar British literature. *The American Journal of Psychoanalysis, 65*(4), 381–403.

Winnicott, D.W. (1969). The use of an object. *The International Journal of Psychoanalysis, 50*, 711–716.

Editor's Introduction to:
'Sleeping beauties': avoidance of the erotic in adolescence

As I introduce the final chapter of this volume, I also draw this book to a close. I have accompanied a variety of analyst–patient pairs in this project to offer reader/clinicians accompaniment in your own work. I feel some regret to bid the assembled cast of characters in this book, 'farewell for now'. Perhaps some consolation is to revisit one last pair – this time myself and 'Sleeping Beauty'.

This chapter presents a challenge quite opposite to that of the 'erotic field' I described in Chapter 2. Here the challenge was an extended absence of passion in the analytic field and in the patient's life. While this avoidance needed space for some time in order to consider the disillusionment that lay beneath it, I felt that at a certain point this withdrawal needed to be 'pierced'. I offer the 'Sleeping Beauty' tale as a way to play with characters in the field. I had to brave challenging my patient's rejection of me and she had to brave the ownership of her own desires.

This chapter and the previous one by Drew Tillotoson are 'brother and sister' chapters in that both explicate the avoidance of turbulence that prevents the full inhabiting of adolescence, as well as a gradual taking hold of adult passions and prerogatives.

DOI: 10.4324/9781003266303-25

13 'Sleeping beauties': avoidance of the erotic in adolescence

Mary T. Brady

Certain adolescents present to us as 'sleeping beauties', seemingly free of severe symptomatology or of the acting out characteristic of adolescence. As analysts we can be lulled to sleep by their somnolence. Seemingly not much is wrong, and yet there is an absence of passion, including in the analytic process. This chapter conveys adolescent turbulence in inverse – too hot to handle and thus slept through – sometimes requiring the analyst to eventually pierce the adolescent's somnolence.

In this chapter I discuss the fairy tale *Sleeping Beauty* as well as my clinical experience with such 'sleeping beauties'. I consider the succession process of adolescence, the psychic isolation (Brady, 2016) experienced during that phase and the splitting required to manage the conflicting desires of adolescence. My aim is to discuss normative aspects of adolescence, which can yet become entrenched and preventive of growth. Persistent and pervasive avoidance of the turbulence of adolescence constitutes a psychic retreat (Steiner, 1993) from the adolescent process. I also aim to discuss the conflicting feelings of the older generation (parents and analysts) towards adolescents.

Since the birth of psychoanalysis, analysts have used myths or tales as a way to capture and convey fundamental truths about human nature and relationships. Likewise, fairy tales have been described (Bettelheim, 1975) as providing a unique way for children to come to terms with the dilemmas of their inner worlds.[1]

Developments in analysis over recent years emphasise the nourishment of the analyst's and the patient's creativity. From an Italian Field Theory perspective, Ferro (1999) describes the use of 'narrative derivatives' to assist the growth of the mind, suggesting that a patient's comment on a fairy tale, film, etc. allows imaginative elaboration of unconscious conflicts in the patient and in the analytic field, which can lay the groundwork for more direct interpretation. The shared elaboration between patient and analyst gradually assists both minds to grow to name and handle conflicts. While the interpretation of conflict is important, the growth of the capacity to handle intense emotions and the processes of reverie in the analyst have become more central in much contemporary psychoanalytic thinking (Bion, 1962; Ogden, 1997; Ferro, 1999).

DOI: 10.4324/9781003266303-26

218   *Mary T. Brady*

I first recap the tale of *Sleeping Beauty* and then link it to the succession process of adolescence. This process occurs in the adolescent, but also reciprocally in the analyst and the parents.

Sleeping Beauty

In the Brothers Grimm's *Sleeping Beauty*, the King and Queen invite seven fairies to come to their daughter's christening and each is given a gold place setting. But alas!' a very old fairy has been forgotten'. The king invites her to be seated but is unable to furnish her gold table setting. This makes the old fairy angry. She spitefully casts a spell, 'When the princess is seventeen years old, she shall prick her finger with a spindle and–she–shall–die!'[2]

Fortunately, a young fairy comes to the rescue. She cannot 'undo what my elder sister has done: the princess shall indeed prick her finger with a spindle, but she shall not die. She shall fall into sleep that will last a hundred years. At the end of that time, a king's son will find her and awaken her'.

Despite the King's command that all spindles be burned, one old woman too deaf to hear the command continues to spin. At the age of 17 Sleeping Beauty comes upon the old woman and wants to try her hand at spinning. She does indeed prick her finger and goes to sleep for 100 years. The good fairy knows that Sleeping Beauty will be frightened when she awakens if she finds herself alone, so she casts a spell on all the others in the castle, except the King and Queen, to go to sleep. The King and Queen depart the castle and later die. An impenetrable wood springs up around the castle, and, of course, a brave, young prince learns of the prophecy. He makes his way to the castle and awakens Sleeping Beauty with a kiss. And in the end, of course, Sleeping Beauty and the Prince wed, move to the Prince's father's castle and live happily ever after.

Succession problems of adolescence

I envision *Sleeping Beauty* as capturing the succession problems of adolescence for both the new and the old generations. In order for the adolescent to attain adulthood, there must be a shift in the generations. As Loewald (1980) tells us, this involves in some sense the murder of the parents. However, I see the psychological murder of the parents as one crucial aspect, but only one aspect of the problem of the passage of generations. In the arduous process of development adolescents want to kill their parents *and* to keep them alive. The adolescent splits off his need to murder the older generation from his love for his parents. In splitting off aggressive parts they are less integrated and feel potentially more dangerous.

The splitting and idealisation fundamental to healthy development in the infant are also characteristic of adolescence. The good object/self is idealised in order to stave off anxiety and confusion. This categorical and rigid separation between good and bad can yield to a gradual reintegration of split-off aspects.

Meltzer (1973) comments that the values of the paranoid–schizoid position are gradually replaced by the values of the depressive position, and egocentricity yields to concern for loved objects in our internal and external world.

> The gradual shift in values has a sweeping effect upon judgment and the estimation in which are held the various attributes of human nature. Thus goodness, beauty, strength, and generosity replace in esteem the initial enthrallment to size, power, success and sensuality.
>
> (Meltzer, 1973: 224)

I have written elsewhere (Brady, 2016) about the physical symptoms (e.g., eating disorders, cutting, substance abuse, etc.) that can emerge in adolescence and express the unnamable physical and emotional tumult of this phase. Here I am considering a different adolescent syndrome: that in which adolescent developmental upheaval is avoided or slept through to a greater or lesser degree. Perhaps all adolescents sleep through that which they cannot deal with to some extent. I think of a late adolescent boy who treated me like a comfortable couch; I would be there when he needed me and he didn't need to think of me otherwise. If he missed a session he did not wonder what I might feel about it. I did not seem to have emerged in his mind as a person in my own right even two years into twice-weekly therapy. I pointed out that I seemed like 'background' to him. He noticed that he treated his own parents in a similar manner. He acknowledged that he had 'won the parent lottery' when he compared his patient, responsible parents with his girlfriend's rather immature mother and father.

We could imagine a range of narcissistic or aggressive reasons for a young person's inability to imagine an analyst as a separate person. But I am thinking of this late adolescent as sleeping through or forestalling the separation process. If I emerge as a separate person for him, then he is also more of a separate person – instead of asleep to any question of separation or loss.

Some adolescents may present with combinations of psychic somnolence and physical symptoms. Could we think of anorexia, for instance, as, in part, a girl's unconscious effort to weaken herself, in order to sleep through the desire to succeed mother? Weakening oneself/sleeping could prevent the physical growth into womanhood that can unconsciously be experienced as killing mother. Such a deadly symptom is surely a fraught combination of violence and protection (Rey, 1994).

Meltzer discusses the 'apprehension' (in both meanings of the word) of beauty in an anorexic patient. Consciously the patient sees the beauty of her object/ mother and the beauty in the world. But, '(I)n the persecutory component of the experience she feels the beauty to be merely a screen for the greedy and cruel fingers of the witch–mother reaching into her to snatch away her vitality and scratch away her beauty' (1973: 226). From this point of view sleep could be a girl's way to withdraw from the witch mother's hatred of her developing beauty and to preserve the beauty of self/mother in a timeless sleep.

220   *Mary T. Brady*

In the poet Anne Sexton's mordant retelling of 'Briar Rose (Sleeping Beauty)', the forgotten old fairy is described much as the above patient's 'witch mother':

> her fingers as long and thin as straws
>
> her eyes burnt by cigarettes,
>
> her uterus an empty teacup
>   (Sexton, 1971/1988: 169)

But, in Sexton's literary rendering, sleep is also submission/escape from a dangerous father:

> I was passed hand to hand
>
> Like a bowl of fruit.
>
> Each night I am nailed into place and forget who I am.
>
> Daddy?
>   (Sexton, 1971/1988: 173)

I consider the experience of 'psychic isolation' (Brady, 2016) to be characteristic of adolescence, as teenagers are often not yet ready to integrate or articulate newfound physiologic capacities and concomitant emotions and fantasies. Erikson's (1959) concept of adolescent 'moratorium' as well as Winnicott's (1965) adolescent 'doldrums' come to mind. The psychological work of adolescence is too great to be gone through in any efficient manner. The adolescent often feels cut off from his or her younger self and not yet able to see a way towards an older self.

The adolescent process cannot be sped up, so the imagery of sleeping for 100 years is apt. Bettelheim comments:

> While many fairy tales stress great deeds the heroes must perform to become themselves, 'The Sleeping Beauty' emphasizes the long, quiet concentration on oneself that is also needed. During the months before the first menstruation, and often also for some time immediately following it, girls are passive, seem sleepy, and withdraw into themselves. While no equally noticeable state heralds the coming of sexual maturity in boys, many of them experience a period of lassitude and of turning inward during puberty which equals the female experience.
>   (Bettelheim, 1975: 225)

This sleep is ultimately pierced by the development towards sexual love, but this transition involves the pain of loss of childhood. A 14-year-old boy starting his first sexual relationship told me he was afraid he would no longer love Christmas with his parents in the same way he always had.

It is familiar and convincing to consider the prick of the needle as representing the dawning awareness of sexual penetration and menstrual/reproductive functioning. This view is persuasive, but the prick with the needle also seems an unconscious association to the first prick of awareness of the desire to supplant the older generation (making the old woman irrelevant by taking over the spinning, or making parents less central by becoming sexually mature oneself).[3] While the imagery of being penetrated and bleeding is more directly relevant to female development, males are also pierced by love and loss.

Sleep, of course, is a state in which dreams occur. We could imagine Sleeping Beauty dreaming her own tale of love and loss. All of these developments take time, so the 100 years are needed before a full awakening can occur. By the end of the story Sleeping Beauty's parents are dead, she awakens to sexual love and she moves to the prince's father's palace. It was interesting to note that the Brothers Grimm have the couple move to the prince's father's palace instead of to their own castle. Perhaps this represents the late adolescent's developmental need that parents remain, while there is a fundamental change of function. Parents are killed and yet survive.

Succession problems for parents of adolescents

Sleeping Beauty begins: 'Once upon a time there lived a king and queen who were very unhappy because they had no children. But at last, a little daughter was born, and their sorrow was turned to joy' (Grimm and Grimm, 1917). The adult world (the king and queen) long for a new generation. We both provide for it (the good fairies) and resent and envy it (the old fairy). Bettelheim sees *Sleeping Beauty* as representing parents' inevitable failure to prevent their child's sexual awakening (1975: 30). Adolescents frequently make parents feel old and irrelevant as they experience themselves as discovering sexuality for the first time.

The old fairy represents the parental generation's hatred of the young for supplanting us and claiming what was once ours – budding sexuality, early promise, physical youth, etc. If parents are not willing to be sidelined to some degree, we cannot take up the promise of parenthood – to be transformed by our love for our children. The young fairy could be the aspect of the older generation that sympathises with the challenges of youth and is able to feel renewed by the cyclical process of life. The King and Queen (in part) inhabit the depressive position. The King and Queen leave the castle after Sleeping Beauty is put to sleep. Parents must leave the territory and position we have previously occupied and go in search of other ways to be ourselves. Despite their seeming power and effort, the King and Queen are not able to protect their daughter from the spell, not able to prevent the progression of generations or their own deaths. On the other hand, the King's rejection of the old fairy (forgetting her 'place') also reflects our potential to split off and deny

222   *Mary T. Brady*

ageing and envy. The older generation's inability to integrate ageing and loss could leave adolescents more fearful to face the succession of generations.

The sleeping servants surrounding Sleeping Beauty evoke the cut-off quality possible between adults and children in the face of adolescents' developing bodies. I have been struck when meeting with some parents of adolescents by how little they know about their children. This is due, in part, to the adolescent's developmentally normative withdrawal from the parents. But not only so – the adolescent's sexual development and subjective emotional states can be more than a parent wants or can bear to have contact with. Likewise, parents can experience their adolescent's changes as a portent of the loss of their youth. The parents of an adolescent boy come to mind. The mother seemed to have gone into a depressive sleep and relegated emotional contact with her son to me. The father, on the other hand, seemed stimulated by his son's adolescence and to be in a full-fledged adolescent state himself.

Aside

My interest in *Sleeping Beauty* was aroused while preparing a Discussion of a paper by Ungar (2014) entitled, 'What remains and what has changed in psychoanalysis'.[4] Ungar suggests that our theory changes in relation to changes in the culture, and that adolescents are the group most affected by rapid cultural changes. She also suggests that adolescents are more alone than ever before. I have discussed an affective sense of psychic isolation as an essential element of adolescence (Brady, 2016). It would seem that all adolescents suffer the strangeness of bodily changes somewhat alone. And yet some elements of adolescent loneliness are contemporary developments. Pressures on contemporary adolescents can leave them very little room for an inner, intimate space. Many adolescents I work with are highly scheduled and are in settings over-focused on external markers of success. Their need for a seemingly timeless sleep, which allows them to absorb their changes, is largely neglected.

The absence of intimate spaces abandons adolescents into more narcissistic formations. Much has been written (e.g., Mondzrak, 2012) suggesting a contemporary culture of narcissism. Part of this culture of narcissism is the idealisation of youth. Consequently, parents may find it harder to parent if they need to deny the loss of their own youth and the transition of generations. Generational differences and conflicts crucial to adolescent identity building may be avoided (slept through).

Ungar provides a clinical vignette of a 15-year-old girl she calls 'Griselda' who says:

> 'I don't get on well with guys – I don't have a single male friend. I don't like the places we go out to at night and I don't drink alcohol – it makes me feel bad right away and the smell of vomit in those places revolts me. I don't dare try a joint …' Ungar recommends that Griselda start analysis, 'based on the idea that she needed to be accompanied during

this adolescent process … And on the fact that she seemed to me to be too involved in the world of adults, without, as she herself said, "finding [her] place"'.

Ungar reports a session in the third year of analysis, in which Griselda (now 18) complains that her friends are not interested in her life but just stop at her house because it is convenient for nightclubs. Ungar interprets that Griselda feels it is difficult for her analyst to understand how bad she felt when faced with such changes. Griselda's 'reaction was quite violent, saying that for sure I didn't understand, that I had already passed through these moments but, as it was such a long time ago, I didn't remember how it felt' (2014: 12–13). Griselda ended this session however, noticing that her boyfriend has started to matter to her.

In the next session Griselda tells Ungar that her boyfriend has received a negative HIV test result and asks: 'can I stop using rubbers now?' Ungar replies that 'it's not just about whether you use a rubber or not' but 'that you are starting your sex life … A lot of issues come up: how you feel, the necessity of intimacy, for example' (ibid.: 13). In an irritated manner, Griselda complains she has nothing more to say: '(T)his free association thing seems just dumb. For example … we can hear the birds singing. So what?' Ungar perseveres and says, 'for example, you could try to think about what comes to mind when you hear the birdsong'. Griselda replies, 'Okay, I've thought of some stupidity: I remembered the film *Sleeping Beauty*. She was dancing in a garden in a pink princess dress and, in the film – I don't know if you saw it – there were two little birds singing, the two of them sitting on a branch, one was pink and the other was light blue'. Ungar interprets to Griselda that 'The time in which Sleeping Beauty is asleep' is similar to Griselda's life – 'a time of suffering when you realise that you are lost in the world of adults and of obligations and responsibilities'. Griselda confirms Dr. Ungar's interpretation, responding: 'How nice it would be to go to sleep and wake up having passed all the bad part. I'm not in any rush to get older, but I never imagined that something that I was really wanting to happen – like finish high school, find a boyfriend, start university – was going to cause such a mess in my life'.

I now discuss my patient, Laura, who I experienced as in a protracted avoidance of adolescent turbulence.

Laura

'Laura', aged 15, came to treatment at the recommendation of her high school counsellor, who saw her as highly needy of adults at school and out of step with her peers. Laura's parents had divorced two years earlier. When I first spoke on the phone with Laura's parents, I discussed with them whether Laura might want to come in first to meet with me to tell her story. Laura's parents felt that she would want to do so. When I met with Laura she was adamant

224   *Mary T. Brady*

that I should not meet with her parents. She seemed cynical about either my or her parents' ability to handle such a meeting in a respectful or protective manner. I acknowledged her concerns but ultimately told her I would need to meet with her parents at least once or twice to ensure that we had a working agreement that would allow the treatment to proceed.

Laura's parents did not want to meet jointly, so I met with them separately. Deep divisions, resentments and a potential to fight over the treatment were evident. Father seemed highly sceptical of treatment for Laura as he felt mother's therapy had not helped her at all and had contributed to the divorce. I thought that he was concerned I would turn his daughter against him. I emphasised the need for the treatment to be a conflict free zone so that Laura could really use it. I was dubious about this arrangement holding, but Laura remained adamant that she did not want her parents' involvement. Thankfully, the parents did not fight over the twice-weekly treatment and continued to support it over the following years. Also, thankfully, the intensity of acrimony between the parents seemed to subside over time and they seemed (to differing degrees) to be able to get on with their own lives.

Laura agreed to twice-weekly therapy grudgingly. I felt that I would need to be the one to hold the value of treatment in mind for her and that she would not risk emotional vulnerability. Early in treatment Laura acknowledged some self-destructive ideas such as a strong feeling of wanting to risk walking in front of an oncoming car. Mainly, however, she seemed quite identified with the adults at her high school and to be avoiding an adolescent process. She was frequently in roles where she had authority over other adolescents who seemed to find her uptight and controlling. She told me: 'I feel like I like people more than they like me'. My experience was that she wanted to feel chosen by me without putting herself on the line.

Despite her minimisation of the treatment, Laura remained in therapy throughout the rest of high school and wanted to continue on the phone on a once-a-week basis when she began college. We continued to meet in person when she returned home for vacations.

While we had both gone to some effort to continue to meet together, Laura continued to diminish the importance of our work. She frequently talked about practical matters, choices of classes, internships, etc. I felt somewhat bored and restricted from a more dimensional, evocative or intimate involvement.

Significant work had been done about Laura's distrust of adults, so I felt I could begin to challenge Laura's minimisation of me. However, my emotional experience was of continuing to be turned down in my invitation to more intimate involvement.[5] Meanwhile, Laura had only minimally entered into romantic relationships with men and not at all with women. Her sexual orientation did not seem evident. 'I am not going there', was her response when issues emerged in her friendships. She was a reasonable student, but often found herself bored by her course work.

I raised the idea of returning to our twice-weekly meetings, but Laura was

'Sleeping beauties'   225

unwilling. In fact, she wanted to take a break from the treatment as she had a summer internship in another state. I interpreted that she was avoiding a more direct emotional involvement with me, but did agree to the break. In our first phone session after the break, Laura cried when she heard my voice. She said that I listened to her in a way that was different from anyone else. Although she was quick to dismiss the importance of her feeling, I thought that she had had a developmental experience of doing without me, but finding that she missed me. I told Laura that while I had been willing to carry the value of our work for some time, I thought her unwillingness to see my importance to her was no longer useful to her. I said that while she frequently viewed my wish to meet more often as an effort to control her, my experience was that she often turned me down. I said I thought that this must also be how other people found her – unwilling to really enter in a relationship. I had been the King and Queen who must let her sleep, but now I felt like the Prince who must insist on her coming to life.[6]

My insistence on intimacy with Laura was followed by her gradually increasing her ability to maintain relationships with friends during conflicts, and then to her first romantic and sexual relationship with a young man. As she spoke of these wonderful and awkward moments, my memories of these times in my own life were stimulated. Although I felt that I needed to pierce my patient's sleep, (the analyst as the Prince), I also found that when Laura had found her own Prince in the external world, I had to be willing to acknowledge this development. I needed to be willing to cede the centrality of my role with Laura, but not so quickly as to leave her waking up by herself.

Discussion

Use of the characters in a fairy tale allows an analyst to play with the different roles the patient unconsciously assigns her. I felt for a time like the King and Queen who must bear the 100-year sleep of a patient who denied her own desires. Eventually I felt that I must break through this denial, penetrating the wood surrounding her, yet at a time when she was psychologically ready for me to do so.

I am not trying to suggest that a clinical situation will unfold like the text of any fairy tale, including *Sleeping Beauty*. I agree with Ferro that: '[t]he characteristic of the psychoanalytic situation is that it confronts two living texts which interreact and transform each other' (Ferro, 1999: 115). Listening to an hour like a fairy tale or a dream though, can sustain the analyst's ability to imaginatively engage with the shifting subjectivities in our patient and in our self.

Campanile distinguishes between subjectivation in adolescence – the ability to recognise and represent what one feels – from subjectivisation, which he calls the process of recognition by the subject of 'the multiplicity and relativity of the subjects that each individual has within himself'. He comments on the

226 Mary T. Brady

double sense of the term subject, particularly in adolescence, the sense of 'an author and of one who is subjugated, subjected to forces and mechanisms that he can learn to see and recognize' (Campanile, 2012: 416). My patient and I evolved from her need to be desired without having to risk desire herself, to braving ownership of her own desires. Such subjective experiences are not static but constantly evolving, as were my own subjective experiences of being with Laura. The elasticity of the fairy tale allows either the analyst in her reverie, or the patient and analyst together, to imagine a changing subjective narrative.

Feminist critiques of *Sleeping Beauty* see the tale as imparting patriarchal social norms (e.g., Semsar, 2014). In contrast, Bettelheim sees the inward turning depicted by Sleeping Beauty and the heroic quest of the Prince as together symbolising the development of a mature self. He proposes that the ability to negotiate an internal reflective space and to prove oneself in the external world are both necessary elements of adolescence. While *Sleeping Beauty* can be interpreted in this psychically bisexual manner, the cultural critique of roles allowed/imagined for girls is crucial. When choices are restricted, girls might have little chance to imagine themselves into an active, heroic character.

Likewise, what happens when there is 'a lack in cultural reverie, a sense of void' (Gonzales, 2013: 117) in gay teenagers' experience of receptivity in their family or culture? Here, the 'animating kiss' of the analyst may be needed to help imagine and enliven the developing gay adolescent's sexuality. The potential avoidance of the emotional turbulence of the adolescent process is relevant for both boys and girls, gay and straight. A genuine awakening in adolescence would involve not just joining stereotypic and proscribed cultural roles, but grappling with these roles to make them one's own or remaking them when they are oppressive.

Concluding comments

The succession of generations poses many challenges for the adolescent. I have used *Sleeping Beauty* to capture the normative adolescent 'doldrums' (Winnicott, 1965), 'moratorium' (Erikson, 1959) or sense of 'psychic isolation' (Brady, 2015, 2016). The extreme avoidance of adolescent turbulence constitutes a psychic retreat. The analyst may eventually need to wake an adolescent from such a sleep.

I have commented on the splitting that can characterise the younger and the older generations' reactions to the passage of generations. *Sleeping Beauty* affords us an opportunity to ponder many splits: desire to kill the older generation and keep us alive; envy/hatred of the younger generation and grateful appreciation of the regeneration they can afford us; sexual awakening and death; fearful apprehension of beauty and deeply appreciative apprehension of beauty; joy and grief.

The deep meanings of *Sleeping Beauty* may be best captured by Meltzer's thoughts on the 'apprehension of beauty' (1973: 225). Meltzer observes a 'failure of apprehension of beauty' in some patients, who lack a 'direct and immediate emotional response', and thus are 'deprived both of confidence in their judgement as well as in the sincerity of their interest' (ibid.: 225). He describes the touching termination of a patient who had lost his father when young:

> He was struggling to hold together within himself the joy and pain of the truth about living and not living things, of the frailty and the feebleness of life forces pitted against the malignant, which so often seemed to be favoured by the great random factor. In other words he was seeming to shift his perception of beauty from the idealized good object to the struggle itself, thus including the malign and the random, along with the good, as participants in the drama, and thus in his love of the world.
>
> (Meltzer, 1973: 226)

Sleeping Beauty offers us a reflection on the possibility of 'apprehending' (both fearing and appreciating) the beauties of the passage of generations and the passage of time, which are central to human existence.

Notes

1 See Bettelheim (1975) for the antecedent versions of the Brothers Grimm version of *Sleeping Beauty*. See also Ben-Amos (1994) for a folklorist's critique of psychoanalytic interpretations of fairy tales. I am not claiming any insight into the author's intentions, nor of the way the tale may have been interpreted when it was written. I am simply advocating the mobile use of the possible meanings of various characters in fairy tales as they lend themselves to the analyst's reverie.
2 Bettelheim makes a case for the 'curse' as referring to menstruation (1975: 232). From this point of view, Sleeping Beauty is overcome by the experience of sudden bleeding and falls into a long sleep. She is protected from premature intercourse by the wall of thorns.
3 While I see the challenge of burgeoning sexuality as crucial to the meanings of *Sleeping Beauty,* psychosexual development is intimately tied to separation issues for both adolescents and their parents. The emergence of adolescent sexuality portends the emergence of the new generation and the older generation going on towards death.
4 Presented 15 November 2014 at the San Francisco Center for Psychoanalysis.
5 There are movements towards and away from intimacy and its accompanying upheavals with many teenagers, but I experienced Laura as consistently and persistently avoidant of both angry and loving emotions. I would agree with Alvarez, that even with children (or young adults), 'chronicity itself has to be addressed' (1992: 57).
6 Alvarez notes that the 'normal mother permits and respects some degree of withdrawal on her baby's part, but she also plays, however gently *an active part* in drawing him back into interaction with her' (1992: 61). I knew that Laura had become disillusioned about intimacy when her family divided, but thought that Laura could become active in reaching towards intimacy in her life.

228 *Mary T. Brady*

References

Alvarez, A. (1992). *Live Company: Psychoanalytic Psychotherapy with Autistic, Borderline, Deprived and Abused Children.* London and New York, NY: Routledge.

Ben-Amos, D. (1994). Bettelheim among the folklorists. *Psychoanalytic Review, 81* (3), 509–535.

Bettelheim, B. (1975). *The Uses of Enchantment: The Meaning and Importance of Fairy Tales.* New York, NY: Random House.

Bion, W.R. (1962). *Learning from Experience.* London: Karnac.

Brady, M.T. (2015). 'Unjoined persons': psychic isolation in adolescence and its relation to bodily symptoms. *Journal of Child Psychotherapy, 41*(2), 179–194.

Brady, M.T. (2016). The Body in Adolescence: *Psychic Isolation and Physical Symptoms.* London and New York, NY: Routledge.

Campanile, P. (2012). "I had twenty five piercings and pink hair when …": Adolescence, transitional hysteria, and the process of subjectivization. *Psychoanalytic Quarterly, 81* (2), 401–418. 10.1002/(ISSN)2167-4086

Erikson, E. (1959). *Identity and the Life Cycle. Psychological Issues Monograph 1.* New York, NY: International Universities Press.

Ferro, A. (1999). *The Bi-Personal Field: Experiences in Child Analysis.* London: Routledge.

Gonzales, F. (2013). Another Eden: Proto–gay desire and social precocity. *Studies in Gender and Sexuality, 14*, 112–121.

Grimm, J., & Grimm, W. (1917). Sleeping Beauty. In Withers, S., Browne, H.S., & Tate, W.K. (Eds.) *The Child's World Third Reader.* New York, NY: Johnson Publishing.

Loewald, H. (1980). The waning of the Oedipus complex. *Papers on Psychoanalysis.* New Haven, CT: Yale University Press.

Meltzer, D. (1973). On the apprehension of beauty. *Contemporary Psychoanalysis, 9*, 224–229.

Mondzrak, V. (2012). Reflections on psychoanalytic technique with adolescents today: Pseudo-pseudomaturity. *International Journal of Psycho-Analysis, 93* (3), 649–666.

Ogden, T. (1997). Reverie and metaphor: Some thoughts on how I work as a psycho-analyst. *International Journal of Psycho-Analysis, 78*, 719–731.

Rey, H. (1994). Anorexia nervosa. In Magagna, J. (Ed.) *Universals of Psychoanalysis in the Treatment of Psychotic and Borderline States.* London: Free Association Books.

Semsar, S. (2014). Sleeping Beauty through the ages. *Ellipsis, 41* (31). http://scholarworks. uno.edu/ellipsis/vol41/iss1/31

Sexton, A. (1971/1988). Briar Rose (Sleeping Beauty). From 'Transformations'. In Middlebrook, D., & George, D. (Eds.) *Selected Poems of Anne Sexton.* Boston, MA: Houghton Mifflin.

Steiner, J. (1993). *Psychic Retreats: Pathological Organizations in Psychotic, Neurotic and Borderline Patients.* London and New York, NY: Routledge.

Ungar, V. (2014). What remains and what has changed in psychoanalysis. Unpublished paper presented at the 'Day with Virginia Ungar', November 15, 2014, San Francisco Center for Psychoanalysis, San Francisco, California.

Winnicott, D.W. (1965). *The Maturational Processes and the Facilitating Environment: Studies in the Theory of Emotional Development.* London: Hogarth Press/Institute of Psycho–Analysis.

Index

abandonment 89, 113, 115, 129, 130
Abel-Hirsch, N. 123
abused adolescents 38
Aciman, A. 77n6
adolescence: Eros and 153–160; frozen 214; prolonged 214; subjectivation in 225; succession problems for parents of 221–222; succession problems of 218–221
adolescents 28; bodily changes in 29–30, 33, 42; boys, adolescent 29, 129, 143; clinical material 35–37; early adolescent girls 41; erotic field 41–42; erotic insufficiency/ erotic playback 33–35; erotic transference and countertransference in treatment of 30–33; loneliness 222; moratorium 220; physical changes of 38; sexually over-stimulated adolescents 38
adult sexuality 12, 14, 19, 196, 203
affectionate transference 3, 122, 187
AIDS 198, 203, 204, 214
aliveness 3, 15, 34, 35, 50, 55, 123, 214
alpha function 37, 58, 93, 94
Alvarez, A. 8, 31, 32, 38, 42, 120, 124, 126, 148, 165, 172, 176, 227n5, 227n6
anal phase 105–106, 110, 111
analyst-and-patient-as-a group 73, 74
analyst-centered interpretation 131
analyst's role 50, 95–96
analytical field theory, erotic transference and 71–76
analytic cure 70
Analytic Engagements with Adolescents: Sex, Gender and Subversion (2018) 48–49
analytic eroticism 34, 51, 52, 54, 55
analytic relationship 34, 38, 39, 60, 68, 93, 186
Anna Freudian way of thinking 18
Anxiety 71, 88, 107, 109; castration anxiety

and love for the father 110, 113–114; separation anxiety and sexuality 111–113
apprehension of beauty 219, 226–227
arrogance and pride 21
astronomical seeing 97n3
Atkinson, S. 31, 32, 43n8
at-one-ment 57, 58, 60, 64, 65, 68–71, 123
atonement 70
attachment: romantic 204; sexuality and 52, 104
attractiveness 21
Autism Spectrum 38
autistic enclave 190
autoeroticism 105

babies: global passionateness of 11; lonely baby 114; love-life of 11
Baranger, M. 4, 123
Baranger, W. 4, 123
Barthes, R. 67–68
beauty, 'apprehension' of 219
becoming-yourself 69
Ben-Amos, D. 227n1
Bernardi, B. 187
beta elements 37, 84, 87, 93
Bettelheim, B. 220, 221, 226, 227n1, 227n2
Beyond the Pleasure Principle (1920) 123
Bick, E. 20
binocular vision in erotic field 82; analyst's role 95–96; child as an erotic resource 96–97; houses 87–90; seeing and being seen 93–95; self-portrait with crossed hands 84–87; sister, lover and wife 90–93
Bion, W.R. 13, 20, 21, 57, 60, 64, 65, 69, 70, 71, 72, 77n7, 82, 83, 95, 96, 97n4, 98n22, 98n23, 99n29, 99n31, 99n32, 123, 140, 142, 148
Bionian model 188
Bionian principle of 'transformation' 74

230 *Index*

Bion's principle of negative capability 74
bisexuality 106, 112, 116–117
Blum, H.P. 165
bodily changes in adolescents 29–30, 33, 42
The Body in Adolescence: Psychic Isolation and Physical Symptoms (2015) 48
body-mind 87
Bollas, C. 164, 165, 215n1
Bolognini, S. 3, 115, 122, 135, 164, 176, 179, 186
bond 69, 70
Bonito Oliva, A. 97
born, being 68
boundary violations, catastrophic prospect of 28
bowel movement 110, 113
boys, adolescent 29, 143
Brady, M. 73
Brady, M.T. 48–55
breast 12, 13, 20, 114, 191, 194
breastfeeding 193
Brenman-Pick, I. 165, 176, 178
'Briar Rose (Sleeping Beauty)' 228
brittle diabetes 141
Britton, R. 15, 19, 172

Campanile, P. 225
Carabba, C. 59
caregiving 85, 86, 87, 92
castration anxiety 110; and love for father 113–114
catastrophic change 142, 210–214
Celenza, A. 6
child-adult asymmetry 190
childhood, end of 29
childhood masturbation 191
childhood sexuality 84, 187, 194; history of psychoanalytic ideas on 10–14; parental objects' role, question of 21; perverse sexuality 16–19
children: as erotic resource 96–97; mother–child relationship 95, 126; nonverbal communication of 95; Oedipal child 15; Oedipal feeling of 19; over-concrete 38; perverse sexuality in 16–19; 'perverse' children 38; physically disabled children 16; post-Oedipal child 15; pre-Oedipal feeling of 19; valorization of 83
A Clinical Lesson at the Salpêtrière (painting) (1887) 63
component instincts 11, 12
confession 66
confession-forgiveness 68

conscious recognition 60, 67
conscious-unconscious relationship 93, 94, 104
Corbett, K. 215n1
Corinthian adoptive parents 18
couch, usage of 29, 32–33
countertransference responses, use of 19–21
Crapanzano, V. 19
creative machine 127
Creativity and the Erotic Dimensions of the Analytic Field (2019) 51
Cresti, R. 98n16

Davies, J.M. 14, 15, 19, 39–40
The Dead Mother (painting) 98n16
deconstruction 62, 128
defecation symptom 109
deficit 33, 52, 128
delayed Oedipal development, clinical example of 21–23
depression 21, 35, 38, 73, 107, 109, 111, 141, 159
depressive cycles 200
depressive position 13, 14, 219, 221
depressive vortex 87
developmental eroticism 52–53
diabetes and mental health 140–142
difference 66, 69, 123
Dimen, M. 42
disappointment, feelings of 130, 132
disgust 16–18
disordered sexuality 8, 16, 18
disordered sexual transferences 31–32
dissatisfaction, feeling of 156
dream elements 37
dreaming the erotic in the service of integration 122–135
Drive Theory 4
dyadic expansion of consciousness 64

early adolescent girls 41
Edwards, J. 13
ego 71
Elise, D. 34, 41, 64
emerging adulthood 214
emotional attunement 69, 123
emotional dulling 39
emotional interaction 95
emotional linking 74
emotional vulnerability 224
enigma 104
Erikson, E. 220
erogenous zones 11

Eros 51, 96, 118, 123, 153–160
The Eros of Parenthood (Noelle Oxenhandler) 51
erotic, eroticized and perverse transference in child analysis 186–187; case 191–195; clinical case 188–190; person of the analyst 191
erotic aliveness 3, 35
erotic chain 104
erotic countertransference 14, 36, 42, 49, 55
erotic deficit 33, 72
erotic desire 50, 86, 90, 91, 97, 104, 202
erotic embodiment 48–49
erotic engagement 53–54
erotic feelings 35, 48, 49, 54, 55
erotic insufficiency 26, 28, 33–35, 50, 53, 72
eroticism 34, 55; analytic 34, 51, 52, 54, 55; autoeroticism 105; developmental 52–53; maternal 34; parental 52
eroticization 73, 187, 190, 192, 193, 196
eroticized transference 10, 30, 32, 57, 60, 72, 73, 114, 115, 186, 188, 190, 193, 194, 196
erotic life 38, 41, 50, 51, 52, 55, 80, 122, 124, 125, 135, 164, 203, 207, 214
erotic playback 33–35
erotic resource, child as 96–97
erotic sufficiency 40
erotic transference 35, 42, 49, 114–115, 164–165, 176, 186, 188, 189, 194; highly explosive forces of 179; and theory of analytical field 71–76; *see also* sexuality and erotic transference
erotic transference and countertransference 14–16; in treatment of adolescents 30–33; with younger children 28
erotic 'madness' 128
erotized transference 115, 164–165
Etchegoyen, R.H. 122, 128, 135, 187
excitation 105
exhibitionism 11, 105, 111

Faimberg, H. 97n1
The Family (painting) 98n12
family romance 82
fantasmatic activity 103
father, love for 113–114
Fear of Breakdown 83
feelings 1–2; of disappointment 130, 132; of dissatisfaction 156; erotic feelings 35, 48, 49, 54, 55; incestuous feelings 38; of

inefficacy 20; Oedipal feeling of child 19; pre-Oedipal feeling of child 19; sexualisation and feeling of love 14; shared meanings and 41
Feldman, M. 165
feminine 63, 116
feminism 62
Ferrari, A.B. 42
Ferro, A. 192, 217, 225
ferrum 60–64
Field Theory 3, 4, 37, 42, 57, 102, 161, 187, 217
Fischer, W. G. 98n18
flirting 15
forgiveness 66, 91
Foucault, M. 63
Fraiberg, S. 99n25
Freud, A. 44n12
Freud, S. 8, 10, 11, 12, 13, 35, 59, 60, 61, 62, 63–64, 65, 66, 67, 74, 82–85, 96, 97n1, 98n14, 99n27, 103, 104, 115, 122, 123, 124, 134, 164, 215n1
Freudian concept of sublimation 13
Frommer, M.S. 215n1
frozen adolescence 214

Gabbard, G. 31, 32, 43n8, 164, 165, 176, 179
Gabbard, G.O. 14
gay 156, 204
gender 2, 41, 113, 191, 192
generational differences 222
'genuine' love 63
Gerrard, J. 14, 15
global passionateness of babies 11
Green, A. 20, 98n16, 104, 123, 124, 128
Green, R. 13
Green, V. 18
Greenberg, J. 127
group relationship 94
guilt-repentance 68
guilt-ridden interpretations 74

Hartmann, S. 42
Hegel, G.W. 59, 60, 65, 67
Hegel's concept of recognition 60
The History of Sexuality (1976) 63
houses 87–90
hyper-activity 115
hyperglycemia 140, 141
hypoglycemia 140

ideo-affective integration 67

232 *Index*

ignis 60–64
Imbasciati, A. 97n1
incestuous feelings 38
inefficacy, feeling of 20
infancy, Kleinian emphasis on 13
infantile sexual fantasies 103
infantile sexuality 12, 16, 103, 117; role of the mother in 104
intellectualization 48, 76
interference 83
internalization 13
intersubjectivity 69, 71
I/you split 68, 74

Jackson, E. 32–33, 53
James, W. 11
Joker (movie) 143
Jones, E. 11
Judith-and-Holofernes situation 74
juvenile onset diabetes 139

Kaës, R. 97n2, 98n13, 99n26
Ki-Duk, K. 65
kissing 12
Klauber, J. 177–178
Klein, M. 10, 12, 13, 19
Kleinian emphasis on infancy 13
Kleinian theory 12, 13, 14
Kohon, Gregorio 132
Kristeva, J. 34, 72

labile diabetes 141
Landreth, G. 142
Laplanche, J. 104
Larrain, M.E. 52
Laufer, M. 43n9, 179
Laznik, M.C. 20
Lena, F.E. 31, 43n8
libidinal co-excitation 104
Liebe, logic of 59, 66–67, 68, 76
Liebeserfahrung 75
life instinct 13, 123
Likierman, M. 12
Loewald, H. 218
Loewald, H.W. 215n2
Lombardi, R. 40, 42
loneliness 89, 154, 199, 222
López-Corvo, R. E. 97n4
love 1, 59, 75, 76; for father 113–114; 'genuine' love 63; sexualisation and feeling of 14; *see also* transference-love
love dangers 207–210
love objects, sexuality and 204

lover 90–93
love relationship 165
loving and affectionate transference 187
Lupinacci, M.A. 12, 19

Maier, C. 149n1
male body, boy's terror and fascination with 139; case example 142–145; diabetes and mental health 140–142
masculine 63
masochism 11
master–servant relationship 65–66
masturbation 84, 87, 90, 91, 92, 110, 112, 114, 191, 193, 194
maternal eroticism 34
meaning-making 83
melancholic terrors 199; catastrophic change 210–214; emergence of the erotic 201–204; love dangers 207–210; Oedipal crisis 204–207; sexuality and love objects 204
Meltzer, D. 127, 187, 194, 196, 219, 226–227
menstruation, early 35
mental coupling 84, 87
mental health, diabetes and 140–142
MFA creative writing programs 210
Molinari, E. 26, 128
mortification 69–70
mother-child relationship 95, 126
mother-infant relationship 64–65, 107
mother's role in infantile sexuality 104
mouth, kissing on 12
Moya, P. 52
Murphy Jones, E. 142

Nannini, N. 98n16
narcissism 111, 222
narcissistic deprivation, sense of 53
narcissistic economy, sexualization in 104
narcissistic egocentric Theban parents 19
narcissistic reassurance 105, 106
narrative derivatives 217
negative capability, Bion's principle of 74
new-born baby, preconception in 13
nonverbal communication of child 95
normal adult sexuality 12
normal baby 11
normal erotic transferences 10
normal sexual transferences 31–32

Object Relations theory 4
Oedipal child 15

Oedipal configuration 103
Oedipal crisis 204–207
Oedipal desire 14
Oedipal development 21–23, 106, 111
Oedipal fantasies 112–113
Oedipal feeling of child 19
Oedipus Complex 11, 31
Ogden, T.H. 2, 3, 34
Oliner, M. M. 106
oral impregnation, fantasy of 109–110
O'Shaughnessy, E. 13
otherness 11, 12, 66
over-concrete children 38
over-stimulating 32–33, 37
Oxenhandler, N. 51

pain and pleasure, link between 85
paraconscious 12
paranoid-schizoid position 13, 219
parental eroticism 52
parental objects' role, question of 21
patients and analyst 73, 74
parents' narcissism 111
Paton, I. 32
Paul, C. 52
penis 13
Person, E. 2, 30, 43n5
Person, E.S. 164
Person's definition of erotic
    transference 164
Pervasive Developmental Disorder 16
perverse-polymorphous 187
perverse sexuality 10, 16–19
perverse sexual transferences 31–32
perverse transference 187
'perverse' children 38
phallic phase 110–111
The Phenomenology of Spirit (1807) 65
Phillips, A. 12
Phillips, S.H. 215n1
physically disabled children 16
Pistiner de Cortiñas, L. 98n11
playing 154
pleasure and pain, link between 85
pleasure–unpleasure principle 103
polymorphous perversity 10–11
positive countertransference 22
post-Bionian field theory 74
post-Oedipal adult sexuality 14, 19
post-Oedipal child 15
post-Oedipal parent 15
post-Oedipal sexuality 10, 14, 16
posttraumatic symptomatology 190

preconception in new-born baby 13
pregenital bisexuality 116
pre-genital period 10
preoccupation 16, 18
pre-Oedipal feeling of child 19
pre-Oedipal origins of sexuality 15
pre-reflexive intersubjectivity 69
pride, arrogance and 21
projective identification 5, 17, 66, 123, 128,
    129, 139, 140, 193, 194
prolonged adolescence 214
proto-mental system 98n22
psychic aliveness 3
psychic isolation 220
psychic learning 94
psychoanalytic seeing 83
psychosexual development 4, 227n3
psychosexuality 103, 104
pubertal self 3
puberty 22, 29, 35, 41

Racker, H. 31
recognition 60, 64–68, 74
Reddy, V. 20
reflexive intersubjectivity 69
Reich, A. 43n6
relational field, theoretical perspective of 84
relational psychoanalysis 64
relationship; analytic 34, 38, 39, 60, 68, 93,
    186; conscious-unconscious 93, 94, 104;
    group 94; love 165; master-servant
    65–66; mother-child 95, 126; mother-
    infant 64–65, 107; romantic 38, 200, 210,
    214; sexual 13, 191, 220, 225;
    therapeutic 33, 64, 65, 83, 154, 177
resistance 2, 61, 64, 73, 164, 192
Resnik, S. 90
rhythm 126
Rivista di Psicoanalisi (1955) 60
romantic partners 204
romantic relationship 38, 200, 210, 214
Romeo-and-Juliet situation 74
Rosenfeld, H. 174, 191, 194

sadism 11, 194
same-sex affection 156
Samuels, A. 33–34, 51
Sandler, A.M. 12
Schröder, K. A. 98n10
Searles, H. 1, 2, 15, 30, 39, 53, 58, 72
Searles, Harold 1
seduction 74; unconscious 104
seductiveness 21

234   *Index*

seeing and being seen 93–95
Segal, H. 13
self-consciousness 65, 71
self-disgust 18
self-esteem 111
self-other dyad 69
self-portrait 91–92
self-portrait with crossed hands 84–87
Semantica dell'amore (poem) 59
sentimentalism 67
separation 91
separation anxiety 111–113, 181n4
separation-individuation 117
Sexton, A. 220, 228
sexual co-excitation 104
sexual fantasies in narcissistic and erotic
    transference 103; anal phase 105–106;
    bisexuality 116–117; castration anxiety
    and love for the father 113–114; erotic
    transference 114–115; oral impregnation,
    fantasy of 109–110; parents' narcissism
    111; phallic phase 110–111; separation
    anxiety and sexuality 111–113; sexuality
    103–105; wolf game 107–109
sexual intercourse 29, 166
sexualisation and feeling of love 14
sexualised transference 164–165, 176
sexuality 4, 10, 51–52, 103–105; adult
    sexuality 12, 14, 19, 196, 203; and
    attachment 104; bisexuality 106, 112,
    116–117; childhood 10–14, 16–19, 21,
    84, 187, 194; disordered 8, 16, 18;
    infantile 12, 16, 103, 104, 117; and love
    objects 204; normal adult sexuality 12;
    perverse 10, 16–19; post-Oedipal
    sexuality 10, 14, 16; pre-Oedipal origins
    of 15; and psychoanalysis 13;
    psychoanalytic conception of 103–104;
    psychosexuality 103, 104
sexuality and erotic transference 163;
    clinical examples 166–177;
    developmental potential of addressing
    180; protective factors 178–180;
    therapeutic equilibrium, maintaining
    177–178; types of 163–166
sexually over-stimulated adolescents 38
sexual relationship 13, 191, 220, 225
sexual self 16, 19–21
sexual self-worth in adulthood 20
sexual symbolism 63
sexual transference and countertransference
    10; childhood sexuality, psychoanalytic
    ideas on 10–14; delayed Oedipal

development, clinical example of 21–23;
    erotic transference and
    countertransference 14–16; parental
    objects' role, question of 21; perverse
    sexuality in a child 16–19; sexual
    self 19–21
shared meanings and feelings 41
shipwreck 62
sin 71
Sinason, V. 16
sister, lover and wife 90–93
Sklansky, M. 44n12
Slavin, J.H. 51
sleeping beauties 217, 218; succession
    problems for parents of adolescents
    221–222; succession problems of
    adolescence 218–221
Sleeping Beauty (fairy tale) 217–218, 221,
    225, 226, 227n1, 227n3
social isolation 199
'soft' porn 51
speculative imagination 96
Strachey, J. 178
striking 61
subjectivation 69, 70, 225
subjectivisation 225
subjectivity 64, 69, 71
sublimation, Freudian concept of 13
succession problems; of adolescence
    218–221; for parents of adolescents
    221–222
surprise 105
symbol-formation 14
symbolic equation and symbol 13
symbolization 13
Symington, N. 175
symptomatology 190, 195

Tattersall, R.B. 141
tensions 11
theatre 61
therapeutic equilibrium, maintaining
    177–178, 179
therapeutic relationship 33, 64, 65, 83,
    154, 177
thirdness 110
Thomson-Salo, F. 52
thoughts, wild 94
Three Essays (1905) 12
TL, concept of 42, 60, 61, 63, 67, 72, 76
toilet training 106
tragedy and life 71
transference-love 30, 59, 122, 164; at-one-

ment 60, 64, 65, 68–71; erotic transference and theory of the analytical field 71–76; *ferrum* and *ignis* 60–64; recognition 60, 64–68
'transformation', Bionian principle of 74
transgressions 61, 73, 157, 164, 175
traversing challenging terrain 48; developmental eroticism 52–53; erotic engagement, negotiating the boundaries in 53–54
Trevarthen, C. 20, 21
true self 67, 105
truth 70
type 1 diabetes (T1D) 140

uncanniness 88
unconscious alliances 98n13
unconscious communication 68
unconscious traumatic memories 95
unconscious 'seduction' 104

Ungar, V. 222–223
unification 70
Urwin, C. 17

valorization of child 83
value 70
virgin territory 33
voyeurism 11
voyeuristic looking 43n8

waking dream 37, 58, 92, 123
Watson, A. 142
Widlocher, D. 117
wife 90–93
wild thoughts 94, 96, 98n23
Winnicott, D.W. 83, 220
wolf game 107–109

young adulthood 204, 207

Printed in the United States
by Baker & Taylor Publisher Services